Derivatives

THE TOOLS THAT CHANGED FINANCE

Derivatives

THE TOOLS THAT CHANGED FINANCE

Phelim Boyle & Feidhlim Boyle

To Bob Merton.

In appreciation of your
trail breaking contributions to
finance

Phelim P. Boyle

August /24/ 2001

Published by Risk Books, a division of the Risk Waters Group.

Haymarket House
28–29 Haymarket
London SW1Y 4RX
Tel: +44 (0)20 7484 9700
Fax: +44 (0)20 7484 9758
E-mail: books@riskwaters.com
Website: www.riskbooks.com

Every effort has been made to secure the permission of individual copyright
holders for inclusion.

© Risk Waters Group Ltd 2001

ISBN 1 899 332 88 X

British Library Cataloguing in Publication Data
A catalogue record for this book is available from the British Library

Risk Books Commissioning Editor: Conrad Gardner
Desk Editor: Martin Llewellyn

Typeset by Mark Heslington, Scarborough, North Yorkshire

Printed and bound in Great Britain by Bookcraft (Bath) Ltd, Somerset

Acknowledgements

Several people have helped us in connection with this book and it has benefited from their comments and their suggestions. Even when we did not follow their advice on a particular point, we were forced to think about how we could do a better job of explaining the issue. These individuals are not responsible for any remaining errors – we are.

Junichi Imai provided excellent technical assistance throughout the project. Darko Lakota and Sahar Kfir read earlier drafts and made many thoughtful suggestions. Peter Christoffersen and Dietmar Leisen gave useful comments on how firms use derivatives. Gladys Yam helped with the proof reading and Lochlann Boyle made suggestions on the syntax. Geoff Chaplin critiqued our discussion of credit risk. Hans Buhlman, Yuri Kabanov and Philippe Artzner provided several historical details.

A number of individuals shared their ideas and experiences with us. These include Sheen Kassouf, Case Sprenkle, Ed Thorp, Mark Rubinstein, Farshid Jamshidian, David Heath, Richard Rendleman, Britt Barter and Tom Ho. Jeremy Evnine gave us a first-hand account of what it was like to be in the trenches during the stock market crash of October 1987.

The authors are extremely grateful to Amy Aldous for taking care of so many details associated with this work in her usual efficient manner. Bill Falloon initially conceived the idea for this book. We would like to thank Martin Llewellyn, our editor at Risk books, for all his hard work on this project.

Feidhlim Boyle would like to thank his dad for the opportunity to work with him on this project. He credits his own interest in and knowledge of derivatives to his father's influence. Feidhlim did much of the early research on the book but during the later stages, when he was a full time MBA student at Cornell, he did not have as much time for the book as he would have liked. He is indebted to Jim Doak and Professor Charles M. C. Lee whose knowledge of investments contributed to greatly to his understanding of markets.

On a personal note, Feidhlim is deeply grateful to Roben Stikeman for all her support and encouragement during the research and writing process.

Phelim Boyle's ideas on derivatives have been shaped by discussion over the years with his students, colleagues and individuals in the investment community. The list is too long to name every person individually. However, he would like to single out Leif Andersen, George Blazenko, Mark Broadie, Ren-Raw Chen, Piet de Jong, Baoyan Ding, David Downie,

David Emanuel, Paul Glasserman, Yann d'Halluin, Houben Huang , Lee Ann Janissen, Sok Hoon Lau, Inmoo Lee, Dawei Li, Sheldon Lin, Chonghui Liu, Jennifer Mao, Jennifer Page, Dave Pooley, Eric Reiner, Yisong Tian, Vishwanath Tirupattur, Stuart Turnbull, Ton Vorst, Tan Wang, Hailang Yang, Dehui Yu and Robert Zvan. He is particularly fortunate to work with and learn so much from Ken Seng Tan and Weidong Tian. Phelim is grateful to his colleagues at the University of Waterloo especially David Carter, Peter Forsyth, Andrew Heunis, Adam Kolkiewicz, Don McLeish, Bill Scott, Ranjini Sivakumar and Ken Vetzal.

Phelim Boyle's greatest debt is to his wife Mary Hardy. She provided sage counsel, strong support and warm encouragement throughout the project.

Contents

Authors

Phelim Boyle grew up in Northern Ireland and was educated at Dreenan School and Queen's University in Belfast. He obtained a PhD in physics from Trinity College, Dublin and subsequently qualified as an actuary. He became enchanted with options in the early 1970s and since then, has published many papers on derivatives. Phelim was the first person to use the Monte Carlo method to value options. Currently he is Director of the Centre for Advanced Studies in Finance at the University of Waterloo, Canada where he holds the J. Page Wadsworth Chair in Finance.

Feidhlim Boyle was born in Dublin and grew up in Vancouver, Edinburgh and Waterloo in Ontario. He received his undergraduate education in political science at Queen's University in Kingston and then a MPhil from Trinity College, Dublin. While attending the Johnson Graduate School of Management at Cornell University, where he received his MBA, he served as a portfolio manager of the Cayuga Fund LLC. Feidhlim has several years of experience in a variety of roles within the equity divisions of ScotiaMcLeod Inc and Goldman, Sachs & Co. He lives in New York.

Preface

Derivatives are tools for transferring risk. They are now widely used in the business world but a few decades ago derivatives were obscure financial instruments. They were mainly used to manage the price risk of commodities like wheat in a market that was relatively small. From these humble rural beginnings, the market expanded spectacularly. Derivatives are now available on an extensive range of risks, from interest rates to electricity prices. There has been a tremendous amount of financial innovation in the design of these products and this has resulted in an extensive variety of contract designs. The derivatives market transcends national boundaries and is now a truly global market. Today the market for derivatives is the largest financial market in the world.

Despite their importance, derivatives are not well understood. One reason is that they have acquired the reputation of being complicated, technical instruments. This view is widespread in the media. In a *Fortune* article, Carol Loomis described derivatives as being "concocted in unstoppable variation by rocket scientists who rattle on about terms like delta, gamma, rho, theta and vega, they make a total hash out of existing accounting rules and even laws."[1] The CBS show "Sixty Minutes" stated also, that: "Derivatives are too complicated to explain and too important to ignore".[2]

The authors agree that derivatives are too important to ignore but do not agree that they are too complicated to explain. The main aim of this book is to explain in simple terms what derivatives are and, in some respects, derivatives are no more complicated than insurance. The average person usually has a good, basic understanding of insurance, therefore we hope it is possible to create the same level of awareness of derivatives.

Derivatives play two fundamentally opposing roles with regard to transferring risk: they can be used to reduce risk and they can be used to increase risk. It depends on how they are used. In this respect, derivatives are like telescopes, they can either increase our exposure to risk or reduce our exposure to risk in much the same way that a telescope can enlarge objects or make them seem smaller. If I look through a telescope in the normal way, it magnifies objects whereas if I look through the other end, it makes them smaller.

Insurance contracts can also be used to shift risk, which makes them similar to derivatives in this respect. For example, if I buy a fire insurance policy on my house, the risk is reduced because if the house burns down I get money from the insurance company. Hence the purchase of the insurance reduces my risk. However, if I were to underwrite insurance, that is, act as an insurance company, and I only wrote a single policy, my risk would be increased. Suppose I underwrote a fire insurance policy on my neighbour's house, then I would increase the risks I face. I would receive a premium of, for example, US$300 from my neighbour as the insurance premium but in the worst case scenario, I could face a large claim should his house burn down. Thus, the same instrument may be used to reduce risk or it can be used to increase risk. Just as in the telescope example, the results depend on which way the contract is used.

Derivatives are widely used by corporations and financial institutions to reduce risk but they may also be used to take on additional risk. For the derivatives market to work properly, we need agents willing to buy derivatives and agents who are willing to sell them. This is a basic requirement for any market to flourish. More generally, risk taking serves a useful economic function in business and society. Entrepreneurs take on risky projects in the hope of improving their fortunes and in doing so they create wealth, which can contribute to society's economic progress.

However, excessive risk-taking can be dangerous because it can lead to large losses and sometimes the bankruptcy of the individuals or firms involved. The term speculation is often used to describe investment strategies that are very risky.[3] Derivatives provide a very effective mechanism for taking on large amounts of risk with a relatively small initial outlay. It is this feature that makes them such lethal instruments for speculation. A number of large-scale financial failures have involved the misguided use of derivatives to take on risky positions. Some of the most infamous include Barings Bank, Orange County and Long-Term Capital Management. Some observers however, have suggested that these failures were due to faulty risk management, flawed controls or poor disclosure and not derivatives themselves.

The two conflicting roles of derivatives are reflected in the public debates on this subject. Proponents of derivatives stress their benefits:

❑ derivatives enable better risk sharing across the economy;
❑ derivatives provide investors with more flexibility to tailor their portfolios to suit their wants; and
❑ prices of derivatives reveal useful information about future events that can lead to better decisions.

On the other hand, derivatives make it very easy to take on large amounts of risk that can lead to large losses. There have been several such derivatives disasters and these are newsworthy events. Perhaps this is one of the main reasons why the media coverage of derivatives focuses so much on their dark side.[4]

Although there are many books on derivatives, we feel there is a gap that our book fills. Existing books can be classified into two main groups. The first group consists of specialised books written for technical audiences. They describe the details of the underlying models and tend to focus on the mathematical models and the technical details. The second group consists of books that are written for a general audience where the focus is often on the derivatives disasters. The aim of our book is to explain derivatives in an interesting and accessible way for a general audience. We outline the key ideas and we describe how these ideas evolved, as this will give the reader fresh insights into the subject. It is these ideas that provide the intellectual lifeblood of the subject and it is these ideas that lead ultimately to the technological innovations. These innovations, in turn, lead to new insights and act as a spur for further developments.

Since this is an introductory book, we have tried to make it more readable by using simple explanations for the important ideas and basic concepts. We hope the reader will find these examples instructive and perhaps entertaining. For instance, we use a tennis match to explain a key concept in modern finance. The outcome of the match is uncertain and, if we create securities that make different payments depending on who wins the match, we can construct a simple financial market. We can use this simple market to show that the prices of these securities must obey certain relationships. The key insight can be summed up by saying that there is no free lunch in finance and our tennis example makes this point very lucidly.

We also discuss the reasons behind the explosive growth in the derivatives market during the past 25 years. We describe the major types of derivative markets and the role they play in the economy. Derivatives are widely used by corporations to reduce their exposure to certain risks and this process is known as hedging. We discuss real examples where firms hedge their risk with derivatives and we also give practical examples to describe how investors can use derivatives to alter their exposure to risk. Once again, our aim is to give the reader the big picture, as it is all too easy in this area to become swamped in the details.

The story of modern derivative pricing began in 1900, with the publication of Louis Bachelier's seminal thesis at the University of Paris. Bachelier's ideas were so far ahead of his time that his work was ignored for 50 years until there was a renewed interest in the subject. During the 1950s and '60s, several people worked on developing a formula for pricing a very important type of derivative known as a call option. A call option is a security that gives its owner the right to buy something in the future for a fixed price.

The work started by Bachelier was completed in the early 1970s by Fischer

Black, Myron Scholes and Robert Merton. These authors discovered the most important formula in the derivatives area; a formula that gave the price of a call option. Merton and Scholes were awarded the Nobel Prize for this work in 1997. We discuss the evolution of the ideas that led to this discovery. We will see that progress towards the solution was made, not directly, but in a series of fascinating twists and turns. The publication of the Black–Scholes–Merton (BSM) results stimulated a flood of new ideas and provided the foundation for new derivative contracts that would eventually become the largest financial market in the world. Indeed there has been an active interplay between the creation of these ideas and their commercial applications.

Many of the new ideas emerged from academic research, but practitioners working in the financial sector also made significant contributions. The work of practitioners is often unrecognised because it is generally not published in the usual academic outlets. In some cases, the new ideas and applications were not publicised because of their commercial potential. The situation here is similar, but less extreme than in cryptography where secrecy is so important that the best code breaking work is destined to remain unknown.[5]

At this point, some caveats are in order. Because we are trying to paint the bigger picture, our discussions of the ideas and their applications is not comprehensive and there are many important contributions that we do not mention. It is also difficult to get the attribution of ideas correct, often when a new idea emerges a number of people have similar insights around the same time. We apologise to the many individuals whose creative work is not cited. Although much of the initial development in the derivatives area took place in the United States, and the US still is the leader in many aspects of derivatives, there is a strong trend towards globalisation. Many markets now operate on a worldwide basis and the increasing importance of electronic trading will reinforce this trend. This book retains a largely North American focus and we are conscious of this bias.

The layout of the rest of the book is as follows. In Chapter 1, we introduce derivatives and explain how they can be used to transfer risk. Chapter 2 explains how the dramatic growth in derivatives came about because of changes in the business world and advances in technology. We describe the major markets and the most important contracts. In Chapter 3 we explain the concept of no-arbitrage or the no-free-lunch idea. Chapter 4 shows how this idea can be put into practice to find the value of a derivative security in terms of other securities. Chapter 5 tells the story of how the BSM formula for the price of a stock option was eventually discovered by tracing the twists and turns of the discovery path from the work of Bachelier to the final formula.

Chapter 6 describes how firms use derivatives to hedge their risk and draws examples from the gold-mining, computer software and insurance industries. Chapter 7 explores how investors use derivatives to satisfy their investment objectives. Chapter 8 analyses three famous derivatives disasters and shows they have some key common features. Chapter 9 explains the nature of credit risk and how derivatives are being used to transfer this type of risk. Those who do the maths in the derivatives business are called financial engineers and in the final chapter we describe this new profession.

1   See Loomis (1994).

2   The programme "Derivatives" was broadcast on March 5, 1995 (repeated on July 23, 1995).

3   Edward Chancellor (1999) analyses the term "speculation" in his book *Devil Take the Hindmost*. Robert Shiller (2000), argues that speculation in the US stock market has driven it up to unsustainable levels.

4   To examine this issue, we analysed the major articles on derivatives published in the *New York Times* during the period 1997 to 2000 and classified them with respect to the overall treatment of derivatives. We discovered that 19% of the articles were positive, 26% were neutral and 55% percent were negative.

5   See Singh (1999).

1

Introduction

A derivative is *a contract that is used to transfer risk*. There are many different underlying risks, ranging from fluctuations in energy prices to weather risks. Most derivatives, however, are based on financial securities such as common stocks, bonds and foreign exchange instruments. This chapter will explain, in broad terms, the following points:

❑ what derivatives are;
❑ how they are used;
❑ how derivatives can reduce risks such as price risk;
❑ how they can also increase risk – the aspect of derivatives that receives most attention from the media;
❑ how some recent derivatives disasters occurred; and
❑ the ways in which some basic derivative contracts such as forwards, options, swaps and futures work.

Derivatives have changed the world of finance as pervasively as the Internet has changed communication. Their growth has exploded during the last 30 years as ever more risks have been traded in this manner. By the end of 1999, the estimated dollar value of derivatives in force throughout the world was some US$102 trillion – about *10 times* the value of the entire US gross domestic product.[1]

Insurance is the traditional method for sharing risks. We will use the concept of insurance when discussing derivatives because insurance is a familiar notion and most people understand it. However, although insurance and derivatives share common features in that they are both devices for transferring risk, there are also distinct differences. The risks covered by insurance are generally different from those that are dealt with by derivatives.

We first need to clarify the meaning of the word "risk". "Risk" has a specialised meaning in an insurance context: it refers to *the chance that a future event might happen with bad consequences for somebody* – for example an airline might lose someone's baggage. This event is uncertain in that it may or may not happen. If it does not happen, you are no worse off but if it does, there is an adverse consequence that could involve an economic loss or something else untoward.[2]

The more usual meaning of "risk" has positive as well as negative undertones. In business and investment decisions risk involves both the prospect of gain as well as the chance of loss. When there is a wide variation in the range of outcomes we say that a project "carries a lot of risk". If there is little variation in the range of outcomes we say that it "carries very little risk". We willingly take on risks all the time – risk taking is a pervasive human and business activity. Individuals and firms undertake risky ventures because of their potential rewards even though there is the possibility of loss. Indeed, we have a basic intuition that high expected returns are associated with high risk.

Insurance risk, then, relates only to downside risk. Business risk, on the other hand, involves both an upside chance of gain and a downside possibility of loss. No one likes pure downside risk and we would like to dispose of it if we could. We can sometimes do this by entering a contract with an insurance company whereby we pay the premium up front and the insurance company reimburses us if a specified event happens. The policy specifies what the payment will be under different outcomes and is one way of eliminating downside risk.

A derivative is also a contract where the ultimate payoff depends on future events. To that extent it is very similar to insurance. However, derivatives are much more versatile because they can be used to transfer a wider range of risks and are not restricted to purely downside risks.

Contracts that serve a useful economic purpose such as reducing or transferring important types of risks are the ones most likely to survive and flourish. Thus, insurance contracts that serve to transfer risks from consumers to insurance companies are pervasive. One of the reasons why derivatives have become so popular is that they enable risks to be traded efficiently. Different firms face different risks   and attitudes to risk vary across firms as well as individuals. These factors increase the gains from trade. The same event may have opposite impacts on two different firms. For example, a rise in the price of oil will benefit an oil-producing company because it receives more money for its product. The same price rise will hurt an airline company because it has to pay more for fuel. However, one can envisage a contract based on the price of oil that would make both companies better off.

The concept behind derivatives is simple. First, the risk is sliced up into standardised pieces, then these pieces are traded in a market so that there is a price for all to see. Those who want to dispose of the risk sell it and those who are willing to take on the risk buy it. The idea is that those players who are most able to bear the risk will end up doing so at market prices. In a competitive market it can be argued that the market price provides a fair basis for exchange.

SOME SIMPLE DERIVATIVES

With advancing technology it is now possible to write derivatives on a broader range of underlying assets and variables. There has been remarkable innovation in the development of new derivatives. In this section we shall look at two simple types of derivatives.

Common stocks

If you own 100 common shares of General Electric you actually own a very tiny piece of this huge company. Common stocks are very flexible vehicles for risk transfer. They are, in fact, early examples of derivatives. Their basic structure illustrates four simple yet powerful concepts that foreshadowed subsequent developments in derivatives:

❏ *Divisibility of the claim*. The division of the total-ownership pie into identical little slices is a very simple way to distribute risk.
❏ *Upside appreciation*. Common stocks do well when the firm does well, so they provide a way to share in the firm's good fortunes.
❏ *Downside protection*. Common stocks provide a way of limiting the investor's downside risk. Because of limited liability, the maximum a shareholder can lose is the initial investment made to buy the share. This protection does not exist under some other forms of ownership such as certain types of unlimited partnership.
❏ *An organised market*. Publicly traded stocks trade on an organised market. The prevailing market prices should accurately reflect their current value.

These four features make common stocks extremely efficient tools for transferring risk. Financial derivatives have magnified such features.

Forward contracts

A forward contract is an important example of a derivative. It is *an arrangement, made today, to buy something in the future for a fixed price*.

Consider the example of buying a house. Normally there is a period between the signing of the purchase contract and my taking possession of the property. This contract to purchase the house is an example of a forward contract. In other words, I agree *now* to buy the house in *three months' time* and to pay the agreed purchase price at that time. The seller also agrees now to sell me the house in *three months' time*. In the jargon of forward contracts, I have *a long position* in the forward contract or, more simply, I am *long the forward contract*. The seller is said to have a *short position* in the forward contract or, more simply, is *short the forward contract*.

A forward contract can be written on almost any type of underlying asset. The owner of a forward contract has the obligation to buy the underlying asset (or commodity) at a fixed date in the future for a fixed price.

The price to be paid for the asset is termed the delivery price or the contract price. This price is fixed at inception and does not change over the term of the contract. In contrast, the price of the underlying asset will change as time passes. If the price of the asset rises a lot over the term of the contract, the asset will be worth more than the contract price at the delivery date. In this case fortune has favoured the person holding the long position because they can buy the asset for less than its market value. However, if the price of the asset falls during the life of the contract, the asset will be worth less than the contract price at the delivery date. In this case fortune has favoured the person holding the short position because they can sell the asset for more than its market value.

The parties have agreed in advance to exchange the asset for the contract price at a fixed rate in the future. However, when the delivery date arrives, one of the parties will show a profit on the contract and the other will show a loss. We will explain later how the contract (delivery) price is determined at the outset so that when the forward contract is set up, the terms of the contract are fair to both parties.

HEDGING AND SPECULATION

Corporations use forward contracts to manage price risk. A gold mining company, Sperrin Corp (a hypothetical company named after a mountain range in Northern Ireland that does contain traces of gold) faces the risk that the price of gold will fall. To protect itself against this risk Sperrin could enter a forward contract to sell gold in one year's time at a fixed price of US$310 per ounce. In other words, the delivery price is US$310.

This forward contract protects Sperrin if gold prices drop below US$310. If the price falls to US$200 an ounce Sperrin will still be able to sell its gold at the prearranged price of US$310. On the other hand, if gold prices rise Sperrin still has to fulfil the terms of the contract. For example, if the price of gold jumps to US$400 an ounce Sperrin has to sell its gold for the contracted price of US$310 per ounce. In other words, Sperrin has given up the right to any price appreciation above the contract price of US$310. In this situation, the other party will be able to make money by buying gold from Sperrin under the forward contract at US$310 and selling it on the cash (spot) market at US$400.

Who might be willing to take the other side of the forward contract with Sperrin Gold? The forward contract might also be attractive to a firm that makes gold jewellery, as the risks it faces are the mirror image of those faced by Sperrin. Suppose the Old Triangle[3] jewellery firm normally buys its gold on the cash market. If the price of gold rises, Old Triangle faces higher production costs. If the price of gold falls the firm's costs decline. Gold price changes have opposing impacts on Old Triangle and Sperrin so they can both reduce their risks at the same time by entering the forward contract. Through the forward contract Sperrin has locked in a fixed price at which it can sell gold in the future and Old Triangle has a contract to buy gold at a fixed price in the future.

This practice of reducing price risk using derivatives is known as *hedging*. In our example, Sperrin is hedging its exposure to gold price risk. Old Triangle is also hedging its price risk. Thus, the same contract can be used as a hedging vehicle by two different parties.

The opposite of hedging is speculating. Speculation involves taking on more risk. An investor with no exposure to the price of gold can obtain this exposure by entering into a forward contract. Many financial markets need risk takers or speculators to make them function efficiently and provide liquidity. Speculation serves a useful economic purpose. It can lead to improved risk sharing and provide a rapid and efficient way of incorporating new information into market prices. Derivatives provide a very powerful tool for speculating as they can increase an investor's exposure to a given type of risk.

OPTIONS
Options are classic examples of derivatives that can be used to increase or reduce risk exposure. *An option is a contract that gives its owner the right to buy or sell some asset for a fixed price at some future date or dates*. A call option gives its owner the right to *buy* some underlying asset for a fixed price at some future time. A put option confers the right to *sell* an asset for a fixed price at some future date.

The owner of the option has the right – but not the obligation – to buy (or sell) the asset. In contrast, under a forward contract one party is obliged to buy (or sell) the asset. Options can be based on a wide range of underlying assets. The asset could be a financial security such as a common stock or a bond. The underlying asset need not be a financial asset: it could be a Picasso painting or a rare bottle of Chateau Margaux.

The terms of the option contract specify the underlying asset, the duration of the contract and the price to be paid for the asset. In option jargon, the fixed price agreed upon for buying the asset, is called the *exercise* price or the *strike price*. The act of buying or selling the asset is known as *exercising the option*. The simplest type of option is a "European" option, which can only be exercised at the end of the contract period. On the other hand, an "American" option can be exercised at any time during the contract period.[4]

Put options provide protection in case the price of the underlying asset falls. Sperrin Corp could use put options on gold to lock in a floor price. For example, suppose the current gold price is US$280 an ounce and Sperrin decides it wants to have a guaranteed floor price of US$285 per ounce in one year's time. The company could buy one-year maturity put options with a strike price of US$285 an ounce. If the price of gold in one year's time is below US$285, Sperrin has the right to sell its gold for a fixed price of US$285 per ounce. For example, if gold dropped to US$250 per ounce Sperrin has the right under the put option to sell the gold for US$285 per ounce and the option is then worth US$35 per ounce. However, if the price were to rise to US$360, Sperrin can make more money by selling its gold at the prevailing market price and would not exercise the option. In this case, the option would not have any value at maturity. The put option gives Sperrin protection against a fall in the price of gold below US$285 while still allowing the gold company to benefit from price increases. In this respect the put option differs from the forward contract. Under a forward contract, the firm still has price protection on the downside but it gives up the benefits of price increases because it has to sell the gold (at a loss) for the contract price.

We will now examine how call options can be used by an airline to reduce the risks of high fuel costs. Assume the current price of jet fuel is US$135 per tonne and American Airlines is concerned about future increases in fuel prices. If American Airlines buys one-year call options with a strike price of US$140 per tonne it has the option to buy jet fuel at a price of US$140 per tonne. We assume the option is "European", which means simply that it can only be exercised at its maturity. If the price of jet fuel in one year's time is US$180 per tonne, the airline can buy the fuel at US$140 per tonne or US$40 below what it costs on the cash market. In this case American Airlines will exercise the call option, which will then be worth US$40 per tonne. On the other hand, if the price of fuel in one year's time has dropped to US$100 per tonne, the airline will not exercise its option. It makes no sense to pay US$140 for fuel when it can be bought in the market for US$100. When American Airlines buys this option contract from a Texan-based energy company it has to pay for the option. The price it pays for the option is called the *option premium*. We will discuss how this premium is determined in Chapters 4 and 5.

Hedgers can use option contracts to reduce their exposure to different types of risk. In the above examples both Sperrin and American Airlines used options to reduce their risk. As is the case with all derivatives, options can also be used to increase risk. Victor Niederhoffer, a legendary trader, provides a dramatic example of how put options can be used to increase risk. Niederhoffer's hedge fund routinely sold put options on the Standard and Poor (S&P) Index. This index is based on a portfolio of the common stocks of large US corporations. When the fund sold the options it collected the option premiums. This strategy worked well as long as the Index did not drop too sharply. However, on October 27, 1997 the S&P fell by 7% in a single day and totally wiped out Niederhoffer's fund. Ironically, Victor Niederhoffer's autobiography was titled *Education of a Speculator*.[5]

SWAPS

A swap is an agreement between two parties to exchange a periodic stream of benefits or payments over a pre-arranged period. The payments could be based on the market value of an underlying asset.

For example, a pension plan that owned 10,000 shares of the Houston-based energy company Enron could enter an equity swap with an investment bank to exchange the returns on these shares in return for a periodic fixed payment over a two-year period. Assume the payments are exchanged every month. Each month the pension plan pays the investment bank an amount equal to the change in the market value of its Enron shares. In return, the plan receives the agreed fixed dollar amount every month; after two years the swap expires. The pension plan still owns its Enron shares. The two parties go their separate ways. During this two-year period the bank receives the same returns that it would have received had it owned the Enron common shares. The pension plan receives a fixed income for two years, thus giving up its exposure to the Enron shares for the two-year period.

Swap terminology

We now describe some of the terms associated with swaps. The duration of the swap contract is called the *tenor* of the swap. In the above example the tenor is two years. The two parties to the contract are called the *counterparties*, following the example, the counterparties are the pension plan and the investment bank. The sequence of fixed payments is called the *fixed leg* of the swap and the sequence of variable payments is called the *variable leg* of the swap.

In a *commodity swap* the payments on one leg of the swap may be based on the market price of the commodity. Sometimes the swap is based on the actual delivery of the underlying commodity. Cominco, the largest zinc producer in the world, is based in British Columbia, Canada. In December, 2000, Cominco entered an innovative swap with a large US energy company.[6] Under the terms of the swap Cominco agreed to deliver electricity to the energy company at a fixed price per megawatt hour. The energy company paid US$86 million for the power. The duration of the swap was from December 11, 2000, to January 31, 2001. During this period, electricity prices were very high in the western US as a result of the California power crisis (which we discuss in more detail in Chapter 2).

Cominco generates its own power from a dam on the Pend Oreille River. Normally, Cominco uses this power to refine zinc in its plant near the town of Trail in southern British Columbia. In the winter of 2000, the price of power in the Pacific North West was so high that Cominco found it profitable to scale back its production of zinc to free up the power. During this period, Cominco reduced its zinc production by 20,000 tonnes. To meet its customers' demands for zinc, Cominco purchased the zinc on the spot market. The employees, who were no longer needed in the zinc-production operations, were deployed on maintenance activities. The revenue from the swap had a major impact on the company's bottom line. According to Cominco officials, the company has a goal of making an annual operating profit from its Trail operations of US$100 million – the revenue generated by the swap almost produced an entire year's projected profit.

Interest rate swaps

Interest rate swaps are very popular financial instruments. They have grown to such an extent that they are the most widely traded derivatives contracts in the world. In an interest rate swap, one counterparty pays a fixed rate of interest and the other counterparty pays a variable, or floating, rate of interest. The payments to be exchanged are based on a notional amount of principal.

Interest rate swaps are useful tools for managing interest rate risk. We can illustrate this use of interest rate swaps with an example involving a savings and loan bank. These institutions, often known as "thrifts", were set up in the US to provide mortgages to residential homeowners. Most of the assets of a typical thrift consist of long-term mortgages, which often pay fixed interest rates, and the liabilities tend to be consumer deposits. The interest rates paid on these deposits vary with market conditions and depend on the current level of short-term rates. This means that the thrift's income and outflow are not well matched. If there is a dramatic rise in the level of rates, the thrift has to pay out more money to its depositors. At the same time its revenue stream remains fixed because its existing assets provide a fixed rate of interest computed at lower rates. The thrift therefore faces a significant exposure to interest rate risk.

The thrift's problem can be neatly solved with an interest rate swap. The parties exchange a stream of fixed-rate payments for a stream of floating-rate (variable-rate) payments. The thrift agrees to pay the fixed interest rate and receive the floating rate. The dealer agrees to pay the floating rate and receive the fixed rate. These floating rate payments provide a much closer match to the amounts the thrift must pay to its depositors.

NEW CONTRACTS

New types of derivative instruments are being introduced all the time. Weather derivatives provide a good example of a recent innovation in this area. Many business organisations have profits that depend on the weather and there is considerable scope for such derivatives as hedging vehicles. For example, a brewery company's beer sales in the summer are strongly linked to the weather. As the temperature increases, more beer is consumed but if it gets too hot the consumption of beer may actually decrease. On the other hand, the yield on many crops may be adversely affected by a long, hot summer thereby reducing farmers' incomes.

If the winter is abnormally cold, a company that sells snowmobiles will experience increased sales. For example, Bombardier, a Quebec-based company that manufactures and sells snowmobiles, has sales that are highly related to the amount of snowfall in its sales areas. Bombardier has exposure to a specific type of weather risk and it was able to hedge this risk by buying a weather derivative, based on the amount of snowfall. Bombardier bought a snow derivative that meant it could offer cash back to customers if snowfall was less than half the norm. In a weather derivative we need to specify precisely the method by which the payment is to be computed: if the contract is to be based on the temperature level or the average temperature level, then the location needs to specified. For example, the traded weather options on the Chicago Mercantile Exchange use the temperature readings at O'Hare Airport as a basis for their Chicago contract.

Power providers and energy utilities have considerable exposure to the vagaries of the weather. If the summer is very hot consumers will turn up the air conditioning and if the winters are very cold there will be a surge in heating demand. These companies can reduce their risk exposure using weather derivatives. For example, consider Hank Hill, a propane distributor. Hank lives in Arlen, Texas and he is concerned that in a very mild winter propane sales will be low, reducing his profit. Suppose that under normal winter conditions his sales are one million gallons but if the winter is very mild he will only sell half this amount, reducing his profit. Hank can protect himself against this risk by buying a weather derivative from Koch Industries. The payoff on this derivative will be based on the actual average winter temperature for Hank's sales region. Panel 1 describes an interesting weather derivative that is designed to protect the revenues of a chain of London pubs from adverse weather conditions.

MARKETS

In the next chapter we will discuss the reasons for the significant growth of derivatives that has taken place in recent years. Much of the initial growth was in the development of exchange-traded instruments, which are standardised contracts that are traded on organised markets such as the Chicago Board Options Exchange (CBOE) or the London International Financial Futures Exchange (LIFFE). The exchanges provide a secondary market for derivatives and current information on market prices. There are a number of safeguards to maintain orderly markets and, in particular, to guard against the risk of default. For example, there are limits on the position any one firm can take. If an investor is losing money on a short position, the exchange will monitor the situation and require additional funds from time to time, known as "margin funds". These include the posting of margins and position limits. The exchange knows the positions of all the participants and can step in if necessary to take corrective action. Kroszner

PANEL 1
ENRON WEATHER DEAL FOR UK WINE BAR CHAIN

LONDON, 6 June – Corney & Barrow (C&B), which owns a chain of wine bars in the City of London, has closed a weather derivatives deal with US energy giant Enron – the first such undertaking by a non-energy company in the UK. The deal was brokered by Speedwell Weather, a division of the UK-based bond software company Speedwell Associates.

Sarah Heward, managing director of C&B Wine Bars, told RiskNews that the deal helps to protect her company against volatility in business caused by spikes and falls in temperature. "This deal protects a total of £15,000 in gross profit, so it is not a huge contract. But it does show that weather derivatives can be used by small companies", says Heward. She was introduced to the idea of hedging her business's volatility with weather derivatives by her own customers. "Many of our customers are market makers – including Speedwell – and we were talking about the volatility in C&B's business. They suggested that weather derivatives might help", she says. Heward acknowledges that for some executives of small companies, convincing their board of the need to use weather derivatives will be difficult. She says it was not a tough pitch for her, as her board members all work in the City of London.

Steven Docherty, chief executive of Speedwell Weather, says that the market responded surprisingly well to the offer of the C&B deal. Once Speedwell had taken some time to research and define C&B's particular problem, the deal itself was closed a couple of days after it was offered, he says. He believes that those involved in the weather derivatives market will view non-energy contracts as a good way of hedging against putting too many eggs in the energy basket. However, he points out that these deals will still need to be aggressively priced.

While Docherty told RiskNews that the weather market has developed more slowly than was expected, he still describes himself as "insanely optimistic". He believes that banks and funds are becoming more interested in weather products and that this will bring a capital markets approach – resulting in aggressive pricing and efficient marketing of weather products, as well as additional liquidity.

(1999) suggests that the control of credit risk is an important achievement of organised exchanges.

The other main market for derivatives is the so-called over-the-counter (OTC) market, which now accounts for about 85% of all derivatives. This market does not have a fixed geographical location, rather, it is formed by the world's major financial institutions. OTC derivatives are extremely flexible instruments and they have been the vehicles for much of the financial innovation in the last two decades. OTC contracts tend to be much longer dated than exchange-traded options: in some cases they last for as long as 30 to 40 years. One of the most critical differences between exchange-traded derivatives and OTC derivatives is that the former are guaranteed by the exchange whereas OTC derivatives are only guaranteed by the issuer. Thus, the investor is subject to credit (default) risk. The longer the term, the higher is the risk that one of the parties will default. Firms and countries that seem strong today may be in default in the future.

DERIVATIVES AND DISASTERS

Inordinate risk taking, however, can have harmful results. Indeed, the term "speculator" has acquired unsavoury associations because of past excesses. In their role as speculative instruments, derivatives have been associated with some of the most famous financial failures in recent years.

For example, in 1995 the venerable British bank, Barings, collapsed with a loss of US$1.4 billion. The scapegoat for this loss was Nick Leeson, the bank's 28 year-old head trader. A characteristic of derivatives is that the price paid to enter the contract is often small in relation to the size of the risk. We call this property *leverage* because a lever gives us the ability to magnify our efforts. Leeson used derivatives to take very highly leveraged positions, betting on the direction of the Japanese stock market. He guessed wrongly and brought down the bank. However, the bank's internal control system proved to be ineffective and Leeson's activities were not supervised. Most of Leeson's pay was in performance bonuses: if he made a large trading profit his bonus would be huge. Leeson therefore had a very strong incentive to take risks.

One of the criticisms of the Barings case was that Nick Leeson was not an expert in the derivatives area. In contrast , Long-Term Capital Management (LTCM), which collapsed in 1998, was advised by some of the brightest minds in the business. LTCM was a very prominent hedge fund that invested the funds of very rich clients and provides a spectacular example of extreme speculation. Note that the word "hedge" in this context does not mean that these funds actually hedge. LTCM tottered on the brink of collapse in 1998 in the aftermath of the Russian debt crisis because it had taken on massive and very risky positions in several markets. Edward Chancellor observes that LTCM "used derivatives wantonly to build up the largest and most levered position in the history of speculation".[7] Paul Krugman describes the role of leverage in the fund's near collapse:[8]

> Rarely in the course of human events have so few people lost so much money so quickly. There is no mystery about how Greenwich-based Long-Term Capital Management managed to make billions of dollars disappear. Essentially, the hedge fund took huge bets with borrowed money – although

its capital base was only a couple of billion dollars, we now know that it had placed wagers directly or indirectly on the prices of more than a trillion dollars' worth of assets. When it turned out to have bet in the wrong direction, poof! – all the investors' money, and probably quite a lot more besides, was gone.

Funds such as LTCM historically operated with very few restrictions and little disclosure. The justification for this state of affairs was that people who invested in hedge funds were presumed to be sophisticated investors who needed less protection. The most frightening aspect of the LTCM affair was the threat its demise posed to the entire financial industry which was already under pressure from the Russian debt crisis. LTCM was such a major player that it had very significant positions with many large institutions. If it fell into disarray, the domino effect could topple the entire financial system. LTCM was rescued by an infusion of US$3.6 billion from a consortium of some of the world's largest investment banks, which had significant exposure to LTCM. The rescue was mounted after it was realised that LTCM would have to default if the banks stood idly by. Disasters such as Barings and LTCM provided a compelling incentive for banks and other financial institutions with large derivatives positions to improve the way in which they managed these positions. This trend was reinforced by regulation at both the domestic level and the international level. Trade associations, motivated by enlightened self-interest, also developed codes of best practice for the derivatives business.

We have seen that derivatives have two contradictory powers. On the one hand they are remarkably efficient tools for reducing risk. At the same time derivatives have an awesome capacity to increase risk through leverage. This dual nature of derivatives can be viewed in terms of two conflicting emotions that can be used to describe attitudes to risk: fear and greed. The common tendency to reduce risk stems from fear of loss. The motivation to take on large amounts of risk and reap high profits is based on greed. Derivatives provide an efficient way to construct a strategy that is consistent with either of these attitudes.

DEFAULT RISK

Default risk has been a factor since the first contracts were arranged and various procedures have been used to deal with it. One is to try to set up the contract so that it provides incentives that discourage default or non-performance. The life of the Russian author Dostoevsky provides an interesting example of a contract with draconian penalties for non-performance. The contract involved an agreement to produce a new book within a given time. Dostoevsky was deeply in debt because of his gambling activities and he was under pressure from his creditors, so, he entered a deal with an unscrupulous publisher named Stellovsky. Under this deal Dostoevsky sold the copyright to all his published books for 3,000 roubles. The deal also stipulated that Dostoevsky would deliver a new novel by November 1, 1866. If he failed to deliver on time, then Stellovsky would also gain the rights to all of Dostoevsky's future books. This created a severe penalty if the book was not produced on time. Dostoevsky with help from a secretary, Anna Snitkin, whom he later married, managed to write the book in under a month and finished it by October 31, 1866. By a twist of irony the new book was called *The Gambler*.

Futures contracts provide a further example of how the design of a derivative contract can help reduce exposure to default risk. These are exchange-traded instruments. The owner of a futures contract has the obligation to buy some underlying asset. In this respect futures contracts are similar to forward contracts but there are important differences between them concerning the realisation of gains and losses. For example, if an investor is long a forward to buy some asset and the price of the underlying asset rises steadily over the contract period, the gain will not be realised until the end of the contract term. In contrast, if the investor owns (is long) a futures contract and the price of the underlying goes steadily up, the gains would be realised on a daily basis and they are posted to the investor's account. By the same token, if a trader sells (is short) a futures contract and the price rises every day, then the loss will have to be settled up each day and the trader loses money every day. The exchange clearing house ensures that losses and gains are settled up on a daily basis. If the prices move dramatically during the day then the settling up can be more frequent. The exchange broker will ask his client to deposit more money (margin) as soon as a position exceeds a given loss. This periodic settling up means that no side of the transaction is allowed to build up a large loss position. If the client is unable to meet the margin call the position may be liquidated to prevent additional losses. The design of futures contracts provides a very sturdy mechanism for reducing default risk.

CONCLUSION

This chapter demonstrated how widely derivatives are used as tools for transferring risk. It described some basic derivative contracts such as forwards, options, swaps and futures, and gave examples of how these contracts are used to reduce different types of risk. It emphasised that derivatives can be used to increase leverage and take on more risk, while pointing out the dangers of unbridled risk taking. There are also important differences between exchange-traded derivatives and OTC derivatives. The next chapter will analyse the reasons for the tremendous growth of derivatives.

1   These figures refer to the notional amounts. Figures are from the Bank for International Settlements (BIS) press release, 18May 2000 ref 14/2000E. The data relate to December, 1999.

2   Sometimes the term "risk" is used to describe the occurrence that triggers the bad consequences. This usage of "risk" to mean "peril" is common in insurance. For example, an insurance policy may be described as offering protection against named "risks".

3   The firm, invented by the authors, gets its name from a song by Brendan Behan: "And the old triangle/Went jingle jangle/Along the banks of the Royal Canal."

4   The terms "European" and "American" are misleading in this respect. They have nothing to do with geography. The names are apparently due to Samuelson, who coined the term European to describe the simpler type of option and the term American to describe the more complicated type of option. Samuelson picked these names because of some Europeans he met during his research on options.

5   See Niederhoffer (1998).

6   At the time of writing the name of the energy company was not public.

7   See Chancellor (1999).

8   Paul Krugman, "What Really Happened to Long-Term Capital Management", Slate, URL: http://slate.msn.com/dismal/98-10-01/dismal.asp (1 October 1998).

2

Markets and Products

This chapter explains why derivatives have become so popular in the last 30 years. It discusses the initial growth of derivatives products on organised exchange markets and the more recent expansion of derivatives on over-the-counter markets. It describes how derivatives now play an important role in deregulated power markets. Different types of derivative contracts are described using diagrams to explain the concepts. The chapter ends with an example showing how a pension plan used derivatives to alter its investment mix.

REASONS FOR GROWTH

The explosive growth in derivatives began during the 1970s when certain key financial variables became more volatile and new types of derivatives were introduced to manage the increased risk. This growth was fuelled by:

❑ deregulation;
❑ growth in international trade;
❑ increased investment abroad;
❑ advances in computers and technology; and
❑ new research ideas that showed how to price options.

This confluence of factors enabled derivatives to grow from their former modest position in the financial landscape to the dominant place they occupy today. In the early 1970s, the increased volatility in financial variables such as interest rates and exchange rates exposed corporations to more risks and increased the demand for vehicles to reduce these risks. During the last quarter of the 20th century there was also a large increase in international trade and foreign direct investment in real assets, associated with a huge expansion of cross-border capital market flows. Derivatives provided investors with efficient instruments for investing in the global economy, and dramatic advances in information technology lowered the costs of storing and transmitting information. This made the rapid development of global markets possible. Finally, fundamental advances in financial theory gave rise to the basic models that provide the foundation for the pricing and risk management of derivatives.

Foreign exchange risk, which had not been a major concern during the previous 30 years, became an important factor in the early 1970s. This added a new dimension of uncertainty to international trade. A system of fixed exchange rates had been in force among the industrialised nations since the Bretton Woods Agreement in 1944. This meant that the price of one currency in terms of another currency remained fixed. For example, the value of £1 sterling remained constant in terms of US dollars. Under this system, a US manufacturer knew at the outset how many dollars it would receive for a payment of, for example, £1 million due in two year's time. If £1 was worth US$2 at the outset, it would still be worth US$2 after two years.

Fixed exchange rates came under increasing pressure due to economic growth in Europe and Japan and a decline in the competitiveness of US exports. In 1971, Richard Nixon severed the fixed link between the US dollar and gold and set in motion the breakup of the Bretton Woods system of fixed exchange rates. This lead to a system of floating exchange rates, where the price of one currency in terms of another varied according to the relative strength of the two countries' economies.

With the advent of floating exchange rates our US exporter would have to convert the £1 million back into dollars at the prevailing exchange rate. If the pound had strengthened against the dollar so that £1 was now worth US$3, the manufacturer would receive US$3 million for the UK currency. Alternatively, if the pound had weakened against the dollar so that £1 was only worth US$1, the manufacturer would receive just US$1 million for the British pounds. Hence the increased risk in international trade.

The advent of floating exchange rates coincided with the increased volatility in interest rates and a sharp increase in oil prices. The stage was set for the development of new derivatives – instruments that could protect firms against these risks.

The Chicago exchanges

The centre of this development was Chicago, whose location as the major hub in the fertile farming lands of the American Midwest had made it the world's leading centre for agricultural and commodity derivatives. Contracts are traded on two major exchanges: the Chicago Board of Trade (CBOT) and the Chicago Mercantile Exchange (CME).

In the early 1970s, both exchanges were anxious to expand their business and were looking for new contracts to trade. In true Chicago style they competed vigorously with each other. In 1972, the CME created the first financial futures contract to trade futures on seven major currencies.

In 1973, the CBOT began trading option contracts on individual stocks. These were the first derivatives to be based on financial assets rather than agricultural commodities.

In 1975 the CBOT introduced its US Treasury bond futures contract, which was to become one of the most active exchange-traded contracts in the world. The bond futures contract enabled corporations to protect themselves against future interest rate movements.

As we have indicated, other factors contributed to the rapid growth in derivatives. In the last 25 years there has been a global expansion in trade due to the relaxation of trade restrictions. Financial markets have been deregulated, especially in Europe and Asia, and cross-border transactions in the basic securities have expanded enormously. For the US, these transactions rose from 4% of GDP in 1975 to 230% by 1998. Other industrialised countries show similar rates of growth during this period. In Germany, for example, cross-border transactions grew from 5% of GDP in 1975 to 334% in 1998.[1]

Advances in information technology and developments in electronic communication mean that vast amounts of data can now be stored very efficiently and transmitted quickly and inexpensively to almost any corner of the globe. These advances in technology have reduced trading costs and lowered the cost of innovation.

In turn this has made it easier to create new types of derivatives. The basic instruments such as standard calls and puts are often termed plain vanilla derivatives. The more complex instruments are sometimes termed exotic derivatives. Later in this chapter, we will describe some of the fascinating new types of derivatives that have been introduced in recent years.

Sometimes a legal restriction can impede innovation and its removal can open the way for the development of new contracts. There is an interesting example of this that led to the growth of financial derivatives. In 1982, the CME introduced the first cash-settled futures contract and this paved the way for an extension of the futures concept to a whole new range of assets. The idea behind the cash settled futures contract is that instead of delivering the underlying asset, the two parties settle the contract by exchanging cash at the delivery date. The first contract with this feature was the CME's Eurodollar futures contract. Cash settlement of futures contracts would have been illegal had they been subject to Illinois state law because they would have been classified as "gambles". However the Commodity Futures and Trading Commission (CFTC), set up in 1974 as the sole regulator of futures contracts, sanctioned the use of this concept. This change in the way that derivative contracts could be settled has had profound implications for the expansion of the market.

We can get a sense of how important this development was if we hypothesise a world where only physical settlement is permitted. For example, consider how we would organise the settlement procedure for an option based on the Standard & Poor's 500 Stock Index. This index corresponds to a portfolio of the common stocks of 500 of the most important firms in the US. Suppose that an option to buy this index could only be settled by physical delivery. In this case, when the option is exercised, the seller of the call would have to deliver to the buyer a physical portfolio that consisted of the entire 500 stocks that made up the index. This would be so inefficient as to be impractical. By settling in cash, the buyer of the option receives a cash amount that has the same value as the index portfolio.

Paradoxically, the existence of regulations can also increase the use of derivatives and provide a spur for financial innovation. Derivative instruments can be used to circumvent regulations or alter the impact of tax law. For example, in many countries there is a limit on the percentage of pension assets that can be invested in foreign securities. Options and futures contracts can be used to neutralise such regulations. We will see later in this chapter how the Ontario Teachers' Pension Plan Board used derivatives to change its asset mix without selling assets that it was required by law to hold.

THE OVER-THE-COUNTER MARKET

In the last chapter, we made the distinction between exchange-traded contracts and over-the-counter (OTC) contracts. Exchange-traded derivatives dominated the 1970s and 1980s but in the last decade the off-exchange or OTC market grew so quickly that it is now much larger than the exchange-traded market. Although the OTC market competes with the exchanges for some of the same business, the two markets have advantages for one another. An institution that writes OTC derivatives will often use an exchange-traded product to offset the risk that it has taken on. For example, a British insurance company might buy a five-year call option on the UK market from a Swiss investment bank to cover option features that it has included in its insurance contracts. This growth in demand can increase trading volumes in exchange-traded products. Moreover, the market prices available from the exchange-traded products provide valuable information for the pricing and risk management of the OTC products.

Sometimes products that start out as highly customised OTC instruments can evolve until they acquire many of the standardised features of exchange instruments. A standardised instrument with clearly specified contractual provisions on default, reduces uncertainty and lowers transaction costs. Interest rate swaps are prime examples. The first swaps were individually tailored agreements between two counterparties. The bid-ask spreads were huge.[2] As time passed, market participants saw the benefits of standardisation and, in particular, of having clear documentation to reduce uncertainty. It was important to reduce legal uncertainty because swaps can involve parties from different legal jurisdictions. Many swap contracts are now standardised and have many of the features of exchange-traded contracts. The bid-ask spreads have shrunk by a factor of 100 to one or two basis points.

The globalisation of the world economy has expanded the use of derivatives. The expansion of international trade has increased the foreign exchange risk in business transactions. Derivatives provide an efficient method of managing this risk. Moreover, equity investments have become much more international. Until 1985, equity investment in most countries took place mainly in the domestic market, with the UK and the Netherlands being notable exceptions. Since then there has been a marked increase in the volume of cross-border equity investment.

In the financial sector, there has also been a restructuring from domestic institutions to global entities. For example, Citigroup now conducts business in virtually every country in the world with interests in banking, insurance and investments. Citigroup was formed by the merger of Citicorp and Travelers Group in 1988. Citigroup is a very broad-based financial services organisation, being the parent company of Citibank, Commercial Credit, Primerica, Salomon Smith Barney, SSB Citi Asset Management Group, Travelers Life & Annuity, and Travelers Property. For such global institutions derivatives provide an efficient mechanism to structure deals to arrange financing and transfer risks.

The OTC derivatives market encourages the creation of new products and innovative contracts; new types of derivatives can be introduced to solve particular problems. However, such creations are more likely to flourish if they solve a generic problem. Such derivatives cover an expanding range of risks and new applications open up for various reasons. For example, there is now a worldwide trend towards deregulation in some industries that were once highly regulated, such as in the electricity industry.

DERIVATIVES AND POWER

Electricity is such an important commodity that governments have traditionally regulated the industry and controlled its price. Typically, the electricity supply for a given region was produced by a single entity. This could be either a state-owned enterprise or a privately owned regulated utility. The price of electricity was computed by a formula based on the utility's production costs with an allowance for profit.

In recent years there has been sweeping deregulation in this industry in many countries. The first country to deregulate electricity markets was Chile, in 1982. Since then deregulation has occurred in several countries in South America, Europe and in many regions of the US and Canada. The aim of these changes is to make the industry more competitive and efficient.

The stereotype of the traditional utility is of a sleepy, inefficient giant passing on its costs to the public. Under deregulation, the monopoly power of the single producer is abolished and a market is established for the supply of electricity. Under the new regime different producers bid to supply the power and this establishes a market price. It turns out that market prices for electricity are significantly more volatile than regulated prices. Hence, both producers of electricity and consumers are exposed to more price risk under the market regime than under the previous regime. New types of derivatives to buy (and sell) power have been created so that this price risk can be better managed.

When you switch on your washing machine, it begins to consume electricity because it taps into an electric current that is being generated by a central power source at a central power plant. If you turn up your air conditioner during a hot and muggy summer day you will use more electricity. We take the existence of the steady supply of power for granted, the price we pay is an average price based on the usage for the month. The total consumption for a given region is the sum of the usage by the households and industries in that region. This consumption varies considerably by time of day, by the season of the year and also with the vagaries of the weather. The total consumption level at a given time represents the total demand for electricity and traditionally this demand is not very sensitive to price.

Electricity cannot be stored and so it has to be produced in sufficient quantities to meet this demand. The electricity is produced at generating facilities and the production involves turning some energy source into electricity.

The supply of electricity is related to the cost of producing it and this cost depends on the technology used to generate it. Once the facilities are in place the costs of producing electricity using nuclear power, coal and hydro power are stable and do not increase much as capacity is increased. Of course, there is an upper limit to the amount these plants can produce. Gas and oil tend to be more expensive and when the system is operating near full capacity it is becomes very expensive to produce additional units of electricity using these fuels. The total amount of electricity produced at a given price is called the aggregate supply. The total supply is not very sensitive to price when the system is not producing at full capacity. However, the total amount of electricity supplied to the market becomes highly sensitive to the price when the system is operating at full capacity. At the higher levels of production the supply becomes inelastic.

Forward contracts on electricity have become very important as soon as the electricity industry becomes deregulated because they can be used to manage price risk. A forward contract to buy electricity is an agreement, made today, to buy a certain amount of power over some future period at a fixed price. The price to be paid for the power is fixed today so that it is locked in at the outset. By entering the forward contract to buy the electricity a firm can guarantee a certain supply of electricity at a guaranteed price.

Power failure

This background will help us understand what happened in California in the winter of 2000. When electricity was deregulated in 1996, the state's investor-owned utilities were compelled to sell their power plants and buy wholesale power. However to protect consumers the law put a cap on the prices they could charge their customers. Throughout the 1990s, California had underinvested in new power plants and transmission lines and during this same time, the state's economy was booming, putting increasing demands on power consumption. By the end of the decade a number of factors had pushed the market price of electricity in California to unprecedented heights. The state's two largest utilities, Southern California Edison and Pacific Gas & Electric Co, teetered on the verge of bankruptcy.

The market price of electricity in California rose because of both demand and supply factors. The summer of 2000 was one of the hottest on record with low rainfall in the west and northwest of the United States. The hot weather increased the demand for power and the low rainfall meant that the availability of hydro-electric power was reduced. This was followed by one of the coldest winters on record: November 2000 was the coldest November nationwide since 1911. The cold winter increased the demand for power. Since there had been very little new generation added in California, Washington and Oregon, the supply was not on hand to meet the increased demand. To make matters worse, well-intentioned environmental legislation restricted the full use of power generation in the region. The confluence of these factors meant that both scheduled and unscheduled power cuts were common.

With hindsight, it is clear that deregulation could have been introduced in a more sensible way. One of the advantages of deregulation is that the market price provides a signal that helps to reduce demand and also bring new production on line. Why did this not happen in California? One of the reasons is that the existence of price caps can distort these signals. As a recent report noted:[3]

In addition, price caps that protect consumers from the signals of higher spot prices do not create any incentive to reduce demand, leading to higher costs in the long run. Price caps will also deter new entry at a time when new entry is the essential to long term solution. Finally, price caps could reinforce any reluctance of California or other states to deal with long term solutions. The existence of the price caps would not have been such a problem had the utilities been able to reduce the risk by hedging it. The natural vehicle here is a fixed-price forward contract. If the utilities had bought electricity in the forward market they could have locked in a price for their power. Forward contracts are efficient risk-management tools for handling a price cap but surprisingly, the California utilities were not allowed to enter long-term forward contracts. As the Federal Energy Regulatory Commission (Ferc) report notes: "The primary flaw in the market rules in California was the prohibition on forward contracts, and the primary remedy is the re-establish-ment of forward contracts".

Elsewhere the Ferc staff report comments:

If California had negotiated forward contracts last summer, or even last fall, it is likely that billions of dollars would have been saved and its two largest utilities might not be facing bankruptcy today.

THE BASIC PRODUCTS

To describe derivatives it is useful to classify them systematically. This can be achieved in different ways. We can classify derivatives:

❑ by type of instrument based on the payoff structure of the contract; or
❑ according to the underlying risk or risks on which the payoff is based.

In this section we start with very basic contracts and then move on to more complex derivatives.

Digital options

The first type of derivative we consider is a digital option where the payoff is either a fixed amount or zero. The payoff depends upon whether the terminal asset price exceeds the strike price or is less than the strike price. For example, a digital call option might pay 100 in three months provided that ABC stock is above 110 at that time. In this case the strike price is 110 and if the terminal asset price is less than 110 at that time, the call pays zero. The corresponding digital put option pays 100 in three months provided that ABC stock is below 110 in three months.

Figure 2.1 shows how the payoff on a digital call option at maturity varies with the price of the asset at maturity. The terminal asset price is plotted on the horizontal axis and the option payoff is plotted on the vertical. Note that the payoff is zero as long as the terminal asset price is below 110. As soon as the terminal asset price rises above 110, the option payoff becomes 100. Figure 2.2 shows how the payoff on the corre-sponding digital put option at maturity varies with the price of the asset at maturity. Note that the payoff is 100 as long as the terminal asset price is below 110. As soon as the terminal asset price rises above 110, the option payoff becomes zero.

Figure 2.3 shows that if we combine these two digital options we get a very simple payoff. The combined package produces a payoff of 100 in three months no matter what happens to the price of the underlying asset. Therefore, the two digital options can be combined to produce a risk-free bond that matures in three months. These two digital options combine like two interlocking pieces of Lego.

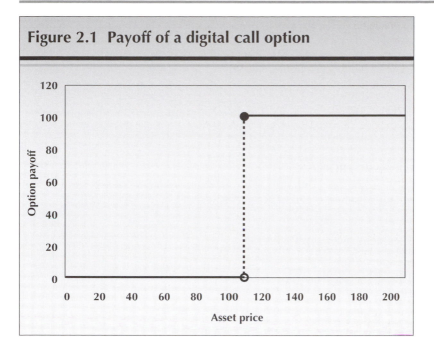

Figure 2.1 Payoff of a digital call option

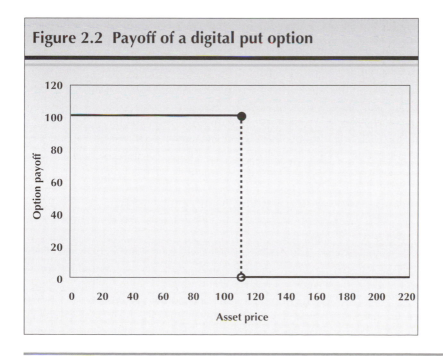

Figure 2.2 Payoff of a digital put option

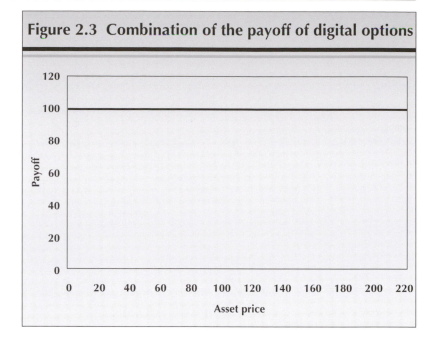

Figure 2.3 Combination of the payoff of digital options

Standard options

Next, we consider a standard or plain vanilla European option. We have already discussed this type of option in Chapter 1. First, we deal with call options. In this case the payoff at maturity is equal to the difference between the terminal asset price and the strike price if this difference is positive. For example, if the strike price is 110 and the option matures in three months then the call payoff is positive if the asset price is above 110 in three months. Otherwise the payoff is zero. Figure 2.4 shows how the payoff on the call varies with the terminal asset price.

Figure 2.5 gives another way of showing how the payoff on a call option is related to the history of the asset price. In this case we plot time along the horizontal axis. The two jagged lines represent two possible paths of the asset price. We see that one path gives a terminal asset price that is greater than the strike price. For this path the call has a positive value at maturity. The second path ends up with a terminal asset price that is less than the strike price. For this path the call is worth zero at maturity.

Now we deal with European put options. In this case the payoff at maturity is equal to the difference between the strike price and the terminal asset price as long as this difference is positive. For example, if the strike price is 110 and the option matures in three months then the put payoff is zero if the asset price is above 110 in three months. The put has a positive payoff if the terminal asset price is below the strike price. Figure 2.6 shows how the payoff on the put varies with the terminal asset price.

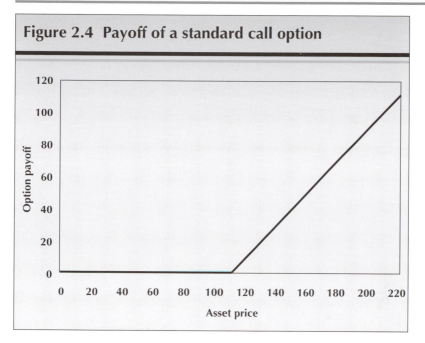

Figure 2.4 Payoff of a standard call option

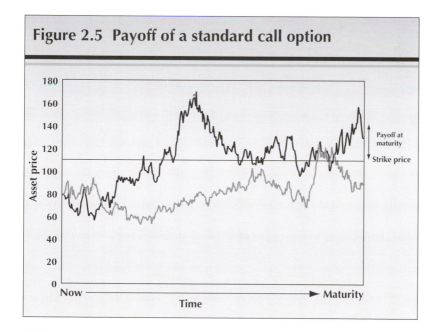

Figure 2.5 Payoff of a standard call option

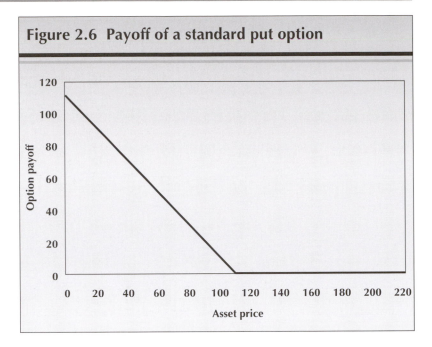

Figure 2.6 Payoff of a standard put option

Figure 2.7 shows how the payoff on the put option is related to the history of the asset price. In this case we plot time along the horizontal axis. As before, the two jagged lines represent two possible paths of the asset price. We see that the path marked in bold gives a terminal asset price that is greater than the strike price. For this path, the put is worth zero at maturity. The second path ends up with a terminal asset price that is less than the strike price. In this case the put payoff is positive and equal to the difference between them.

Straddles

The basic contracts can be packaged together to produce different payoff profiles. One of these combines a basic European call and the corresponding European put. The two option contracts are based on the same underlying asset and have the same strike price. An investor who purchases this package is said to be "long a straddle". This position has a payoff profile similar to that given in Figure 2.8. The payoff increases as the terminal asset price moves away from the strike price. On the other hand, an institution that sells this particular package is said to be "short a straddle". The profit profile in this case is displayed in Figure 2.9.[4] This position loses money for big asset moves; the larger the move the more is lost. We will see in Chapter 9 how Nick Leeson managed to lose a great deal of money using straddles.

Figure 2.7 Payoff of a standard put option

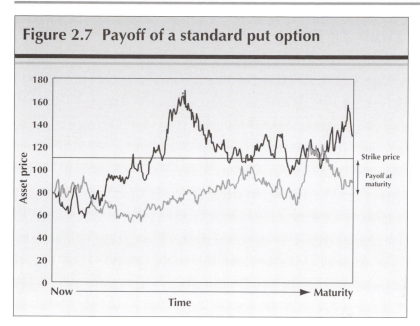

Figure 2.8 Payoff of a long straddle

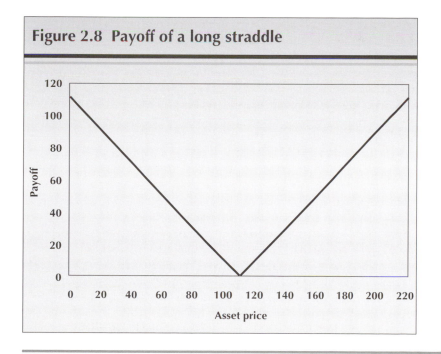

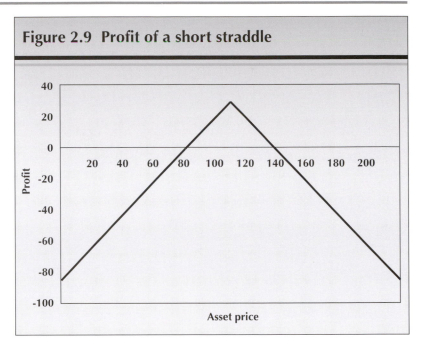

Figure 2.9 Profit of a short straddle

Lookback options

In a standard option the strike price is fixed and the price used to determine the contract value at maturity is the asset price at maturity.[5] We can create new contracts by extending these features. For example, the strike price need not be fixed but can be based on the actual price path of the asset. In the same way, the price used to compute the option value need not be restricted to the terminal asset price but can be related to the values taken by the asset over some time.

In a lookback option, the payoff at maturity is based upon the highest (or lowest) asset price realised over the term of the contract. The maturity payoff on a lookback call option is equal to the difference between the highest asset price, realised over the life of the option and the final asset price. In theory, the asset price could be observed at each instant to calculate its highest or lowest value although in practice this monitoring is carried out at periodic intervals. The prices could be observed daily or weekly or at any other specified time interval. Figure 2.10 illustrates how the payoff on a lookback call option is determined for a particular asset price path given by the jagged line. The maximum realised asset price is denoted by the horizontal line at the top of the figure. The maturity payoff is given by the distance between the two arrowheads on the right-hand side of the graph.

A lookback put option receives a payoff equal to the difference between

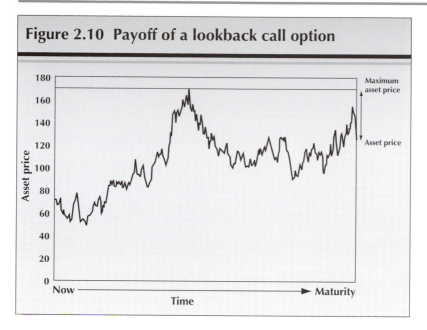

Figure 2.10 Payoff of a lookback call option

the final asset price and the lowest asset price realised during the life of the option. Figure 2.11 illustrates a lookback put option for a particular asset price path given by the jagged line. The minimum realised asset price is denoted by the horizontal line near the bottom of the diagram. The maturity payoff is given by the distance between the two arrowheads on the right-hand side of the diagram.

There is an investment maxim that advises investors to "buy high and sell low". Of course the problem with this advice is to figure out when the market is high and when it is low. With lookback options it would appear that investors now have the tools to realise this dream. However, the prices charged for these contracts will reflect their value, and therefore lookback options tend to be relatively expensive. As is often the case in life, you do have to pay for what you get.

Bermudan and American options

We mentioned the distinction between European options and American options in Chapter 1. The owner of a European option can buy or sell the asset for the strike price when the option matures. In contrast, the owner of an American option can buy or sell the asset for the strike price at any time during the life of the option contract. These terms continue to confuse the beginner because any traces of a geographic association that might have existed have been washed away.

A Bermudan option lies midway between a European option and an

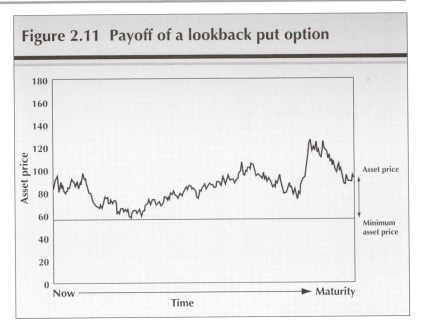

Figure 2.11 Payoff of a lookback put option

American option. The owner of a Bermudan call option can buy the underlying asset for the strike price on any one of a fixed number of dates during the term of the option contract. Similarly, the owner of a Bermudan put option has the right to sell the asset for the strike price on any one of a fixed number of dates during the term of the option.

Asian options

In an Asian option the payoff at maturity is based not on the asset price at maturity but on the average of asset prices over a specific time interval. This average can be formed by using daily, weekly or monthly observations. Suppose we have an Asian call option with a strike price of 100 and that the four prices that make up the average are 92, 135, 131 and 130. The average of these four prices is 122 and so the payoff of the contract at maturity is 22. Figure 2.12 shows the price path that generates these prices. The fact that Asian options are based on the average of the asset prices over a period makes them well suited to hedge periodic transactions. For example, a firm that has regular transactions in a foreign currency can use Asian options to hedge this risk. This is because when the firm converts its revenues from its foreign operations into its home currency, it does so based on the average exchange rate. In Chapter 6 we will explain how Microsoft uses Asian options to hedge its foreign currency risks.

The Asian option we have just described, has a fixed strike price and its payoff is based on the average of the asset prices over the term of the

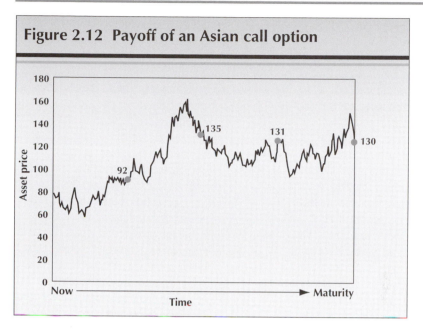

Figure 2.12 Payoff of an Asian call option

contract. This type of Asian option is termed a fixed-strike Asian option. In contrast, under a floating-strike Asian option the strike price is based on the average of the asset prices taken during the term of the contract. Suppose we have a floating-strike Asian call option with the four prices that make up the strike price as follows: 92, 135, 131 and 130. In this case the floating-strike price is 122 (the average) and the payoff at maturity under this contract is 8. This is because the payoff is equal to the difference between the final asset price (130) and the average (122).

Barrier options

Another extension of the standard contract occurs when the payoff depends upon whether or not the asset price crosses a particular level or barrier during the life of the option. These contracts are called barrier options and come in many varieties. The criteria to define the crossing of the barrier must be set out carefully in the contract specifications. This is because there can be incentives for dealers to deliberately push the asset price across the barrier.[6] The barrier may be monitored continuously or discretely. The practice in foreign currency options is to use continuous monitoring whereas the convention in most other markets is to use discrete monitoring.

There are various forms of barrier options. For instance a knock-out option is a barrier option that behaves like a standard option as long as the asset price does not cross the barrier during the life of the option. If the asset price crosses the barrier the option expires, which is why it is called a knock-out option. If the barrier is set below the starting asset price, it is a down-and-out option. Figure 2.13 shows how the payoff on a down-and-out call is computed for two particular price paths. If the asset price does not cross the barrier (the bolder line) during the life of the contract the option is never knocked out and it has a terminal payoff just like a standard call option. In the case of the other price path, the barrier is breached (barely) and the option expires worthless. If the barrier is set above the starting asset price it is an up-and-out option.

A knock-in option is an option that becomes activated if the asset price crosses the barrier. If the price crosses the barrier the contract behaves like a standard option contract. A down-and-in option is a knock-in option where the barrier is below the initial asset price. An up-and-in option is a knock-in option where the barrier is above the initial asset price.

A package consisting of an up-and-out call plus the corresponding up-and-in call has the exact same payoff at maturity as a standard call. Hence, the price of the package must be equal to the price of a standard call. We can view these two barrier options as a standard call divided into two parts. Each of these parts is worth something so the price of an up-and-in call is less than the price of the standard call. Barrier options are therefore cheaper than their plain vanilla counterparts.

Barrier options may be used to take account of specific aspects of a firm's hedging requirements. For example, an airline might be concerned that a deterioration in the political situation in the Middle East might drive up

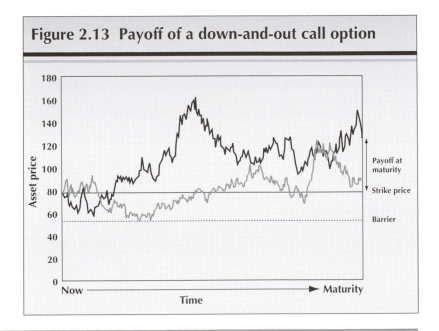

Figure 2.13 Payoff of a down-and-out call option

the price of fuel. If the firm buys an up-and-in call option on oil where the barrier is set at a level beyond today's price, then the protection kicks in if there is an oil price hike above the barrier.

Spread options

So far, we have only considered derivatives on a single underlying asset. A whole new suite of products can be created if the payoff is based on two or more assets. With just two assets we can see the range of possibilities. The payoff could be based on any combination of the two assets, such as the average of their prices or the difference between their prices at maturity. The payoff could be based on some weighted combination of their prices such as 40% of the first asset plus 60% of the second asset. Other specifications include the maximum of the asset prices at maturity or the corresponding minimum. The possibilities are endless.

An option where the payoff is based on the difference between two prices is known as a spread option. These options have found applications in the energy industry. Oil refineries use crude oil as an input to produce heating oil, petrol and other products. Their profits depend on the difference between their costs and their output prices. The crack spread, which denotes the difference between the price of gasoline and the price of crude oil, is a measure of their profit margin. Crack-spread options are based on this difference and are natural hedging tools for oil refineries as they enable refineries to control their margins and stabilise their profits.

Basket options

Options that have a payoff based on the average or weighted average of several underlying assets are known as basket options. (An option on a stock market index is a good example of this.) The market value of the index at any time is a weighted average of the prices of its individual components. Basket options can include any given set of assets. For example, the basket could be based on the stock market indices of the so-called Group of Ten industrial countries.[7] Basket options are also used to hedge foreign currency risk. A company such as Microsoft has a significant part of its total revenue denominated in non-US dollar currencies. A basket (portfolio) of foreign currencies can be constructed to reflect Microsoft's forecast exposure to these currencies. The company can use options on this basket to hedge its exchange rate exposure.

Other options

New contracts can be constructed by splicing elements of these options together. For example, we can design a contract where the payoff is based on the most recent average of the asset prices and allows for early exercise. This hybrid contract is known as an American Asian option. We could also add a barrier feature as well. There is virtually no limit to the complexity of these instruments. However, the mutations that endure are those that fulfil some need or serve some economic purpose. The economic counterpart of Darwinian selection is at work.

FURTHER EXTENSIONS: DERIVATIVES BASED ON DERIVATIVES

We can also classify derivatives in terms of the underlying asset. At one time, the underlying assets were mainly agricultural commodities. Subsequently, derivatives were written on commodities such as precious metals. Derivatives are now written on a wide variety of assets and commodities. The possibilities expanded enormously with the introduction of derivatives on financial assets such as individual equities, stock market indices and bonds. New derivatives can also be created by "piggy-backing" on existing derivatives, eg, options written on futures; the range of applications is being extended all the time.

By writing an option on an interest rate swap, we create what is called a "swaption". We discussed swaps in Chapter 1 and interest rate swaps account for about one quarter of all derivatives contracts in terms of notional amounts. A swaption is a contract that gives its owner the option to enter an interest rate swap in the future. Swaptions are widely used by corporations and financial institutions to manage interest rate risk. We will give examples in Chapters 6 and 7, which explain how swaptions can be used to manage interest rate risk.

Sometimes options are added to, or embedded in, another derivative. For example, some futures contracts have additional options embedded in the contract. A futures contract to deliver a commodity, grain for example, commits the long position to buy the grain and the short position to sell the grain under the terms of the contract. If the terms of the futures contract specify that the grain can be delivered at one of a number of locations, the contract is said to contain a *location option*. If the terms of the contract specify that one of several different grades of grain can be delivered to fulfil the contract, it is said to contain a *quality option*. These options are known as delivery options. For example, the US bond futures contract, traded on CBOE, permits the short position to deliver any one of a set of US government bonds. These options provide additional flexibility to the party that has to deliver the commodity (or asset).[8]

TRANSFORMING TEACHERS

The Ontario Teachers' Pension Plan provides a striking example of how derivatives can be used in innovative ways to reduce risk and increase return. This plan provides retirement pensions for teachers in Ontario. It is one of the largest public pension plans in Canada with total assets (in 2000) of C$70 billion. Before 1990, the plan was only allowed to invest in non-marketable securities issued by the government of Ontario. These securities provided funds for building highways and other government projects.

All the assets of the pension plan were in the same type of security so there was no diversification and no exposure to common stocks. In 1990, the plan's assets only covered 85% of its liabilities. There was a shortfall of C$3.6 billion between the assets it held and what the plan required to meet its promised benefits. The plan was in very poor shape; it had a large deficit and its investments were not diversified.

In 1990, the management of the fund was privatised with the appointment of the Ontario Teachers' Pension Plan Board, a new chief executive officer Claude Lamoureux was also hired to manage the plan. Under his leadership, the plan's asset mix was transformed and derivatives played an important role in this transformation. By law, the plan was not allowed to sell its Ontario debentures. However, the fixed-rate coupons on these debentures could be effectively transformed into floating-rate payments using interest rate swaps.

The Teachers' Plan swapped the fixed income from its Ontario debentures for floating-rate income. Then the floating-rate payments were swapped in exchange for the returns on equity indices. These equity swaps enabled the plan to cleverly (and legally) circumvent the foreign content restrictions of the Canadian Federal Income Tax Act.[9] By the end of 1999, the surplus in the plan had grown to C$9 billion and the effective asset mix contained 65% equities.

The Ontario Teachers' Plan 1999 annual report explains why the plan is an active user of derivatives:[10]

> Derivative contracts play a large part in our investments programs. We use derivatives for active or index equity investing in the US, internationally and in Canada because they are a quicker and cheaper way to gain market exposure and rebalance our portfolios than buying actual stocks. Using derivatives also minimises market disruption. As a result, we are one of Canada's largest traders of equity based futures and options.
>
> Derivatives enable us to manage interest rate risk and foreign exchange volatility through swaps, forwards futures and options. They also help us to ensure that all assets contribute fully to total returns.

The Teachers' Pension Plan is an example of a derivatives story with a happy ending, in contrast with the widely publicised disaster stories.

CONCLUSION

In the first part of this chapter we saw that the derivatives revolution was the result of the convergence of some very powerful influences. The initial rapid growth of derivatives took place on the exchanges but the OTC markets later surpassed this. The exchanges have developed effective ways to control default risk and provide transparency, whereas the OTC market is more creative and flexible in coming up with new concepts and product ideas. Each market covets the advantages of the other: the OTC market would benefit from more transparency and better credit protection whereas the derivatives exchanges would like more flexibility to expand their operations into new markets. The two market structures benefit each another: we have seen that innovations in one market can stimulate expansion in the other. Both markets have been fertile incubators of new ideas.

The second part of this chapter described the main types of derivative. A useful way to classify derivatives is to start with the simplest type of contract design. More complex designs are created by generalising different aspects of this simple contract. Another way to classify derivatives is in terms of the underlying asset, and on this basis, too, the scope of the market has increased. We noted the power of these instruments to generate new products by combining different concepts in a more complex security. Finally, we explained how the Ontario Teachers' Pension Plan used derivatives to reinvent itself.

1   Bank of International Settlements' 69th Annual Report. May 1999, (Basle: Switzerland).
2   The bid-ask spread is the difference between what the investor can buy the security for and the price at which they can sell the security. Market markers charge a spread in order to pay for their operations.
3   Response of the Staff of the Ferc to Questions Posed at December 20, 2000 Western Governors Association Denver Meeting, http://www.ferc.fed.us/electric/bulkpower.htm.
4   Figure 2.9 shows how the profit on a short straddle position depends on the asset price when the position matures. If a trader enters a short straddle, they receive cash, representing the prices of the call option and the put option that make up the straddle. Their profit is largest when the asset price, at maturity, is equal to the strike price of the two options because in this case, they do not have to make any payments at maturity. Figure 2.9 shows that the position loses money if the asset price at maturity is far away from the strike price. Incidentally, Figure 2.9 is not the exact image of 2.8 as 2.9 shows the profit on the position and Figure 2.8 only shows the payoff at maturity.
5   Lookback options were first proposed in 1979 by Goldman, Sosin and Gatto.
6   For a discussion of the importance of defining the barrier event see Hsu (1997).
7   There are actually 11 countries in the Group of Ten (G10). They are: Belgium, Canada, France, Germany, Italy, Japan, the Netherlands, Sweden, Switzerland, the United Kingdom and the United States.
8   In the late 1990s, these delivery terms have been modified in response to strong pressure from the futures regulator. On 19 December 1996, the Commission formally notified the exchange of its findings that the delivery terms of the corn and soybean contracts no longer accomplished the statutory objectives of permitting delivery at such delivery points and differentials as would tend to prevent or diminish price manipulation, market congestion or the abnormal movement of the commodities in interstate commerce.
9   These restrictions limited the amount of foreign (non-Canadian) equities in the plan.
10 Ontario Teachers'Pension Plan Board, 1999 Annual Report. URL: http://www.otpp.com/web/website.nsf/web/annualreport.

3

Why There Are No Free Lunches

The idea that there are no free lunches – that you cannot get something for nothing – is critical in pricing derivatives. If we have two investments that have the same payoffs in the future then they must sell at the same price. If this were not the case then it would give rise to a very simple way to make a risk-free profit. Such opportunities do not exist (or only exist fleetingly) in financial markets.

This idea accords well with our experience and intuition. Financial economists refer to the "no-free-lunch" idea as the *no-arbitrage* principle. Roughly, it states that you cannot make a sure profit if you start with an empty wallet. Arbitrage exists if we can make sure profits with no risk and no money down. The no-free-lunch/no-arbitrage idea is one of the cornerstones of modern finance theory.

MARTINA HINGIS VERSUS VENUS WILLIAMS

We will use a tennis match to understand how the no-arbitrage principle works. Suppose that in three months Martina Hingis is to play Venus Williams. You make a bet today with a bookmaker that Venus Williams will win the match. If Williams wins the match you will receive US$100, however, if Hingis wins the match you will receive nothing.

Your best friend also makes a bet with the same bookmaker that Hingis will win the match. If she wins your friend will receive US$100, but if Williams wins your friend is out of luck and will get nothing. If you paid US$60 for your wager and your friend paid US$39, the bookmaker collects a total of US$99.

If the bookmaker can invest this money in a government security known as a Treasury bill[1] so that after three months it will grow into US$100, they carry no risk. Irrespective of who wins the tennis match, the bookmaker has just enough money to cover the winning bet.

The package consisting of the two bets, has exactly the same payoff in three months as the three-month Treasury bill. The payoffs are exactly matched. Both the betting strategy and the investment have the same initial cost (US$99) and yield the same payoff in three months' time.

This is an illustration of the no-arbitrage principle, which implies that two investment strategies that have the same payoffs in the future should have the same current prices.

If the bookmaker just charges at these prices they will not make any money but will not lose any money either. In the real world, a bookmaker would add on something to the cost of the bets to make a profit on the transaction. If they add on too much then their competitors could undercut them by charging lower prices and they could still make a profit. Thus, competition will drive the prices down but there is clearly a limit. The total amount charged for the two bets should be at least US$99, otherwise the bookmaker will definitely lose money. We see that, in this example, there is a range for the sum of the prices of the two bets. The lower limit of this range, US$99, is established by the bookmaker's desire not to lose money and the upper limit is determined by competition. As the market becomes more competitive the difference between these two limits becomes smaller.

We can modify the example so that the bets on the outcome of the tennis match are more like traded financial securities. The Venus Williams (VW) security is a contract that entitles its owner to US$100 if Williams wins the tennis match and zero otherwise. Similarly, the Hingis (MH) security is a financial instrument that pays US$100 if Hingis wins and zero otherwise. We also assume that both of these securities are publicly traded with their current market prices readily available on the Internet. The University of Iowa Business School operates an electronic market of this type, where investors can buy and sell securities whose contract payoffs depend on future events such as the outcome of political elections.[2]

In such a market the forces of supply and demand determine the price. If the two tennis securities are traded on an electronic market, we will have market prices for each security at every instant. The no-arbitrage principle gives us the total of these two prices.

If an investor buys both tennis securities the package will produce a certain payoff of US$100 in three months. They could also obtain a sure payoff of US$100 in three months by buying a three-month Treasury bill. This portfolio of the two tennis securities has exactly the same payoff as the three-month Treasury bill. The no-arbitrage principle tells that the current price of the package of the two tennis securities has to be equal to the price of the Treasury bill.

The reason why the no-arbitrage principle holds is that if it did not hold, an investor could make certain profits with no risk and no money down. To see this, suppose that the current price of the VW security is US$60 and the current price of the MH security is US$20, so that the combined price of the pair is US$80. At these prices an investor can make sure profits.

Here is the strategy. First, she sells the Treasury bill short. Let us explain what selling short means. When an investor sells an asset short they sell it today for its market price with the promise that they will buy it back in the future. When they sell the Treasury bill short they receive US$99 but they promise to buy it back in three months for its then market price (US$100).

The short sale means that the investor has US$99 available for immediate investment but has made a commitment to pay US$100 in three months.

The investor is now positioned to make money on the two tennis securities. They buy both securities for a total cost of US$80, leaving them with an immediate profit of US$19. Now they own the two tennis securities and, because one of the players has to win, this package will pay US$100 in three months. These proceeds will be just enough to cover the US$100 that they must pay to liquidate their short position in the Treasury bill. The investor has made a sure profit of US$19 and arranged affairs so that the cashflows they will receive in the future are exactly enough to cover the amount they have to pay. At these market prices our investor has made a clear profit of US$19 without having to risk a single cent of their own. However, we assert this cannot happen due to the no-free-lunch rule.

Why are we confident that the free lunch opportunities won't exist in practice? Let us look at some of the implications of the above prices. Suppose that there actually was a free lunch and that the prices of the tennis securities were US$60 and US$20. What would happen? Investors would buy pairs of these securities because they are such an obvious good deal. If an investor purchased 10 pairs they would make US$190 and if they bought 100 pairs they would make US$1,900. Other market players would also see that this is a good money-making idea. There would be a rush to buy these securities and, as a consequence, the price would rise until the combined price of the two securities reached US$99 and, at this price, the incentive to buy the securities would disappear. If the combined price of the two tennis securities is US$99, then the strategy we described earlier will not yield a profit.

As long as the combined price is less than US$99 there is a free lunch to be had. Astute investors will queue up to buy. The no-free-lunch principle is an economic consequence of the actions of profit-seeking individuals. If a free lunch opportunity ever presents itself, investors will immediately eliminate it by their own actions in trying to exploit it. In financial markets there are many astute and sophisticated investors roving the finance landscape, seeking to make arbitrage profits.

The no-free-lunch principle can be applied to find the price of a security in terms of the prices of related securities. In the tennis example, the sum of the prices of the VW security and the MH security must be equal to the price of the Treasury bill. That means that if we know the price of any two of these, the no-free-lunch principle gives us the price of the third one. For example, the payoff on the MH security can be replicated using a combination of the Treasury bill and the VW security. The MH security has the same payoff as a long position in the Treasury bill and a short position in the VW security. This combination pays out zero if Williams wins because the inflow of US$100 from the bill is matched by the payment we have to make on the VW security. Should Hingis win, the combination has a total inflow of US$100 because there is no payment on the VW security in this case.

A numerical example shows how this works. Suppose the VW security trades for US$60 and the Treasury bill trades for US$99. We can work out that the MH security must sell for the difference: 99 – 60 = 39. If an investor were willing to sell the MH security for a different price, say US$30, we could make a sure profit. We would sell short the government bond, which gives us US$99 with a commitment to pay US$100 in three months. We then buy the MH security for US$30 and the VW security for US$60. The total cost is US$90 but we have US$99 on hand so there is US$9 left. In three months, one of them will win and so we will collect US$100. This is exactly enough to cover the US$100 we owe on the Treasury bill. At these prices we can make a sure profit of US$9 on the strategy. It looks too good to be true and it is. This argument demonstrates that the price of the MH security cannot be less than US$39.

We can also show that the price of the MH security cannot be greater than US$39 if the VW security trades for US$60 and the bill price is US$99. For example, suppose investors are willing to buy the MH security for US$41. We can make a sure profit at these prices. We sell both tennis securities, producing a total inflow of US$101. We use US$99 to buy the Treasury bill. The bill costs US$99 but we have US$101 available so there is US$2 left. In three months we will receive US$100 from the bill and this is exactly enough to make the payoff on the winning security. So, at these prices we can make a profit of US$2 on each transaction. The same logic as before shows the price of the MH security cannot be *greater* than US$39. It was shown above that the price of the MH security cannot be less than US$39. Hence, the price has to be exactly US$39.

REPLICATION

The technique of mimicking the payoff of a particular instrument using a package of other securities is known as *replication* and it plays a key role in derivatives pricing – for example in the Black–Scholes–Merton model of option pricing.[3] We will see in Chapter 4 that we can replicate the payoff on a European call option using a package consisting of the underlying stock and a bond.[4] The no-free-lunch principle dictates that if this package pays off the same amount as the call option at maturity then it must have the same current price as the call option.

The process of replicating the payoff from one security by using a combination of other related securities is also known as *hedging*. The concepts of hedging and pricing are intertwined. Indeed, the only derivatives that we can price using the no-free-lunch principle are those that we can also hedge.

Another consequence of the no-free-lunch principle is that the value of a package must be equal to the sum of the individual parts. We can apply this idea to public companies whose shares are traded on exchanges like the New York Stock Exchange. A company's balance sheet consists of the things it owns (its real assets) and the things it owes to other claimants (its financial liabilities). Examples of real assets would be real estate, factories and computers. Common stocks and bonds represent the most common types of financial liabilities. If a rich investor buys all the common stock and all the bonds he will own the company outright. If the market value of the stock is US$100 million and the market value of the bonds is also US$100 million then the no-free-lunch principle tells us that the market value of the assets should also be US$200 million. If it happened that the market value of the assets was US$250 million, then a wealthy investor could buy the entire company for US$200 million and sell off the assets at their market value of US$250 million, making a profit of US$50 million. This would be a whale of a free lunch.

The same idea lies at the heart of an important concept in finance: in a perfect world, the relative amounts of stock and bonds that a firm uses do not affect the market value of the firm. It is conventional to refer to stock as equity and bonds as debt. Stockholders and bondholders differ significantly in their relationship with the company. Stockholders jointly own the company. The price they pay for their stocks is the price of buying a little piece of the company. Owners of bonds are creditors. This means that they have lent money to the company that the company must repay according to some agreed schedule. The mix of common stock and equity and debt is called the firm's *capital structure*.

Merton Miller and Franco Modigliani, provided the first clear demonstration that a firm's capital structure does not affect its market value – in other words, that a firm could *not* change its total market value by changing the relative amounts of its common shares. However, for this result to be true, there must be no taxes or bankruptcies. In the real world of course, we do have taxes and firms can (and sometimes do) go under. It is very common in financial economics to make simplifying assumptions like these. We know that the precise conditions required for the Miller–Modigliani law are not found in the real world, but the result does provide a useful benchmark. This notion of the irrelevance of capital structure has been very influential in corporate finance and it helped earn Miller and Modigliani the 1985 Nobel Prize in economics.[5]

ARBITRAGE AND TRANSACTION COSTS

The no-arbitrage result stems from the insight that two identical items should trade for the same price. Sometimes, however, even if the items are identical there are other factors that can cause price differences.

To illustrate this we use an example from a Seinfeld episode called *The Bottle Deposit*.[6] This story features two characters in the series: Kramer and Newman. Kramer has noticed that the refund on empty pop cans is 10 cents in Michigan as opposed to 5 cents in New York. He reasons that if he could arrange to collect enough cans in New York and transport them to Michigan he would make a bundle. Kramer decides to involve Newman in the scheme. In true Seinfeld fashion, nothing ends up happening. Kramer's grand plan does not take account of the trouble and hassle involved. In other words, he does not allow for the expenses – usually termed transaction costs in finance. These are costs involved in getting the cans to Michigan. Normally these would include the truck rental, petrol and payment to the driver of the truck. There is also the labour involved. Kramer tries to reduce these costs through devious schemes with his accomplice Newman. However, there is still no free lunch even in Seinfeld's world.

We can see that if the costs of doing this deal are low the disparity in prices will not grow too high. For example, if cans collected on the Upper West Side of New York City around Columbia University could be sold for 50 cents more in Time Square this situation would not persist very long. In this case the distance is about four miles and the price differential is quite high. The Kramers and the Newmans would take action to exploit this price difference. The transaction costs are relatively low and the actions of arbitrageurs would force the price difference to come down. Used cans in the Upper West Side would become more sought after and their price would increase. The demand for cans in Time Square would also fall. Profit-seeking agents would eliminate the price difference.

The Kramer-Newman story indicates that price differences can exist and we can still have the no-free-lunch result. If there are no costs involved in exploiting a price difference then the price difference will quickly disappear. However, if there are transaction costs involved (getting a mail van, driving to Michigan, petrol, lost work opportunity), then the amount of the price difference will correspond to the transaction costs incurred in arranging the deal. Indeed, the agent with the lowest level of transaction costs will determine the size of the price difference. This person can still exploit the arbitrage opportunity if they make a profit after carrying out the deal and accounting for all the associated costs. The price will quickly settle at the level where there is no free lunch (arbitrage) for anyone after all the costs are factored in.

In financial markets the transaction costs, such as commissions and other expenses associated with trading, have come down considerably in recent years. These costs are very low for large financial institutions and their trading actions ensure that market prices do not provide any arbitrage opportunities except for a fleeting instant.

THE FOREIGN EXCHANGE MARKET
One of the most efficient financial markets is the foreign exchange market. The largest foreign exchange markets consist of the leading currencies such as the US dollar, the Japanese yen and the euro. For large institutions

such as banks and investment houses, the dealing costs in these markets are extremely low.

If a US investor converts US$100 into Canadian dollars and then exchanges the Canadian currency for French francs and finally converts the French francs back into US dollars, this strategy should not generate profits. If we know the exchange rate between the US dollar and the Canadian dollar and the exchange rate between the Canadian dollar and the French franc, this fixes the exchange rate between the French franc and the US dollar. For example, if US$1 is worth C$1.50 and C$1 is worth Ffr4 then Ffr6 must be worth US$1 (1.50 × 4). The investor who started with US$100 will receive C$150, which in turn is worth Ffr600. To avoid arbitrage, these French francs must be worth US$100 so the exchange rate is Ffr6 to US$1. If the exchange rate in the last step was Ffr5 to the US dollar, the Ffr600 would be converted into US$120 and in one round trip the investor would make a clear profit of US$20.

This result tells us that exchange rates are free of arbitrage. We see that if we start with one dollar and exchange it through a sequence of currencies and back to dollars, then in the absence of any trading costs we must get back exactly one dollar. Unless this happens we can obtain a free lunch. The Frenchman Augustin Cournot (1801–77) gave the first statement of this result in 1838.[7] Cournot's conclusion was that if we transform one unit of the home currency around any circular path of other currencies back to our home currency we get exactly one unit of our own currency, if and only if, there is no arbitrage. The exchange rates are arbitrage-free if their product around any cycle equals one. This gives rise to the term "Cournot cycle".

ARROW–DEBREU SECURITIES

The tennis securities that we discussed earlier are examples of contracts named after Kenneth Arrow and Gerald Debreu. Arrow and Debreu shared the 1974 economics Nobel Prize for their work in the economics of uncertainty. *An Arrow-Debreu security pays one unit if and when a certain event occurs and zero if this event does not occur.* The VW security is equivalent to a portfolio of 100 Arrow–Debreu securities based on the event that Williams wins the match. Arrow–Debreu securities are the most fundamental building blocks in finance. We can combine them into packages or portfolios to perfectly replicate the payments on any derivative.

Arrow–Debreu securities can be used to replicate the payoff on a European put option – the right to sell an underlying security at the end of the period. Consider a put option written on the Dow Jones Industrial Average Index (DJIA) with one month to maturity. At the time of writing, the Dow Jones level was around 11,000 but let us just take it to be 100 to simplify the numbers. Assume the strike price (the price at which the option is exercised) is US$100. If we buy the put today its value at maturity will depend on the index level at that time. If the index drops to 95 the put will be worth five; if the index drops to 50 it will be worth 50, but if the index finishes above 100 the put will expire worthless.

Assume there is a complete set of Arrow–Debreu securities corresponding to every level of the index, from 1 to 100 and higher. To make our example easier suppose the index level is only recorded at round numbers such as 50, 92, 95, 100. Security 92 pays one unit if the Dow Jones index is at 92 in one month and zero for other index levels. If the index does end up at 92 our put will then be worth eight and a package of eight units of Security 92 would also be worth eight if the index level were 92. There are in total, 100 index levels that lead to a positive put value at maturity. We can construct a package of Arrow-Debreu securities that will have precisely the same value as the put. This package consists of one unit of Security 99, two units of Security 98, three units of Security 97 and so on. This package will replicate the payoff on the put. By the no-arbitrage principle the current price of the package must be equal to the current price of the put option.

We pointed out in Chapter 1 that derivatives facilitate the transfer of risk. In this connection a complete set of basic Arrow–Debreu securities would provide a very extensive arsenal of tools for risk transfer. These securities would carve the risk up into its most elemental pieces. The tremendous amount of financial innovation that has taken place in the last 25 years is taking us closer to this goal but there are practical limitations on how far this division can proceed. If we chop the risk up too finely the price of the little pieces become too small and the costs of establishing and maintaining the market would be too high.

Prices and information security

The prices of Arrow–Debreu securities also provide information about how likely the market views a certain event. We have already referred to the Iowa market. The University of Iowa runs a market based on the outcome of the US presidential election. If it is more likely that a Democrat will win the White House the security that pays one dollar if the Democrat wins will be more valuable than the corresponding Republican security. Interestingly, these markets are better predictors of the results of elections than are public opinion polls. In our tennis example, if the VW security trades for more than the MH security, this means that the market believes that Williams has the better chance of winning the match.

Our tennis example also showed how the payoff pattern of a security could be replicated using other securities. The treasury bill and the package of the two tennis securities will both be worth US$100 in three month's time. The price of the package will remain equal to the price of the Treasury bill as time goes by. As time passes, the prices change but the prices will change in such a way as to preserve this relationship. Prices change as new information becomes available and the market incorporates this information into prices. For example, if it is announced that one of the players has sprained her ankle this will affect her chances of winning and this information will influence the prices.

If Alan Greenspan, Chairman of the US Federal Reserve at the time of writing, announces a drop in US interest rates, this will have an effect on the price of the Treasury bill. Greenspan's pronouncements have no effect on the outcome of the tennis match but the drop in interest rates translates into a rise in bond prices so, even though this news has no effect on the likely outcome of the tennis match, it will affect all three prices. The price of the government bond will rise. In order to preserve the no-arbitrage relationship this will induce a corresponding rise in the sum of the prices of the two tennis securities.

In the other markets, such as commodity markets and stock markets, prices also change as a result of new information. If there is a severe frost in Florida, orange juice prices will rise. The market knows that a reduced crop in Florida will lead to a smaller supply driving up the prices. Indeed, Richard Roll, a UCLA finance professor, found that orange juice futures prices increased even before the cold weather arrived. In fact, he found that the futures market was a better predictor of the weather than the official weather forecast. This can be explained by the fact that trading firms can afford to invest more in meteorologists and weather services than the government.

The dramatic effects of the Gulf War on crude oil prices provides another example of how quickly information is impounded into market prices. Just before the Gulf War in 1990, the price of oil soared as the likelihood of an invasion of Iraq increased. The uncertainty surrounding future oil price movements also increased dramatically. This uncertainty is measured by the volatility of future oil price measurements. We will discuss volatility in Chapter 4.

We have seen that the MH security can be created by constructing a portfolio consisting of the Treasury bill and the VW security. The market price of the MH security will be the market price of this portfolio. If the MH security were not traded so that the only traded securities were the Treasury bill and the VW security, an investor could effectively create the MH security. Suppose that for some reason it is more efficient for an investment bank to create the MH security (for example the investment bank could have negligible trading costs). The bank can sell this security to a customer and use the money received to set up a portfolio that will pay US$100 if Hingis wins the tennis match. We have noted that this process of replicating one security with a portfolio of other securities is called hedging. Financial institutions such as investment banks and brokerage houses routinely hedge their positions. The MH tennis security can be perfectly hedged at the outset using a one-time trade. However, for most derivatives hedging is more complicated because the replicating portfolio has to be adjusted as time passes. We will explain in more detail how this is carried out in Chapter 4.

HANGING CHADS: WHAT IF THERE IS NO WINNER?

We can use the tennis securities to illustrate the importance of defining the circumstances under which payment is made and how this can have implications for the replication argument. Until now, we have implicitly assumed that one of the following two events must occur: either Williams wins the match or Hingis wins the match. There is another possibility that has not been discussed yet: the tennis match might not take place for some reason. If we factor in this possibility what happens to the arbitrage argument?

To explore this issue we note that unlikely outcomes sometimes do occur. The US presidential election in 2000 provides a striking example. The results were to be announced on 7 November. Before this date there was no doubt that the results would be known then. Suppose that three months earlier, securities corresponding to the two candidates, Al Gore and George W Bush, traded on an electronic market. These securities are like the tennis securities. The AG security promises to pay US$100 on 7 November if Al Gore wins the most votes in the electoral college.[8] The GWB security promises to pay US$100 on 7 November, if Bush wins the most votes in the electoral college. Using the same reasoning as before, a portfolio of the AG and GWB securities should trade for the price of the three-month Treasury bill. However the Florida vote count was contested and the outcome was not resolved until 13 December.

To make matters more precise we could introduce a third security. In the tennis example this security would pay US$100 if, for any reason, it was not possible to name a winner of the match on the appointed day. We will call this security the rare event security (RES). A portfolio consisting of the VW security, the MH security and the RES security would surely pay US$100 on the appointed day.[9] We could also create a similar security to ensure that all the possible election outcomes were covered. These examples indicate that it is important to define the terms of these securities very precisely.

The central message of this chapter was the importance of the no-free-lunch principle. It underpins many of the methods now used to price derivatives and it also gives a method for hedging the derivative. Indeed the hedging comes first. We can only accurately price what we can hedge and we can only hedge using other traded securities.

1 A Treasury bill is a security, issued by the government, which pays its owner a fixed maturity amount on a specific future date. An investor who buys a three-month Treasury pays for it now and receives the maturity amount in three months. Because these securities are obligations of the government they are viewed as riskless.

2 For a description of the Iowa Electronic Markets see: URL: http://www.biz.uiowa.edu/iem/.

3 We discuss this famous model in Chapters 4 and 5.

4 We discussed call options in Chapter 2.

5 Modigliani and Miller published this seminal paper in 1958 in the *American Economic Review*. Miller related a story about winning the prize that illustrates the dangers of oversimplification. A journalist once asked him to explain in lay terms what the main idea of his award winning research was. Miller gave an explanation of the capital structure irrelevance principle. The journalist looked very confused and requested a simpler explanation. Miller then explained it again in simpler terms but the journalist was still confused. Finally, Miller explained that if there is cake on the table and he cut it in two parts, no matter where he cut the cake, the size of the cake would not change. The journalist, who now understood the explanation, expressed surprise that this insight was considered sufficiently profound to garner a Nobel Prize.

6 A popular US television comedy series about a group of comic, if neurotic, New Yorkers.

7 Augustin Cournot was educated at the École Normale Supérieur in Paris and at the Sorbonne, becoming a Professor of Mathematics at the University of Lyons and later the Rector of the Dijon Academy at Grenoble. In 1838, he published *Recherches sur les Principes Mathématiques de la Théorie des Richesses*, wherein he discussed the basics of mathematical economics. He was a pioneer in merging these two previously distinct disciplines.

8 Under the US system, the presidency is not decided by the popular vote but by electoral votes, with each state given at least three electoral votes and additional votes based on its population. The candidate who wins the largest number of votes in the state is entitled to count all of the state's electoral votes.

9 For now we are ignoring the risk that the institution that has issued the security will default and be unable to pay the promised amount at maturity. We are assuming the government Treasury bill bond also carries no risk of default, although there have been cases where governments have defaulted on their obligations. We discuss default risk in Chapter 9.

4

Pricing by Replication

This chapter details how we can price a derivative. We can price a derivative if we can find a portfolio of other securities that will have the same future cashflows as the derivative. If we can construct such a portfolio then we can use the no-arbitrage principle to find the price of the derivative security. We show how this idea works in some simple cases.

A WORD ON MODELS

We often simplify things to obtain a clearer understanding of what is important in a given situation. In different branches of science, we often make idealised assumptions to produce a simple model that provides a clear insight of how the world works. In the same way, we use models to represent what is really going on in financial markets. By making simplifying assumptions, we can concentrate on the important variables. Emanuel Derman, a leading finance practitioner, describes the role of models in these terms.[1]

> Models are descriptions of idealized worlds; they are only approximations, if even that, to the real hurly-burly world of finance and people and markets. Even in engineering, that's true. Models don't describe the real world. They describe an approximation to the real world at best. But you try to use them to give you a value for something in the real world.

This chapter will show how we can find the prices of some basic derivatives using simple models. Specifically, we will discuss forward contracts and European options. In each case we will construct a replicating portfolio that has the same payoff as the derivative at maturity. Then we apply the no-arbitrage principle to obtain the current price of the derivative.

In the case of the forward contract, the replicating portfolio does not need to be adjusted as time passes. However, in the case of the option we will generally have to adjust the portfolio with time. As we will see later, the adjustments will depend on what happens to the price of the underlying asset. This means that we need assumptions about – or a model of – how the asset price moves. The model we use to describe how the asset price moves is a very simple one and yet it is able to provide profound insights.[2]

PRICING FORWARD CONTRACTS

We begin with forward contracts, as they are among the simplest derivatives. Recall from Chapter 1 that the owner of a forward contract is obliged to buy an asset on the delivery date. The owner of the forward contract has to pay the pre-arranged contract price in exchange for the asset.

The no-arbitrage principle can be used to estimate the contract price. We do this by constructing a portfolio that has exactly the same payoff as the forward contract on the delivery date. This portfolio is known as the *replicating portfolio*. The portfolio that replicates the forward contract consists of positions in the underlying asset and a risk-free security. The Treasury bill that we discussed in Chapter 3 is an example of a riskless security. It pays a fixed amount of money at a fixed date in the future without any risk. To make matters simple we assume that the underlying asset makes no cash payments such as dividends.

We will show that the replicating portfolio consists of a long[3] position in the underlying asset and a short position in a risk-free bond.[4] This risk-free bond matures at the delivery date of the forward contract and it pays an amount equal to the contract price. It should be noted that at this point we do not know the value of the contract price – this is what we are looking for. We can regard the contract price as a quantity that will be determined later.

We now check what this portfolio is worth on the delivery date of the forward contract. The value of the portfolio, at contract maturity, will be the market value of the asset at the delivery date less the amount of the contract price. However, this value corresponds exactly to the market value of a long forward position. The market value of the long forward position at delivery is equal to the market price of the asset minus the amount that has to be paid, namely the contract price. The replicating portfolio has therefore lived up to its name: it has replicated the forward contract at the delivery date.

We now show that this approach enables us to find the contract price. From the no-arbitrage rule we know that the initial market price of the replicating portfolio must be equal to the initial market value of the forward contract. However we know the initial market value of the forward contract. When a forward contract is set up it is designed so that it does not favour either party, there is no cash transferred at inception and the initial market value of the contract is zero. By the no-arbitrage rule, the initial market value of the portfolio that replicates the forward contract is also zero. The initial market value of the replicating portfolio just contains one thing that we do not know: the contract price. We are now able to find it.

A numerical example may help to clarify this point. Consider a newly initiated forward contract with a delivery date one year from today. The current market price of the underlying asset is US$100. Assume the risk-free interest rate is 5%. The contract price can be computed using the above argument. We have explained that the market value of the replicating portfolio is zero. However, this means that the current market value of the asset (US$100) is equal to the current market value of a risk-free bond that pays the contract price in one year. They are both equal to US$100 and therefore the current value of a bond that pays the contract price is also equal to US$100. The risk-free interest rate in this market is 5% so the maturity value of the one-year bond is US$105. Hence the contract price under the forward contract is US$105. The contract price is equal to the accumulated amount obtained by investing the initial asset price over the term of the contract at the risk-free rate. We can compute it from the initial price of the asset and the risk-free interest rate. This simple formula works quite well in practice.

A MODEL FOR STOCK PRICE MOVEMENTS

One of the aims of this chapter is to describe a model that can be used to find the price of options. We will consider only European options to buy (or sell) some underlying asset.

We will need a model of how the asset price moves in order to price the option. The reason why we need such a model will become clearer as we proceed but here is a quick explanation.

We will construct the replicating portfolio that will eventually lead us to the current price of the option. The replicating portfolio that mimics the option's payoff needs to be adjusted to reflect changes in the asset price over time and we will need to keep track of its composition over time. To track the composition of the replicating portfolio we need to make some assumptions about how the asset price changes. The numerical example that follows illustrates the nature of the assumptions we use.

Suppose that, in our model, the asset price is just recorded at fixed time intervals. These intervals could be one hour, one day, one week, one month or one year. This type of model, with observations at periodic time intervals, is known as a *discrete time model*. Our first numerical example is based on annual observations. The initial price of one unit of the asset is US$100 and each year the asset price either goes up by US$20 or drops by US$20. We display the possible asset prices at the end of the first two years in Figure 4.1. After one year there are just two possible asset prices: US$120 if the price goes up and US$80 if the price falls. After two years we see there are three possible prices. If the price rises in the first two years the price will be US$140 (100 + 20 + 20). If the price falls in the first two years the price will be US$60 (100 − 20 − 20). The third possible price is US$100 and there are two ways this can happen. The first way is if the stock price rises by US$20 in the first year and drops by US$20 in the second year. The second way is if the asset price drops by US$20 in the first year and rises by US$20 in the second.

The random walker

The pattern of asset prices displayed in Figure 4.1 is an example of what is called a *random walk*. There is a very simple and intuitive way to construct a random walk. An individual called the Random Walker (RW) starts at a fixed point, called the origin. RW always moves in a straight line that runs directly in a north-south direction. He takes either one step to the north or one step to the south and every step is one yard long. Assume that he rests for one minute after each step; he is a very slow walker. RW decides which direction to go in by tossing a coin. If the coin comes up heads he takes a step to the north; if the coin comes up tails he takes a step to the south. After one minute he will have taken exactly one step and he will be one yard from where he started. He will be either one yard north of the origin or one yard south of it depending on the outcome of the coin toss. After two minutes he has taken two steps and there are just three possible places where he could be. His position could be either two yards to the north of the origin or two yards to the south of the origin, or he could be back at the origin depending on the outcome of the two coin tosses.

Random walks have played an important role in the history of probability. This simple model provides a very accessible path to very deep and important results.[5] We will again encounter the random walk in the next chapter, where we will see that it played an important role in the birth of modern option pricing. The random walker we introduced in the last

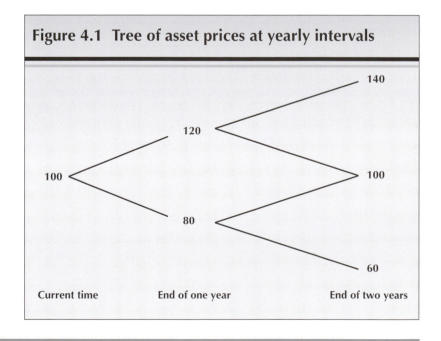

Figure 4.1 Tree of asset prices at yearly intervals

140

120

100   100

80

60

Current time   End of one year   End of two years paragraph always walks in a straight line. If he keeps walking in this way he will keep revisiting the starting point.

There is a charming story about random walks coming back to where they started that concerns the famous mathematician George Polya. This story was told to us by Hans Buhlmann, a former president of the Swiss Federal Institute of Technology in Zurich, where Polya once worked and Dr Buhlmann heard it from Polya himself. Indeed it appears that Polya first coined the phrase "random walk" and he used the German term *Irrfahrt im Strassennetz.*

PANEL 1
POLYA'S RANDOM WALK

When he was a young academic at the Swiss Federal Institute of Technology (better known by its German initials ETH), George Polya was living at Pension Zuerichberg near the hill called Zuerich-berg. This area provides attractive walks in the woods very near to the city of Zurich. Polya's best friend also lived in this pension. One weekend, his friend's fiancée visited and the couple went off for a walk in the nearby woods. Polya himself also went for a walk in the woods and to his embarrassment, he met the couple not just once but twice. When Polya went back to his room he started to reflect on what had happened.

"I got the idea that this might not have been such an improbable event as it had seemed *a priori*. I started the study of the probability of the event that two persons walking at random independently would meet each other."

Polya started by studying the problem of a two-dimensional random walk. The walker is walking in a city with a rectangular system of streets. At each corner, the walker tosses a coin to decide whether to go forwards or backwards and another coin to decide whether to go right or left. Polya was able to prove mathematically that in this two-dimensional random walk it was almost certain that the walker would come back to their original starting point. Polya also proved that in a three-dimensional random walk the walker would almost never return to their original starting point.

We can identify our model of the asset price movements with a specific random walk. The starting point is set to be 100 (corresponding to the initial asset price of 100) yards. Think of the walker, in this case, as a giant who tosses the coin before deciding whether to move due north or due south. The northwards step is 20 yards long and the southward step is also

20 yards in length. To start the walk, the giant tosses the coin and takes a step north or south depending on the toss. Then he rests for a year before repeating the process. The possible paths taken by the giant will correspond to the price paths of the asset.

A ONE-PERIOD MODEL TO PRICE OPTIONS

We now show how to find the value of a one-year option when the asset price behaves as described in Figure 4.1. We first consider a one-year European call option on this asset. The strike price of the option is US$100. The one-year interest rate in this market is assumed to be zero. This means that, if the initial bond price is US$100, the bond price one year later will be the same. In reality interest rates are not zero but positive. We make this assumption to simplify matters.

We will sometimes refer to the underlying asset as the *risky asset* because its price after one year is uncertain. In contrast, we will sometimes refer to the bond as the *riskless asset* because its future price is known.

To find the price of this call option, we construct a portfolio that has exactly the same payoff as the call option at maturity. From the no-arbitrage assumption this portfolio has the same current value as the call option. If this were not the case we could make riskless profits and become enormously wealthy.

We know the value of the asset in one year in each of its two possible final states. The value of the call option also depends on the asset price at that point. If the asset price has increased then the call value is US$20 (120–100). On the other hand, if the asset price has dropped to US$80 it makes no sense to exercise the call and so the value of the call option will be zero.

This means that we now know the value that we wish to replicate at the year end in each of the two states. The basic building materials for the replicating portfolio are the asset itself and the one-year riskless bond. We know the prices of these assets at year end in each state. If the asset price goes up to US$120, the bond is worth US$100 and the call option is worth US$20. If the asset price goes down to US$80 the bond is still worth US$100 but now the call price is worth zero. These payoffs are displayed in Figure 4.2.

To replicate the option payoff we need to construct a portfolio of the asset and the riskless bond that will be worth US$20 if the asset price rises to US$120 after one year and zero if the asset price falls to US$80 after one year. It turns out that we will be able to find such a portfolio. One very painful way would be to use what is known as a *trial-and-error method*. Under this method, which we do not recommend, we would construct a portfolio by guessing how much to put in the asset and the bond and then calculate the value of this portfolio after one year. We would check whether or not the value of the portfolio corresponds to the payoff under

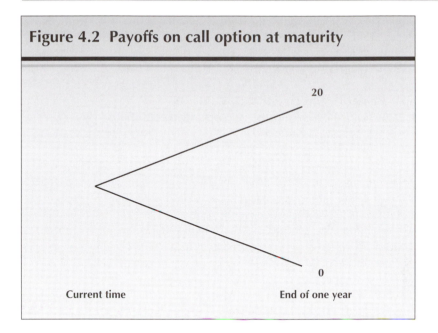

Figure 4.2 Payoffs on call option at maturity

20

0

Current time

End of one year

the option contract. It is most unlikely that we would guess correctly and so under this method we would go back and guess again until we find the portfolio that exactly matches the payoff of the call option.

Suppose our first guess is that the portfolio consists of two units of the risky asset and one unit of the riskless asset. This portfolio would be worth US$340 after one year if the asset price rose to US$120. The US$340 corresponds to two units of the risky asset, at US$120 each, plus one unit of the riskless bond because

$$2(120) + (100) = 340$$

The same portfolio would be worth US$260 after one year if the asset price dropped to US$80. The US$260 corresponds to two units of the risky asset, at US$80 each, plus one unit of the riskless bond, because

$$2(80) + (100) = 260$$

Hence the portfolio has a payoff of US$340 if the asset price rises and a payoff of US$260 if the asset price falls. As the corresponding call option payoffs are US$20 and zero, we see that this portfolio overprovides in each state. The portfolio *does not replicate* the payoff of the call option.

Our first guess produced a portfolio whose payoffs were larger than those of the call option. We now make a second guess as to the composition of the replicating portfolio. Consider a portfolio that consists of a long position in the risky asset and a short position in the risk-free asset. Assume also that the portfolio involves the purchase of five units of the risky asset and the short sale of four units of the risk-free asset. If the risky asset's price were to rise to US$120 after one year, this portfolio would then be worth US$200. The US$200 corresponds to five units of the risky asset, at US$120 each, minus four units of the risk-free bond, worth 100. We have

$$5(120) - 4(100) = 200$$

This same portfolio would be worth zero after one year if the asset price dropped to US$80. This is because a long position of five units of the risky asset, at US$80 each, minus four units of the risk-free bond gives a combined market value of zero:

$$5(80) - 4(100) = 0$$

Hence, the portfolio has a payoff of US$200 when the risky asset's price rises and zero when it falls. The corresponding payoffs under the option contract are US$20 and zero. We still have not obtained a portfolio that matches the option payoff.

However this last "guess" can guide us to the desired portfolio, which will produce payoffs that exactly match those of the call option.[6] The last portfolio gave a payoff of US$200 if the risky asset's price were to move to US$120 after one year, and a payoff of zero if the price of the risky asset were to drop to US$80 after one year. What we require is a portfolio that generates a payoff of US$20, if the risky asset's price moves to US$120 after one year, and a payoff of zero if the price of the risky asset drops to US$80 after one year. We see that our last guess produced payoffs that *are 10 times too big*. This suggests that if we scale down our portfolio by a factor of 10 it will do the job.

Our third guess, then, will be a portfolio that is one-tenth the size of the portfolio in our second guess. This portfolio consists of a long position in the risky asset that involves buying 50% of one unit of the risky asset because one tenth of 5 is 50%. The portfolio will also involve a short position of 40% of the risk-free bond, because one tenth of 4 is 40%. The payoffs of this portfolio will match exactly the payoffs of the call option.

Table 4.1 shows that the portfolio that has a long position of 50% of the risky asset and a short position of 40% of the riskless asset has the same payoff at maturity as the European call option. In the Appendix we show how to find the replicating portfolio in this case without resorting to inspired guesswork.

Table 4.1 Payoffs on replicating portfolio and call option at option maturity

Risky asset price	Bond value	Replicating portfolio	Option payoff
120	100	0.5(120) – 0.4(100) = 20	20
80	100	0.5(80) – 0.4(100) = 0	0

We have constructed a portfolio whose value is exactly equal to the value of the call option, irrespective of whether the stock price goes up or down. We know that the market value of this portfolio must be equal to the market price of the option at inception. The initial market value of the replicating portfolio is equal to 10. This is because 50% of the initial asset price (US$100) minus 40% of the initial bond price (US$100) is equal to 10. We have

$$0.5(100) - 0.4(100) = 10$$

The initial value of the call option price must also be 10.

We now explain why this must be the case. Suppose, for example, the current market price of the call is equal to US$11. An investment bank could sell this option and collect the price of the option (the US$11). The bank could then set up the replicating portfolio, which will cost it US$10; the bank would make an immediate profit of US$1. When the option contract matures, the bank's replicating portfolio provides the right amount to pay off what it owes on the option contract. If the asset price goes up to US$120 the bank owes US$20 to the investor who bought the option. However the value of the bank's replicating portfolio is also US$20. In the same way if the stock price drops to US$80 then the bank does not owe anything under the option contract. In this case the value of the replicating portfolio is also zero. Hence, this transaction produces a sure immediate profit of US$1. Naturally the bank would take advantage of this money machine if it did not violate the principle of no-arbitrage, which means the price of the call cannot be US$11. The same argument also shows that the price of the call cannot be greater than US$10.

A similar argument demonstrates that the option price cannot be less than US$10. Suppose, for example, the market price of the call option at inception is US$8. To make arbitrage profits in this case the bank should set up a short position in the replicating portfolio that will yield an immediate cash inflow of US$10. The bank then buys the call option in the market for US$8 leaving a profit of US$2. This is a clear profit for the bank because the amounts the bank has to pay on the portfolio that it has set up, are perfectly offset by the payoff it receives from the call option it has bought. If the stock price rises to US$120 the bank's call option is worth US$20. The amount it owes on the portfolio is also US$20, which means that the books balance. If the stock price drops to US$80 then the call is worth zero but the value of the replicating portfolio is also zero so, once again, the two amounts are equal. Thus if the market call price is US$8 the bank makes arbitrage profits. Indeed this same argument can be used to show that the market price of the call cannot be less than US$10. We have also shown that the market price of the call cannot be greater than US$10 and so it must be exactly US$10.

The steps used above to obtain the current price of the call option illustrate the general method that is used to price derivatives using the no-arbitrage principle:

❑ First, we set up a replicating portfolio that has the same values as the derivative at maturity.
❑ Then we use the no-arbitrage argument to assert that the current value of the portfolio must be equal to the current value of the derivative.

The same approach that we used in this very simplified example can also be used in more complicated settings to obtain the replicating portfolios that correspond to various derivatives. The current value of the replicating portfolio corresponds to the current price of the associated derivative and the construction of the replicating portfolio shows how to generate a structure with exactly the same payoff as the derivative.

A TWO-PERIOD MODEL TO PRICE OPTIONS

Our last example was deliberately simplified to focus on the key concepts. We will now indicate how it can be generalised. Previously, we used a one-year time period but this is too large a measurement interval, it is more accurate to use smaller time intervals. Hence, we will use six-month time steps to show the procedure.

We divide the term to maturity of the option into two six-month periods. During each six-month period, assume that the risky asset's price can either go up by US$10 or down by US$10. This means that after the first six months, the asset price will be either US$110 or US$90. If it increases to 110 then the two possible asset prices at the end of the year are US$120 or US$100. If, after six months, the asset price is US$90 then after one year it will be either US$100 or US$80. Thus after two periods (12 months), there will be three possible asset prices: US$120, US$100 and US$80. Note that an upward movement followed by a downward movement gives us the same price as a downward movement followed by an upward movement – both correspond to the mid-value of US$100. We again emphasise that these asset price dynamics have been picked for simplicity.[7]

It is convenient to display the possible prices as in Figure 4.3. This is known as a *tree diagram* because it resembles a fir tree lying on its side with the top pointing to the left. Time runs from left to right. There are three time points corresponding to the current time, six months later and one year later. At time zero the asset price is US$100. Six months later, there are two possible asset prices and one year later there are three possible asset prices. Recall that, in the first model with just one period, there were just two possible asset prices after one year. Now we have three possible asset prices after one year.

We can price a call option with this two-period model using the same type of approach that we used for the one-period option. Assume that the strike price of the call option is once again US$100. The basic idea is to break the two-period problem into smaller one-period problems. From the tree diagram, we can see that there are three little one-period problems. At the end of the first period there are two of them. Figure 4.4 shows the topmost little tree for the last six months of the period. In this case, the starting asset price is US$110 and the two ending asset prices are US$120 and US$100. Figure 4.5 shows the bottom tree for the last six months when the starting asset price is US$90 and the two ending asset prices are

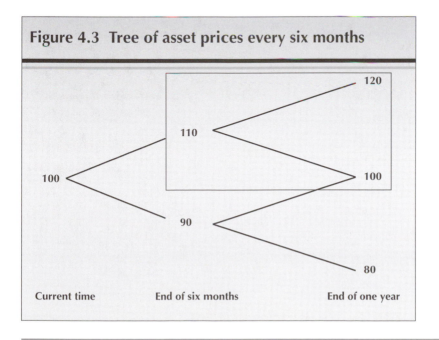

Figure 4.3 Tree of asset prices every six months

100

110

90

120

100

80

Current time   End of six months   End of one year

US$100 and US$80. We work from right to left because we know the value of the replicating portfolio at option maturity: the end of the second period.

We now concentrate on the tree in Figure 4.4. We see that the call option values at the option maturity are either US$20 or zero. The interest rate over this six-month period is again assumed to be zero. Our task is to find the replicating portfolio of the risky asset and the riskless asset that produces the same payoff as the call option. The replicating portfolio should be worth US$20 if the risky asset price rises to US$120 and worth zero if the price drops to US$100.

The details are given in the Appendix but we can show the idea behind the approach as follows.

We note that the replicating portfolio is known, when we have two pieces of information. These are the number of units of the risky asset and the number of units of the riskless asset.

We also know that the market value of the replicating portfolio has to be equal to the option payoff both when the risky asset price rises and also when the risky asset price falls.

This provides two conditions that enable us to discover the two things we need to know. Each of the two conditions is an example of a linear equation. We explain the concept of a linear equation in Panel 2 using the connection between the temperature in centigrade and the temperature in Fahrenheit as an example.

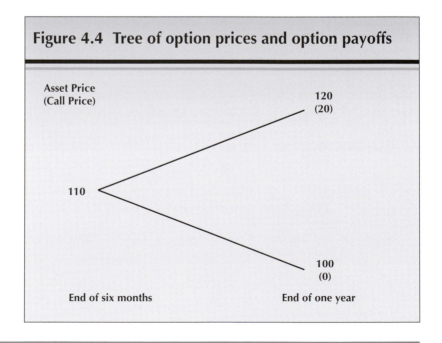

Figure 4.4 Tree of option prices and option payoffs

Asset Price
(Call Price)

110

120
(20)

100
(0)

End of six months   End of one year

PANEL 2
TEMPERATURE CONNECTIONS

Temperature can be measured in centigrade or in Fahrenheit. In the United States, temperature is measured in Fahrenheit and in Canada it is measured in centigrade. These are just two different scales and on a winter's day it is just as cold in Windsor as it is across the border in Detroit. If C denotes the temperature in centigrade and F denotes the temperature in Fahrenheit the relationship is

$$F = \frac{9}{5} C + 32$$

When C is equal to zero, we see from the formula that the corresponding value of F is 32. This is because

$$32 = \frac{9}{5} 0 + 32$$

So zero degrees centigrade is the same as to 32° Fahrenheit.
   We also see that if C = 100 then F equals 212.

$$212 = \frac{9}{5} 100 + 32$$

Hence, 100° centigrade is the same as 212° Fahrenheit.

The replicating portfolio corresponding to Figure 4.4 consists of a long position of one unit of the risky asset and a short position of one unit of the bond. We can confirm that this portfolio is worth US$20 if the risky asset price rises to US$120 and that it is worth zero if the risky asset price falls to US$100. The market value of this portfolio at the left-hand node of Figure 4.4 when the asset price is US$110 is therefore US$10. This is because

$$(110) - (100) = 10$$

Applying the no-arbitrage principle, we know that the market value of the replicating portfolio at this node will also be the market price of the call option at this node.

   We now turn our attention to the second tree in Figure 4.5. We see that the call option value at the option maturity is zero if the asset price is US$100 and that it is also zero if the asset price is US$80. Our task is to find the replicating portfolio of the risky asset and the riskless asset that produces the same payoff as the call option. The replicating portfolio should be worth zero if the risky asset price rises to US$100 and worth zero

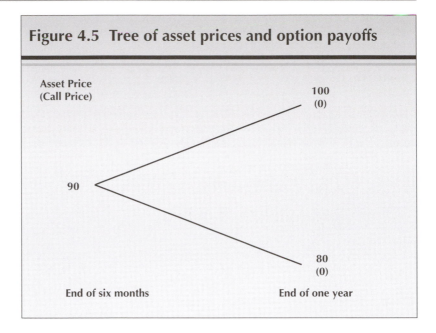

Figure 4.5 Tree of asset prices and option payoffs

Asset Price
(Call Price)

100
(0)

90

80
(0)

End of six months   End of one year

if the price drops to US$80. The replicating portfolio in this case is very simple, if a little strange. It consists of zero units in the risky asset and zero units of the riskless asset. Such a portfolio must be worth zero six months earlier at the left-hand node of Figure 4.5.

The stage is now set for the final step. We now focus on the little tree that starts with a stock price of 100 at time zero. Figure 4.6 shows the call values that we have obtained from our analyses of the previous two trees. The tree in Figure 4.6 covers the interval from current time to six months from now. At the top node, when the risky asset price is US$110, we have found that the call value is US$10. At the bottom node, when the risky asset price is US$90, we also know that the call value is zero. The bond is worth US$100 at inception and it is still worth US$100 six months later because we are working with a zero interest rate.

We now have all the ingredients for a standard one-period problem. We construct a replicating portfolio whose value matches that of the call option in each node at time one. We just give the result here and leave the details to the Appendix. In this case, the replicating portfolio consists of a long position of 50% of the risky asset and a short position of 45% of the riskless asset. We can confirm that this portfolio gives the correct payoffs:

$$0.5(110) - 0.45(100) = 10$$

$$0.5(90) - 0.45(100) = 0$$

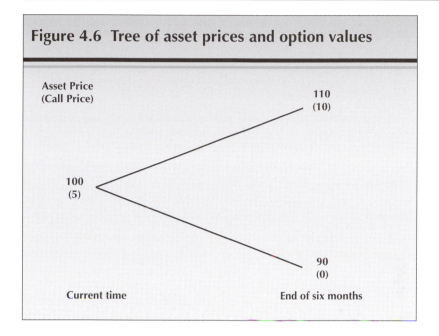

Figure 4.6 Tree of asset prices and option values

Asset Price
(Call Price)

110
(10)

100
(5)

90
(0)

Current time   End of six months

To prevent arbitrage, the market value of this portfolio at the initial time must also be the market value of the call option at time zero. The market value of this portfolio is US$5 at the initial time. Hence the market value of the call option is also US$5.

We could also use this approach to find the market value of the corresponding European put option, (assuming that the strike price of the put option is also US$100). If we use the same model for the movements of the asset prices as given in Figure 4.3 we can find the portfolio that replicates the put option for the three little trees as we did before. We will not wade through the details, instead we will just give the result. It turns out that the initial price of the European put option in this case is also US$5.

THE REPLICATING STRATEGY

The two-period example, we have just worked through, demonstrates that the amounts of the risky asset and the riskless asset in the replicating portfolio need to be changed at each intermediate node. The intuition is that as we reach each node, new information becomes available and this information needs to be reflected in the replicating strategy. The total market value of the replicating portfolio does not change during this rebalancing. The clearest way of seeing is to work through the tree in Figure 4.3, beginning at the initial point and track what happens to the replicating portfolio in this case.

Recall that the replicating portfolio starts with a long position of 50% of

DERIVATIVES

the risky asset and a short position of 45% of the riskless asset. The market value of the portfolio at this stage is 5. Six months later, the risky asset price will be either 110 or 90. In both cases, we need to adjust the positions in the replicating portfolio. If the risky asset price is 110, the value of the replicating portfolio will be 50% of 110 (less 45% of 100: ie, 10). Our earlier analysis showed that when we are at this node we will need to revise the replicating portfolio. The revised portfolio consists of a long position of one unit in the risky asset and a short position of one unit of the riskless asset. The market value of this revised portfolio is also 10 and this is exactly the right amount. The amount invested in each asset is different before and after the revision. We have

$$0.5(110) - 0.45(100) = 1(110) - 1(100) = 10$$

We now consider the other possibility, where we assume the risky asset price drops to 90 after six months and examine how the replicating portfolio needs to be adjusted. The value of the replicating portfolio will be zero at the bottom right hand node of Figure 4.6, because 50% of 90 is equal to 45% of 100. Our earlier analysis shows that as we head into the next tree, (Figure 4.5) we need a replicating portfolio that consists of zero in each asset and so the market value of the revised portfolio is also zero. The market value of the replicating portfolio does not change when we rebalance the positions, but the positions in the two assets do. We have

$$0.5(90) - 0.45(100) = 0(80) - 0(100) = 0$$

The replicating portfolio provides exactly the same payoff as the option at the maturity date if it is rebalanced according to the prescribed strategy. The adjustments to the portfolio at the intermediate times do not require any infusion of cash and do not produce any excess cash either. This property is called *self-financing*. The entire cost of manufacturing the option payoff is given by the initial price of the replicating portfolio. Of course, in practice an institution would want to make a profit, this scenario is idealised to keep matters simple.

In our two-period tree model, it is assumed that the possible future asset prices are those given on the tree and, indeed, they are the only possible stock prices at these future times. This is a strong assumption and in the case of an actual stock, such an assumption will not be correct. For example, the stock price of a company like Nortel changes moment by moment and there is a wide range of values that it could take six months from now. If we divide the total time interval into a large number of periods, it will automatically increase the range of possible stock prices. This replaces the one big tree with a new set of little trees. We can do a much better job of representing how an actual stock price moves if we use small time steps.

64

If the stock price process is represented using a large number of little time steps, then the replicating strategy will involve more frequent adjustments. The maturity payoff from the replicating portfolio will correspond to the payoff under the option contract. This process of replicating the payoff is called dynamic hedging. Sellers of derivative contracts such as investment banks often use dynamic hedging strategies to replicate the payoffs they have promised to their customers.

As the number of time steps becomes larger, we say the discrete time model *converges* to a *continuous time model*. In the case of the discrete time option model, the expression for the option price tends to the famous Black–Scholes–Merton (BSM) formula as the number of time steps becomes large. The BSM price also corresponds to the value of a replicating portfolio. This replicating portfolio will correspond exactly to the price of the call option at maturity. The portfolio must be rebalanced every instant of time from its inception to option maturity, ie, the replicating portfolio must be adjusted continuously.

In reality, it is not possible to adjust a portfolio at every instant. However, this does not mean that a model based on this assumption is of no use. It is common in the natural and social sciences to make strong assumptions to simplify the real world. Often the assumptions that underpin our models are idealistic and frequently they are clearly false.

CONCLUSION

This discussion brings us back to a theme raised by Emanuel Derman in the quotation near the beginning of this chapter. He noted that models describe an approximation to the real world at best. The pricing model, we have discussed in this chapter, is based on some simplifying assumptions but it gives us a foretaste of the main topic of the next chapter.

The next chapter will discuss the Black–Scholes–Merton option pricing model. This model is the most important intellectual development in option pricing and it provides the theoretical foundation for the modern expansion in derivative instruments. Furthermore, their approach provided the fountainhead for a torrent of subsequent theoretical advances in this area. These advances made it possible to price and replicate new types of derivative instruments.

1   Emanuel Derman, 1998, "Roundtable: The Limits of Models" at www.derivativesstrategy. com/magazine/archive/1998.

2   The model assumes that the asset price will move up or down at the end of each period. This model has a long and illustrious history in finance dating back to the work of Louis Bachelier over 100 years ago. We discuss Bachelier's contributions in Chapter 5.

3   Recall that if an investor has a long position in an asset they own the asset.

4   We explained short selling in Chapter 3. If an investor sells an asset short, they sell it today, collect its market price and promise to buy it back in the future.

5   Michael Steele (2000) paid tribute to the random walk model as follows: "Already rich in

unexpected and elegant phenomena, the random walk also leads one inexorably to the development of Brownian motion, the theory of diffusions, the Itô calculus and myriad important applications and developments in finance, economics and physical science".

6 Actually we cheated. This last portfolio is not based on a guess but was constructed to guide us to the solution. A little mathematics, given in the Appendix, shows how we can obtain the portfolio directly without any guesswork.

7 In this case we have added constant amounts at each step (+10 or –10). This gives an additive process. One of the problems with this process is that eventually we would get negative stock prices. To avoid this we should use a multiplicative process, which is theoretically superior. Under a multiplicative process, the stock price would either increase by 10% or decrease by 10% over each six-month period. However, for present purposes the simple additive process is adequate.

APPENDIX

The purpose of this Appendix is to show how to obtain the composition of the replicating portfolio.

First, we find the replicating portfolio for the one-year call option based on Figure 4.2. Recall that the option payoff is equal to US$20 if the asset price moves up to US$120 and that the option payoff is zero if the risky asset price drops to US$80. The riskless bond is always worth US$100 because we have assumed that the interest rate is zero.

At this stage, we do not know the number of units of the risky asset in the replicating portfolio and so we will use a common mathematical ploy when something is unknown. We denote it by X. The number of units of the risky asset is therefore represented by X.

We also do not know the number of units of the riskless bond in the replicating portfolio and so we denote this number by Y.

However we *do* know the value of the replicating portfolio in two different situations. These two conditions will permit us to find numerical values for both X and Y.

First, assume that the risky asset price rises to US$120. In this case, the replicating portfolio consists of X units of the risky asset and Y units of the riskless asset. The total value of this portfolio is:

$$120X + 100Y$$

However, because this portfolio replicates the payoff of the call option, which happens to be US$20, we have

$$120X + 100Y = 20$$

This gives a relationship between X and Y and we will use this relationship in finding the solution.

We will follow the same course of action for the other possibility.

Assume that the risky asset price drops to US$80. In this case, the value of the replicating portfolio is:

$$80X + 100Y$$

However because this portfolio replicates the payoff of the call option, which happens to be zero, we have

$$80X + 100Y = 0$$

At this stage we have two relationships involving X and Y. They are:

$$120X + 100Y = 20$$

$$80X + 100Y = 0$$

These relationships are termed equations. They are linear equations, which are referred to in Panel 2, by analogy with the temperature in degrees Fahrenheit to the temperature in degrees centigrade. Each of these equations is still true if it is multiplied by any number. Thus if we were to multiply the first equation by 3 and the second by 4 we would obtain:

$$360X + 300Y = 60$$

$$320X + 400Y = 0$$

If we keep our original first equation and multiply the second equation by −1 we obtain:

$$120X + 100Y = 20$$

$$-80X - 100Y = 0$$

The last two equations are both true and any combination of them must also be valid. Hence, if we add the last two equations the result is still true because when we add them, the terms in Y cancel ($100Y + -100Y = 0$) and we obtain the following equation, which just involves X:

$$40X = 20$$

Hence

$$X = \frac{20}{40} = 0.5$$

Once we know X we can go back to find Y. We do this by substituting the value of X into any one of the two equations. If we use the first equation we have:

$$60 + 100Y = 20$$

This can be written as

$$100Y = -40$$

Hence Y is equal to -0.4 or -40%. In investment jargon, this negative sign means we sell the bond short.

We will now show that we obtain the same value for Y if we use the second equation:

$$40 + 100Y = 0$$

This means that

$$100Y = -40$$

so that again we have $Y = -0.4$. Thus, we have obtained the amounts in the replicating portfolio. The number of units of the risky asset, X, is 0.5. The number of units in the riskless bond is -0.4.

Computation of replicating portfolio for Figure 4.4

We now use the same approach to find the replicating portfolio for the one-period call option based on Figure 4.4. The option payoff is equal to US$20 if the asset price moves up to US$120, and the option payoff is zero if the risky asset price drops to US$100. The riskless bond is always worth US$100.

As before, we let X denote the number of units of the risky asset in the replicating portfolio and we let Y denote the number of units of the riskless asset in the replicating portfolio. If the price of the risky asset rises to US$120, the portfolio is worth US$20 and if the price of the risky asset drops to US$100 the call is worth zero. Thus, we have

$$120X + 100Y = 20$$

$$100X + 100Y = 0$$

If we multiply the last equation by -1 and add the two equations we obtain:

$$20X = 20$$

meaning that $X = 1$. When we substitute this value of X in the second equation we obtain:

$$100Y = -100$$

This means that $Y = -1$, so the replicating portfolio consists of a long position of one unit in the risky asset and a short position of one unit in the riskless bond.

Computation of replicating portfolio for Figure 4.6
We repeat the same procedure to find the replicating portfolio for Figure 4.6. The value we need to replicate is 10 if the asset price moves up to US$110 and zero if the asset price drops to US$90. The riskless bond is always worth US$100.

We let X denote the number of units of the risky asset in the replicating portfolio and let Y denote the number of units of the riskless asset in the replicating portfolio. Thus, we have

$$110X + 100Y = 10$$

$$90X + 100Y = 0$$

If we multiply the last equation by -1 and add the two equations we obtain:

$$20X = 10$$

meaning that $X = 0.5$. When we substitute this value of X in the second equation we obtain:

$$100Y = -45$$

which means that $Y = -0.45$. The replicating portfolio therefore consists of a long position of 50% of the risky asset and a short position of 45% of the riskless bond.

5

The Quest for the Option Formula

This chapter describes the history of option pricing starting with Louis Bachelier's seminal work in 1900 and culminating some 70 years later in the ultimate solution by Black, Scholes and Merton. We will see that Bachelier's work was neglected for almost 50 years until the renaissance of interest in option pricing in the 1950s. During the next 20 years, there were several notable attempts to solve the problem and we will see that some of them came very close to the solution. We explain some of the technical terms more fully in the Appendix to this chapter.

LOUIS BACHELIER'S CONTRIBUTIONS[1]

To set the stage for our discussion of Bachelier's contributions it is useful to summarise some ideas from the last chapter. We have noted that, to value a derivative, you need assumptions about how the underlying asset price moves in the future as well as a method for converting the future value back to the current time. The replicating portfolio, which is maintained by dynamic hedging, has the same payoff as the derivative at maturity. The no-arbitrage argument shows that the current price of the derivative is equal to the current value of this portfolio. We can use this argument to form a portfolio of the underlying asset and the derivative that replicates the riskless asset. A portfolio of a long position in a stock and a short position in the option can therefore be constructed so that it is risk-free. Note that this portfolio must earn the risk-free rate to preclude arbitrage.

We also saw in our discussion of the discrete time model that, to construct the replicating portfolio, we need to know the distribution of future stock prices. So an important ingredient of an option formula is an assumption about how stock prices move over time.

Bachelier made a number of important contributions to the modelling of stock prices and the mathematics of uncertainty in his brilliant thesis. Specifically, he modelled stock price movements in discrete time as a random walk. (We discussed random walks in Chapter 4.) We saw that we can generate a random walk by tossing a coin at each step. The coin then determines the direction of the stock price movement. If the coin comes up heads the stock price rises and if the coin comes up tails the price falls.

We saw in Chapter 4 that the stock price path will trace out a random walk if the price moves are generated by a sequence of coin tosses. The bold line in Figure 5.1 shows the stock price path for one particular sequence. When we make the number of tosses very large and the individual stock price jumps very small, this path becomes extremely erratic. As the time steps become smaller, the path traced out eventually corresponds to a particular type of movement called Brownian motion. Brownian motion is named after the English botanist Robert Brown, who studied the movement of pollen grains suspended in water. Bachelier showed that the random walk could be used to generate Brownian motion. This was five years before Einstein used Brownian motion to study the movements of dust particles suspended in water.

Bachelier's model of stock price movements essentially assumed that stock prices follow the so-called *normal distribution*.[2] This is the well-known bell curve shown in Figure 5.2. The model gives realistic movements of stock prices over a very short time period but it is not a realistic model of stock prices over a long time because a stock price that follows a normal distribution could become negative. In reality, a stock can end up worth nothing, but its price can never become negative. This is a consequence of the limited liability provision. Hence the lowest possible value of a common stock is zero.

We can adjust the Bachelier model to overcome this drawback by using *the rate of return* on the stock, rather than the actual stock prices used by Bachelier. If the stock price at the start of the year is US$100 and it is

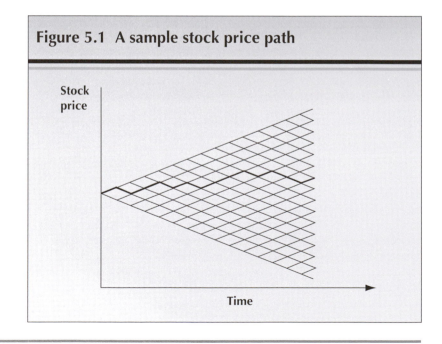

Figure 5.1 A sample stock price path

Stock price

Time

US$120 at the end of the year then the rate of return is 20%. If the stock price at the start of the year is US$100 and it is US$80 at the end of the year, then the rate of return is –20%.

If the log of 1 plus the return on the stock follows a normal distribution we say the stock price follows a *lognormal model*. We provide an example of a lognormal distribution in Figure 5.3. The height of the graph indicates how likely a future event is. We see that in this case the most likely return is around 15%. The advantage of the lognormal model over the normal model in this context is that the lognormal model does not give rise to negative stock prices. Paul Samuelson, who also made important contributions to the development of the option formula, used the lognormal model to represent the stock price distribution.

Bachelier tested his theoretical model using actual options traded on the Paris Stock Exchange. As these options had short maturities, ranging from one day to a maximum of 45 days, Bachelier's use of the normal distribution gave reasonable results. In his thesis, Bachelier developed a very simple formula to price options where the asset price was equal to the strike price. In Bachelier's terminology such options were known as *simple options*. Bachelier stated that "The value of a simple option must be proportional to the square root of time."[3] This formula is still valid as an approximation for the prices of many short-term options.[4]

It is clear from his thesis that Bachelier used his practical experience in

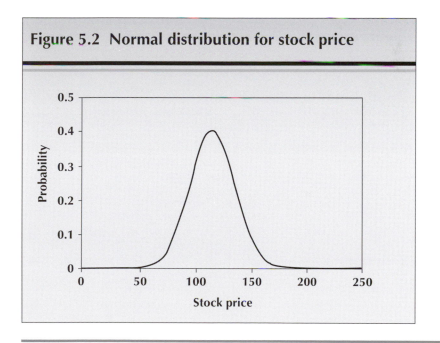

Figure 5.2 Normal distribution for stock price

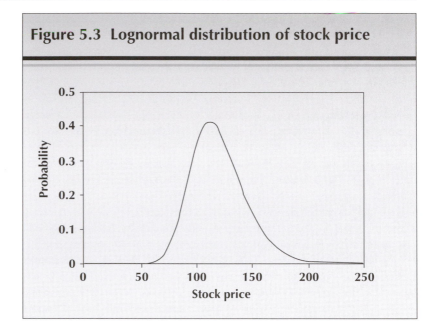

Figure 5.3 Lognormal distribution of stock price

formulating his ideas. For example, he contemplated possible strategies that would generate an arbitrage profit:

> Several years ago I noticed that it was possible, while admitting the above fact, to imagine operations in which one of the traders would make a profit regardless of eventual prices.

After explaining how this strategy could be implemented he noted that there would be no free lunch. "We will see that such spreads are never found in practice."

Bachelier's important scientific contributions to option pricing and probability were not recognised during his lifetime. Indeed, until recently little was known about the father of the modern option pricing theory. Paul Samuelson immediately recognised the importance of the work when he stumbled upon Bachelier's thesis.[5]

> In the early 1950s I was able to locate by chance this unknown book, rotting in the library of the University of Paris, and when I opened it up it was as if a whole new world was laid out before me. In fact as I was reading it, I arranged to get a translation in English, because I really wanted every precious pearl to be understood.

Bachelier's work became more widely known with the publication of Paul Cootner's 1964 book, which contained an English translation of the entire thesis.

ARBITRAGE, WARRANTS AND BEN GRAHAM

The publication of Bachelier's thesis was followed by a 50-year lull in the development of a scientific model to price options. However, during this time important changes were taking place in the world of practical finance. Financial markets became more important in economic life and nowhere more so than in the United States, where the stock market had suffered the Great Depression and was poised to take off.

In 1915, a 21 year-old analyst with the Wall Street firm of Newberger, Henderson & Loeb spotted an arbitrage opportunity.[6] The Guggenheim Exploration Company, which held large positions in the shares of several copper-mining companies, was planning to dissolve and distribute its holding to its shareholders. These mining shares were traded on the New York Stock Exchange. The young analyst noted that the price of the copper shares to be received in the package was higher than the price of Guggenheim's stock. He recommended that Newberger buy Guggenheim stock and sell short the copper shares in the package. This strategy was adopted and proved highly profitable for the firm and several of its clients. Of course, as the market became more efficient such arbitrage opportunities became harder to find. The young analyst was Benjamin Graham who was later to co-author a classic book on security analysis.[7] He founded the school of value investing and became the teacher and mentor of Warren Buffet.

Graham became a partner in the firm in 1920 and ran what we would now call the firm's proprietary trading desk.[8] Graham believed that convertible bonds were good value in relative terms. A convertible bond is a package consisting of debt and an embedded call option to buy a firm's common stock. Graham would buy convertible bonds and sell short call options to hedge the price risk. If this portfolio is suitably constructed the impact of the stock price movements on the convertible bond and the short call option will offset each other. Hence this strategy can eliminate the price risk stemming from the stock price movements. Graham also used short positions in the stock as well as put options to hedge the risk. The idea of combining different securities in a portfolio to hedge out the risk of the underlying asset, lies at the very heart of modern option pricing.

The call option embedded in a convertible bond is a type of warrant. A warrant is basically an option issued by a company on its own stock. In some ways they are like call options. The main differences stem from the fact that warrants are issued by the company itself and tend to be long-term contracts. In the 1920s, warrants became popular in the US but they fell into disrepute in the 1930s when they became associated with market manipulation. They were shunned by the New York Stock Exchange until 1965 when AT&T issued warrants.

We will see that many of the researchers who contributed to the development of option pricing in the 1960s picked up their interest in this topic from their own market experience. Paul Samuelson, who was destined to play a key role in this development traces his interest in warrants to an investment newsletter to which he subscribed in about 1950.[9] Sheen Kassouf was already investing in the market when he went back to Columbia in 1962 to study for a PhD about valuing warrants. Ed Thorp was also preparing to invest in warrants before he teamed up with Kassouf in 1965.

PAUL SAMUELSON

Paul Samuelson, made a number of fundamental contributions to the pricing of warrants. He was already very interested in these securities when he discovered Bachelier's thesis. It will be recalled that Bachelier had assumed that asset-price movements follow a normal distribution and that Samuelson assumed that the returns on the underlying stock followed a *lognormal distribution*. He was able to derive a formula for the warrant price. This formula contained a number of variables. Two of these variables were the expected return on the stock and the expected return on the warrant. (We discuss the expected return in the Appendix to this Chapter.) These were unknown variables and it was difficult to estimate them. If Samuelson had found a way to obtaining values for these two variables, he would have solved the option-pricing problem.

The key to determining the values of the two unknowns was the no-arbitrage concept. Samuelson had the key in his hands because he had already used the no-arbitrage idea.[10]

SPRENKLE, BONESS AND COOTNER

In 1958, Case Sprenkle, an economics graduate student at Yale was searching for a thesis topic. He attended a seminar given by Paul Samuelson on the subject of option pricing and this gave Sprenkle the idea for his own dissertation.

Harry Markowitz had developed his model of portfolio selection in 1952. It provided a precise method for investors to select an optimal portfolio of stocks. In order to implement Markowitz's model the investor needed estimates of the expected returns on the different stocks and a measure of the risk of each stock. This measure of risk is known as the *variance* and we describe it in the Appendix.

Sprenkle's idea was to use the options and warrants market prices to infer investors' expectations about the returns and variance of common stocks. He developed a pricing formula that contained these parameters and used statistical techniques to back out the market's estimates. The extraction of expectations from derivatives prices was quite perceptive and this approach emerged as a powerful tool once these markets were more fully developed.

Case Sprenkle's formula for the price of a warrant also contained two unknown parameters.[11] One of these was the expected return on the stock and the other was a discount factor related to the risk of the stock.

Meanwhile, James Boness was also working on deriving a formula for stock options in his thesis at the University of Chicago under the chairmanship of Lawrence Fisher. Boness, too, assumed that the distribution of stock prices was lognormal. His solution to the expected rate of return question was to assume that investors discounted the expected proceeds from the option at the expected rate of return on the stock. His final formula is tantalisingly close to the Black–Scholes–Merton (BSM) formula, except that it contains the expected return on the stock where the BSM formula contains the riskless rate.

Boness also performed another useful service by translating Bachelier's thesis into English. This translation of Bachelier's thesis formed the centrepiece of an influential collection of research papers that was edited by Paul Cootner. Cootner's book, published in 1964, was entitled *The Random Character of Stock Market Prices*. It brought the major papers on stock price movements together in one volume as well as the key papers on option pricing and warrant pricing. This volume became essential reading for every serious scholar in the field. Cootner wrote superb introductions to each of the four sections of the book. His first paragraph conveys the intended scope of the work:

> Wherever there are valuable commodities to be traded, there are incentives to develop markets to organize that trade more efficiently. In modern complex societies the securities markets are usually among the best organized and virtually always the largest in terms of sales. The prices of such securities are typically very sensitive, responsive to all events both real and imagined that cast light on the murky future. The subject of this book is the attempts by skilled statisticians and economic theorists to probe into this process of price formation.

THORP AND KASSOUF

In 1965, two young professors met at the University of California's newly established campus at Irvine. Sheen Kassouf was an economist and Edward Thorp was a mathematician. They soon discovered their common interest in warrant pricing. Kassouf analysed market data to detemine the key variables that influence warrant prices. Based on this analysis he developed an empirical formula that explained warrant price in terms of these variables. Kassouf collaborated with Thorp to write a book called *Beat the Market*. It discussed the hedging of warrants using the underlying stock and developed a formula for the ratio of shares of stock to options needed to create a hedged position. This important idea was used by Black and Scholes in their celebrated 1973 paper.[12]

Thorp and Kassouf knew that the conventional approach of projecting the terminal payoff under the warrant and discounting back the positive part involved two troublesome parameters: the expected rate of return on the stock and the discount rate.

Thorp and the option formula

While Ed Thorp was thinking about these issues he was also trading warrants, which he believed were overvalued. His strategy was to buy the stock and sell the warrants short. As time passed the price of the stock changed and so too did the price of the warrant. Thorp noted that in these circumstances the portfolio could be adjusted by changing the investments in the two assets. He explored how this dynamic adjustment could be done in an actual market and noted the relationship between the stock price and the warrant price as circumstances changed. In a paper published in 1969, but written in 1968, it is clear that he understood dynamic hedging.[13]

By 1967, Thorp was aware of Cootner's book and the various warrant models that were based on taking the expected value of the payoff. Thorp had previously concluded that if he assumed a lognormal distribution for the asset, this produced a plausible formula for the warrant price. However his formula still contained the two bothersome parameters: the expected return on the stock, which Thorp called m, and the discount rate needed to convert the payoff at expiration back to current time, which he called d. As he experimented with the warrant formula, Thorp noticed that a simple way to eliminate the two parameters was to set both the expected return on the stock and the discount rate equal to the riskless rate. The resulting formula is, of course, the same as the Black–Scholes formula.

Thorp goes on to note that, not only does he not have a proof of the option formula but he does not even know if it is the right formula. At this point however, it provided the practical tool he needed. He describes his experiences using the formula:

> I can't prove the formula but I decide to go ahead and use it to invest, because there is in 1967–68 an abundance of vastly overpriced (in the sense of *Beat the Market*) OTC options. I use the formula to sell short the most extremely overpriced. I have limited capital and margin requirements are unfavorable so I short the options (typically at two to three times fair value) "naked," i.e. without hedging with the underlying stock. As it happens, small company stocks are up 84% in 1967 and 36% in 1968 (Ibbotson), so naked shorts of options are a disaster. Amazingly, I end up breaking even overall, on about $100,000 worth of about 20 different options sold short at various times from late '67 through '68. The formula has proven itself in action.

Was Ed Thorp the first person to discover and use the Black–Scholes formula? We find the evidence persuasive.[14] Thorp had both the background experience in hedging warrants and the mathematical ability to make such a discovery. He also had a strong incentive. When asked why he did not go public with this key result he replied that he was planning to set up a hedge fund and that this result would provide a competitive edge.[15] Thorp's work does not diminish in any way the contribution of Black, Merton and Scholes. They were the first to prove the result and they were the first to publish it. As Thorp himself notes:[16]

> BS was a watershed – it was only after seeing their proof that I was certain that this was the formula – and they justifiably get all the credit. They did two things that are required: They proved the formula (I didn't) and they published it (I didn't).

MEANWHILE BACK IN BOSTON

The story now moves back to MIT. By the late 1960s, Robert Merton was working with Paul Samuelson as his research assistant and graduate student. In 1969 they published a paper on warrant pricing that took a somewhat different approach.[17] They went back to the basic economic idea that in equilibrium the price adjusts so that supply is equal to demand. Samuelson and Merton were able to use this approach to obtain a relationship between the values of the warrant at successive time steps. Their approach, with some additional assumptions, provides another method of reaching the Black–Scholes formula. Samuelson and Merton came close to discovering the option formula. Some of the concepts they used have a very contemporary flavour and are now part of the toolkit of modern derivative pricing.[18] The equilibrium approach requires us to make more assumptions than the no-arbitrage approach but it is more versatile in that it can be applied to a broader class of problems.

FISCHER BLACK

The final steps in solving the option puzzle were made in papers by Fischer Black, Myron Scholes and Robert Merton.[19] The fascinating story of how they arrived at the formula has been told by Peter Bernstein in his book *Capital Ideas*.[20] We will sketch the details of their contributions and achievements.

In 1965, Fischer Black joined the consulting company Arthur D Little in Boston, where he met Jack Treynor who stimulated his interest in finance. Treynor was also a creative individual and made a contribution to the disovery of the so-called *capital asset pricing model* (CAPM). This model is derived from the basic idea that in any market the price is determined by the balancing of supply and demand. It tells us how the expected return on any common stock is related to the expected return on a portfolio that contains all the stocks in the market: the so-called market portfolio. We describe it more fully in the Appendix. Black became intrigued with the concept of equilibrium.

Black's fascination with this essentially economic concept was unusual in view of his background. Black had majored in physics as an undergraduate and his PhD was in applied mathematics at Harvard. He had never taken a formal course in economics or finance in his life.

Black was a remarkable individual. Jack Treynor has summarised Black's contributions as follows: "Fischer's research was about developing clever models – insightful, elegant models that changed the way we look at the world."[21]

Emanuel Derman, who was a colleague of Fischer Black's at Goldman Sachs & Co, has given an insightful account of Black's approach:[22]

> To me, Fischer's approach to modeling seemed to consist of unafraid hard thinking, intuition and no great reliance on advanced mathematics. This was inspiring. He attacked puzzles in a direct way, with whatever skills he had at his command, and often it worked.

Black became interested in the problem of pricing warrants after he teamed up with Treynor. He explored the relationship between the expected rate of return on the warrant and the expected rate of return on underlying stock. Over each short time period, Black assumed that these returns would conform to the CAPM, which was originally developed for common stocks.

Black was able to use the CAPM to derive an equation for the option's price. (We provide further details of Black's derivation in the Appendix to this Chapter.) The equation involved a relationship between the option price and its rate of change with respect to time as well as the asset price. Such equations are known as *differential equations* and have been used for a long time in physics and mathematics but until that point, had not been used much in finance. Black's final equation for the option price did not contain some of the variables he had started with. This meant that the eventual formula would not depend on these variables. The only risk term remaining was the total risk of the stock as measured by its volatility. Black was fascinated to note that the option price equation did not include the stock's expected return nor indeed any other asset's expected return.

BLACK AND SCHOLES

At this point Black had made significant progress. The solution to the differential equation would be the option price. He tried to produce a solution but noted that he was not familiar with the standard solution methods.[23] Black put the problem aside but started working on it again in 1969 with Myron Scholes, who was also interested in the warrant problem. Scholes had obtained a PhD in finance from the University of Chicago, where his mentor had been Merton Miller. In 1968, Scholes had joined MIT as an assistant professor of finance. Together Black and Scholes would solve the problem and produce the most acclaimed formula in finance.

Black has described the thinking that guided them toward the solution. His equation indicated that the option formula depended on the stock's volatility and not its expected return. The implication was that the formula could be derived using any expected return. So, they pretended that the expected return on the stock was equal to the riskless rate.[24] They also assumed, as had the other researchers in the 1960s, that the stock's returns were lognormal. This meant they could compute the expected value of the option at maturity. However this was not the option's current price – only its expected terminal value.

Black and Scholes then had an important insight. They could treat the option's expected return in the same way as they had dealt with the stock's expected return. They could assume, for valuation purposes, that it too had an expected return equal to the riskless rate. So, they could convert the expected final value of the option to its current value by discounting it at the riskless rate and when they did so they discovered the option formula. They confirmed that the formula satisfied the differential equation that Black had derived earlier. The task started by Bachelier was now complete.

HARNESSING THE POWER OF ITÔ CALCULUS

While Black and Scholes were working on their formula, they had several discussions with Robert Merton who was also working on option valuation. One of Merton's important contributions to finance was to introduce rigorous mathematical tools to deal properly with the modelling of uncertainty in continuous time. This framework was known as *stochastic calculus* and was developed by mathematicians. The most important contribution to this development was made by a Japanese mathematician, Kiyoshi Itô who gave a precise mathematical framework for modelling the evolution of uncertainty over time.[25]

Itô's work provided a rigorous mathematical foundation for the ideas of Bachelier and provided Merton with the perfect instrument for the analysis of stock price movements in continuous time. Merton also used this approach to model how individuals select investments over time. He extended the static one-period models to the much more sophisticated continuous time models.

Merton showed how the Black–Scholes model could be derived without the use of the CAPM. Merton's approach corresponds to setting up a portfolio of the stock and the option and dynamically adjusting this portfolio over time. Thanks to his use of the Itô calculus, Merton was able to do this in continuous time. By adjusting the portfolio at every instant, all the random fluctuations can be hedged away. From the no-arbitrage principle, this portfolio must earn the riskless interest rate. However, it would seem that this approach has a Catch 22 feature: to work out the correct amount of the option to hold in the portfolio we need to know how the option

---

PANEL 1
ITÔ USES MUSIC TO DESCRIBE HIS WORK

In precisely built mathematical structures, mathematicians find the same sort of beauty others find in enchanting pieces of music, or in magnificent architecture. There is, however, one great difference between the beauty of mathematical structures and that of great art. Music by Mozart, for instance, impresses greatly even those who do not know musical theory; the cathedral in Cologne overwhelms spectators even if they know nothing about Christianity. The beauty in mathematical structures, however, cannot be appreciated without understanding of a group of numerical formulae that express laws of logic. Only mathematicians can read "musical scores" containing many numerical formulae, and play that "music" in their hearts. Accordingly, I once believed that without numerical formulae, I could never communicate the sweet melody played in my heart. Stochastic differential equations, called "Itô Formula", are currently in wide use for describing phenomena of random fluctuations over time. When I first set forth stochastic differential equations, however, my paper did not attract attention. It was over ten years after my paper that other mathematicians began reading my "musical scores" and playing my "music" with their "instruments". By developing my "original musical scores" into more elaborate "music", these researchers have contributed greatly to developing "Itô Formula". In recent years, I find that my "music" is played in various fields, in addition to mathematics. Never did I expect that my "music" would be found in such various fields, its echo benefiting the practical world, as well as adding abstract beauty to the field of mathematics. On this opportunity of the Kyoto Prize lectures, I would like to express my sincerest gratitude and render homage to my senior researchers, who repeatedly encouraged me, hearing subtle sounds in my "Unfinished Symphony".

(Extract from Lecture by Professor K. Itô (1998) on occasion of being awarded the Kyoto Prize, the most prestiguous scientific award in Japan.)

---

changes as the stock price changes. But it is the option price that we have to find in terms of the things that affect it.

There is a way out. When setting up the hedge it is enough to assume that the option depends on the current stock price and time to maturity. Both of these variables will change as time passes. It turns out we can derive an equation for the option price. The equation involves the option price directly and also includes other terms that depend on the option price. For example, one of these terms shows how the option price changes as the stock price changes. If the stock price moves by a dollar, this term shows how much the option price moves in response. The details of the derivation are beyond the scope of this book but when the dust settles we have an equation for the option price, which is exactly the same differential equation that Black had derived and that Black and Scholes had solved. The hedging argument, developed by Merton, led to the same equation and to the same formula for the option price. When Black and Scholes published their paper in 1973, they first derived the formula using Merton's approach.[26] Their original approach, based on the CAPM, was also included.

Merton also published a remarkable paper in 1973, which included a number of important extensions of the Black–Scholes model. Merton constructed a rigorous and general theory of option pricing based on the foundation of no arbitrage and the Itô calculus.[27] He showed just how far the no-arbitrage assumption can go, in deriving relations among different securities. Merton derived the Black–Scholes model under more general conditions than Black and Scholes originally specified. An option's value depends on the dividends payable on the asset over the option's future lifetime. Merton showed how to handle this in the valuation. He also predicted when a rational investor should exercise an American option and showed how to value American options (see Chapter 2).

In 1973, therefore, with the publication of these two seminal papers, the classic option valuation problem – a problem that had baffled some of the greatest minds in the finance profession – was solved. It had taken a long time and the efforts of many bright minds. The biggest obstacle was how to handle the expected rates of growth and the rate to be used to discount. The solution was simple: blindingly simple, but also deceptively simple. The option could be valued as if all the assets earned the riskless rate. The expected return on the stock and the expected return on the option did not appear at all.

Since the publication of these two papers, there has been an explosive growth in derivatives and this growth is related to the intellectual advances in the field, inspired by the BSM solution. New pricing and hedging technologies fuel this growth and, at the same time, the quest for the solution of practical problems has inspired new ideas. As Merton himself noted:[28]

> While reaffirming old insights, the continuous time model also provides new ones. Perhaps no better example is the seminal contribution of Black and Scholes that, virtually on the day it was published, brought the field to closure on the subject of option and corporate liability pricing. As the Black–Scholes work was closing gates on fundamental research in these areas it was simultaneously opening new gates: in applied and empirical study and setting the foundation for a new branch of finance called contingent claims analysis.

The BSM formula is so important that it has been included as part of the Appendix to this chapter.

APPENDIX
Statistical concepts: expected value and variance

This Appendix contains four sections dealing in more detail with some technical topics that have been mentioned in this chapter. The first section deals with basic statistical concepts. The second describes the capital asset pricing model. The third summarises Black's derivation of the equation for the option price and the last section gives the actual formula itself.

We will explain the concepts of expected value and variance using a simple example. The expected value corresponds to the familiar notion of average and the variance is a measure of the uncertainty associated with a set of uncertain outcomes. The set of uncertain outcomes is said to form a distribution, eg, the prices of a certain stock one year from now or the number of heads in four tosses of a coin. In the coin example, the number of heads could be zero, one, two, three or four and we will now use this example as an illustration.

Suppose we are interested in how likely it is that we will observe a given number of heads in the four tosses. For example, suppose we wish to know how likely it is that we will observe exactly one head in the four tosses. A natural approach might be to take a coin and perform a large number of experiments, in which each experiment consists of a sequence of four tosses. If we count the number of experiments that produced exactly one head and compare this to the total number of experiments, the ratio of these two numbers will give us an estimate of how likely it is to obtain one head. There are two difficulties with this approach: first, we might get tired of repeating such a boring task; second, it is not clear how many experiments we should conduct. Should we run the experiment 100 times or a 1,000 times? However, if we used a computer to simulate this experiment then we could run it a million times and this would give us a very good estimate of how often we could expect to find exactly one head.

The number of experiments that produce exactly one head divided by the total number of experiments provides the relative frequency of this event. In this example, the relative frequency of the event in question will approach 25% as the total number of experiments becomes large. If we are now asked to predict how likely it is that, in a single experiment of four tosses we will get exactly one head, we can assume that there will be a 25% chance of this happening. We can rephrase this as follows: there is a 25% probability of obtaining exactly one head in a series of four tosses of a fair coin.

In this case, we can work out why the probability is 25%. The first toss has two possible outcomes: either heads (H) or tails (T). The second also has two outcomes: either (H) or (T). In same way, the third has two

Figure A1   16 possible outcomes for a series of four tosses of a coin

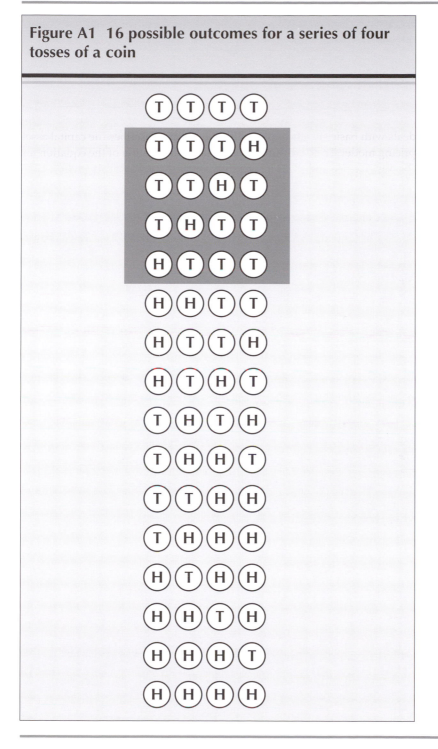

outcomes and so does the fourth. Since each toss can have two outcomes, there are in total, 16 different possible patterns. We record the distinct outcomes in Figure A1, where the number of different patterns with exactly one head are shown in bold. The total possible number is 16 and the ratio of four to 16 is 25%. Hence the probability of obtaining one head in four tosses is 25%.

We apply the same logic to find the probability of obtaining zero heads, two heads, three heads and four heads. If a series of four tosses produce no heads, then all four must show tails and there is just one way that this can happen. Therefore, the probability of obtaining no heads in a series of four tosses is one divided by 16 or 6.25%. In the same way we can find that the probability of two heads is the ratio of six to 16 (37.5%), the probability of three heads is four over 16 (25%) and the probability of having all four turn up heads is one over 16 (6.25%). Note that the sum of all the probabilities is exactly one (100%).

Armed with these probabilities we can compute the expected number of heads. This is the average number we would obtain if we conducted a large number of experiments, where each experiment consists of four tosses. The expected number of heads, for our example, is given by:

$$0.0625(0) \ + \ 0.25(1) \ + \ 0.375(2) \ + \ 0.25(3) \ + \ 0.0625(4) \ = \ 2$$

Hence, the expected number of heads is two. This number is also known as the *expected value* of the distribution or the *mean* of the distribution.

Table A1 Details of steps in computing the variance of the distribution of heads

Number of heads	Probability of this number of heads	Difference between number of heads and expected value	Difference squared	Product of column 4 and probability
0	0.0625	−2	4	0.25
1	0.25	−1	1	0.25
2	0.375	0	0	0
3	0.25	1	1	0.25
4	0.0625	2	4	0.25

The variance measures the dispersion of a distribution around its expected value. To obtain the variance, we first find the difference between each outcome and its expected value; we square these differences and take the expected value of these squared differences. As an example, we now compute the variance of the distribution of the number of heads in four tosses. The main steps in computing the variance are outlined in Table A1. The first column gives the number of heads and the second gives the probability of obtaining this number of heads. The third column shows the difference between the number of heads and the expected number of heads, eg, if the number of heads is zero this difference is negative two. The fourth column shows the square of this difference. The last column is obtained by multiplying the second column by the fourth column and the final step is to add the numbers in the final column. In this case, the sum is 1, so the variance of this distribution is 1.

The variance corresponds to the expected value of the square of the distance from the mean. If the observations are all tightly bunched around the mean, then the variance will be smaller than if the observations are widely dispersed. The standard deviation is defined to be the square root of the variance. In this example, the standard deviation also happens to be 1 but this is because the variance is 1. If the variance is 9, the standard deviation would be 3. In the case of the normal or bell curve distribution, as shown in Figure 5.2 about 68% of the observations lie within one standard deviation of the mean.

In finance applications, we are often interested in the distribution of the rate of return of an asset and its associated standard deviation. In option applications, we often refer to the standard deviation of the return as the volatility of the return. The BSM formula depends, critically, on the volatility of the return on the underlying stock.

The capital asset pricing model

The *capital asset pricing model* (CAPM) tells us how the return on a stock relates to the return on the market as a whole. The market can be represented by a well-diversified portfolio of common stocks or a representative stock market index. Such a well-diversified portfolio is called the market portfolio. Suppose we pick a particular stock, eg, stock A. If the market goes up we expect that the price of stock A will also go up and likewise, if the market falls we expect the price of stock A to fall. The degree to which stock A moves will depend on how sensitive it is to movements in the market.

We need to introduce two concepts before we explain the capital asset pricing model. The first is the *beta* of a security, which represents the sensitivity of the security's return to the market return. If a stock has a high beta, its return is very sensitive to the market return and if it has a low beta its return is less sensitive to the market as a whole. The second concept is the *excess return* on a security, which is defined to be the return on the security over and above the riskless rate. Thus, the excess return on the riskless security itself is zero. If a stock earns 12% per annum and the riskless rate is 5%, the excess return on this stock is 7%. The *expected excess return* on a security is the average rate we expect to earn on a stock in excess of the riskless rate.

The CAPM states that the expected excess return on a security is equal to the beta of the security, multiplied by the expected excess return on the market. A numerical example may help at this stage. Suppose that stock A has a beta of 2, we expect the market to earn 15% and the riskless rate is 5%. In this case, the model predicts that stock A has an expected return of 25%. This is explained thus:

$$\textit{Expected return on stock A} = 0.05 + 2(0.15 - 0.05) = 0.25$$

However, if we have another stock, (B) that has a beta of 0.8, then the CAPM predicts it will have an average return of 13%. This is because:

$$\textit{Expected return on stock B} = 0.05 + 0.8(0.15 - 0.05) = 0.13$$

The CAPM expresses a very simple and powerful intuition. It demonstrates that there is a relation between return and risk and it shows that beta is the right measure of risk to use in this context.

The CAPM holds for combinations of securities in a very simple way. If an investor puts US$50,000 in Enron and US$50,000 in IBM, the beta of their portfolio is simply the average of the betas of these two stocks. By the same logic, the model holds for portfolios of securities including the market portfolio of all the securities. The beta of the market portfolio is therefore unity. We can go long and short securities to mix matters up so that we end up with a portfolio whose beta is zero. For example, if two stocks, C and D, each have the same beta, we can construct a portfolio with a zero beta by going long stock C and going short stock D. Fischer Black used the concept of a zero beta portfolio to derive the equation for the option price.

Summary of Black's approach

Black used the CAPM to formulate expressions for the expected return on the option and the expected return on the stock. The stock's expected return was equal to the riskless rate plus another term, proportional to the beta of the stock. Similarly, the option's expected return was equal to the riskless rate, as well as a risk term proportional to the beta of the option. This would seem to be a rather unpromising start as the ultimate option formula does not depend on these factors. The correct formula does *not* depend on expected returns nor does it depend on the betas. The returns on the option and the stock however, should always move in the same direction since owning the option is similar to a levered investment in the stock. Hence, they move in a synchronised fashion and their movements are also related to the market movements. There is a direct relation between the beta of the option and the beta of the stock that means we can value the option using only the beta of the stock.

The basic idea of Black's derivation lies in the construction of a portfolio that has zero beta. This portfolio consists of a short position in the call option and a long position in the right amount of the stock, to minimise the risk of the position. This was the strategy advocated by Thorp and Kassouf (1967) in *Beat the Market*. There are two criteria that could be used to select the right amount of stock to hold. One is to use the delta of the option, where delta corresponds to the change in the option induced by a dollar change in the stock. The other is to adjust the stock position so that the beta of the portfolio is zero. The result is that for short time periods, both criteria lead to the same stock position since the beta of the portfolio is zero, its *expected* return must also be equal to the riskless interest rate.

Black also knew that the key variables which affect the option's price as time passes are changes in the stock price and the passage of time itself. This insight, (together with the ideas of Professor Itô) can be used to derive a direct expression for the expected return on the option that is related to changes in the stock price and the passage of time. However, since the portfolio is a combination of the stock and the option we can also find the expected return on the portfolio if we know the expected returns on its component pieces. When we include these two pieces of information, the final expression for the expected return on the portfolio does not contain the stock's expected return. Now we can set the expected return on the portfolio equal to the riskless rate because the portfolio has a beta of zero. This gives us an equation that must be satisfied by the price of the option.

Black's analysis resulted in an equation for the option's price. The equation involved a relationship between the option price and its rate of change with respect to time as well as the asset price. His equation is an example of a *partial differential equation*. We have stressed that the final equation did not contain some of the variables he had started with because they had dropped out along the way. This meant that the eventual formula for the option price did not depend on these variables. The beta of the stock did not appear. The only risk term remaining was the total risk of the stock as measured by its volatility. Black was fascinated to note that the option price equation did not include the stock's expected return, nor indeed any other asset's expected return.

The Black–Scholes–Merton formula

The BSM formula gives the price of a standard European call option in terms of five inputs. These inputs are:

❏ the current asset price;
❏ the option's strike price;
❏ the volatility of the asset's return;
❏ the time to option maturity; and
❏ the riskless rate.

It is conventional to use the following notation for these variables:

❏ S: current asset price;
❏ K: strike price;
❏ σ: volatility;
❏ T: time to maturity; and
❏ r: riskless rate.

It is more intuitive to present the formula in steps. First, we consider a zero coupon bond which matures on the same date as the option and has a maturity payment equal to the strike price. The current price of this bond, B is given by

$$B = Ke^{-rT}$$

The Black–Scholes formula can be written in terms of a long position in the stock and a short position in this bond as follows:

$$\Delta_1 S - \Delta_2 B$$

where Δ_1 and Δ_2 are functions of the five variables that determine the option's price. By writing the formula in this way, we see that it corresponds to a portfolio of Δ_1 units of the stock and Δ_2 units of the bond. Indeed, this shows how the current call price can be related to the replicating portfolio that we discussed in Chapter 4.

The BSM formula tells us what the values of Δ_1 and Δ_2 are in terms of the five input variables that determine the option's price. To do so we need to take a little detour to introduce a function that is obtained from the normal distribution.

If we have a normal distribution that has an expected value of zero and a standard deviation of 1, it is called the *standard normal distribution*. Figure A2 shows the shape of this distribution. The total area that lies underneath the standard normal curve in Figure A2 is equal to 1. Hence, if we pick any number on the horizontal axis, say at a distance d from the origin and draw a vertical through this point, the area to the left of the line under the curve will be a positive number less than 1. This area is denoted by the $N(d)$ and it has an important probabilistic interpretation.

Here is the interpretation. Suppose I want to determine the probability

Figure A2 Standard normal distribution

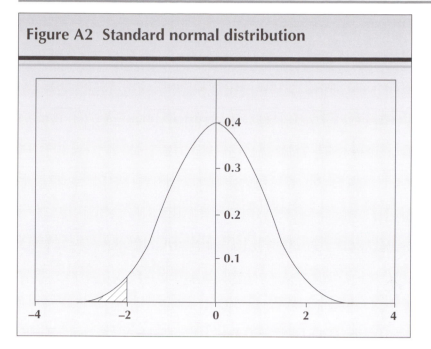

that a number picked at random from the standard normal distribution is less than d. This probability is given by the quantity $N(d)$, which as we saw is the area under the normal curve to the left of the line through d. A few numerical examples may help. If d is zero then since the normal curve is symmetrical around zero and the whole area under the curve is 1, the area to the left of zero must be one half, ie, $N(0)$ equals one half. Most of the area under the standard normal curve is concentrated in the region of two standard deviations on either side of the mean (zero in this case). This means that most of the area lines in the region are bounded by the vertical lines through –2 and +2. So, the probability that a number picked at random from the standard normal distribution is less than 2 is quite high; in fact it is 0.9772. We can confirm this from standard tables of the function $N(d)$, which gives $N(2) = 0.9772$. In the same way, the probability that a number picked at random from a standard normal distribution is less than –2 is very small; in exact terms it is 0.0228 since $N(-2) = 0.0228$. The shaded area in Figure A2 is therefore 0.0228.

Both Δ_1 and Δ_2 in the BSM formula can be written in terms of this function N. In fact

$$\Delta_1 = N(d_1)$$

where d_1 is equal to

$$\frac{\log \dfrac{S}{B} + \dfrac{1}{2}\,\sigma^2 T}{\sigma \sqrt{T}}$$

In the same way,

$$\Delta_2 = N(d_2)$$

where d_2 is equal to

$$\frac{\log \dfrac{S}{B} - \dfrac{1}{2}\,\sigma^2 T}{\sigma \sqrt{T}}$$

Putting things together the BSM formula for the standard European call option is:

$$N(d_1)\,S - N(d_2)\,B = S\,N(d_1) - B\,N(d_2)$$

This formula tells us not only what factors influence the call option price. We now give a numerical example. Suppose we have a European call option based on the inputs below.

Table A2 Inputs for a European call

Variable	Symbol	Numerical value
Stock price	S	100
Strike price	K	135
Stock return volatility	σ	20% per annum
Time to option maturity	T	Five years
Riskless rate	r	6% per annum

If we substitute these numerical values into the Black–Scholes formula we obtain the following values:

Table A3 Black–Scholes values

Symbol	Numerical value for this example
d_1	0.22337
d_2	−0.22384
$N(d_1)$	0.58838
$N(d_2)$	0.41144

In this case the discounted value of the strike price, B is equal to 100.01. Hence the BSM option price is:

$$100(0.58838) - 100.01(0.41144) = 17.69$$

In this case, the replicating portfolio consists of a long position of 58.838% shares of stock and short position of 41.144% units of the riskless bond. The formula can be used to show what happens to the option price if one of the inputs is changed. For example, if the volatility is 19% instead of 20% and the other four inputs remain the same, then the option price drops to 16.82.

1   See Bachelier (1900).
2   If a price follows Brownian motion in continuous time, then over any discrete time interval its distribution is normal. See Feller (1968).
3   Bachelier's thesis, p. 45 as reprinted in Cootner (1965); also reprinted by Risk Books (2000) with an introduction by Andrew Lo.
4   For example, if we consider a three-month call option with representative parameters the square root formula of Bachelier gives prices that are remarkably close to those obtained by the modern Black–Scholes–Merton formula. See Boyle and Ananthananarayanan (1979) for the derivation of the square root approximation to the Black–Scholes formula.
5   As reported in the transcript of the PBS television programme "NOVA 2704: The Trillion Dollar Bet". (Broadcast February 8, 2000.)
6   Editorial, 1968, *Financial Analysts Journal* (January/February), pp. 15-6.
7   Graham and Dodd: *Security Analysis*.
8   The proprietary trading desk trades the firm's own money as distinct from its customers' money.
9   See Bernstein (1992), p. 115.
10 Samuelson (1965) had considered the idea of using the no-arbitrage principle: "Mere arbitrage can take us no further than equation (19). The rest must be experience – the recorded facts of life".
11 There is a description of Sprenkle's formula in Black and Scholes (1973).
12 Black and Scholes (1973) note that, "One of the concepts we use in developing our model is expressed by Thorp and Kassouf".

13 See Thorp (1969).

14 This evidence is based on extensive correspondence with Ed Thorp in June and July 2000 and a study of his published papers and notes.

15 Telephone interview with Ed Thorp, 20 June 2000.

16 E-mail from Ed Thorp, 26 July 2000.

17 See Samuelson and Merton (1969).

18 Samuelson and Merton (1969) derived a formula where the warrant price is expressed in terms of its discounted expected value. The expectation is taken with respect to what the authors termed the utility probability density which in modern terms is the risk neutral measure.

19 See Black and Scholes (1973) and Merton (1973).

20 See Bernstein (1992).

21 See Treynor (1996).

22 See Derman (1996).

23 See Black (1989).

24 The word "pretend" is used advisedly. The expected return on the stock will be higher than the riskless rate. Indeed the capital asset pricing model states that this must be so. The use of the riskless rate here does not mean that any investor actually believes that the expected return on the stock will be this rate. It is a useful trick but one that puzzles even the best students.

25 See Itô (1951).

26 See Black and Scholes (1973).

27 See Merton (1973).

28 See Merton (1990).

6

How Firms Hedge

This chapter discusses hedging and risk management. It explains how a firm's risk management programme can be related to its broader goals and describes value-at-risk (VAR), a simple method for measuring a firm's risk exposure that is now widely used by banks and corporations.

We will then discuss three specific case studies to illustrate how derivatives are used for risk management:

❑ the way in which Microsoft, the largest software company in the world, uses derivatives to manage various risks that it faces;
❑ how firms in the gold-mining industry use derivatives to deal with price risk; and
❑ a situation where the neglect of a specific risk threatened the solvency of a UK insurance company.

INTRODUCTION TO HEDGING AND RISK MANAGEMENT

Before we start describing *how* firms hedge it is useful to discuss *why* firms hedge. There is no doubt that risk reduction is a major part of the story but this assumption misses some important dimensions of the answer.

We need to distinguish between two types of risk. First, there are *core business risks*. These risks arise from the operations of the business. In general, firms have expertise in dealing with their core business risks and they tend to assume these risks because they expect to make a profit from doing so. The second type of risk is sometimes called *financial risk*. This includes foreign exchange, equity price and interest rate risks. Firms usually do not have special expertise in managing financial risks in-house and they often use derivatives for this purpose.

We gain a better understanding of the reasons why firms hedge if we can show how these activities can be related to the firm's overall objectives. It is generally accepted that one of a firm's major objectives is to maximise the value of its common shares. Kenneth Froot, David Scharfstein and Jeremy Stein have provided a clear rationale for risk management by showing how risk management can be linked directly to maximising the value of the common shares.[1]

The authors make three main points:

❑ *Good investments are the key to creating corporate value.* The cash required for these investments can come from new common stock, new debt or the firm's own money.

❑ *Raising money on the stock market is costly.* Furthermore, there are often self-imposed limits on the amount of debt that a company will raise because too much debt can be dangerous. Hence the preferred way is to use the company's own internal funds.

❑ *The cashflow that comes from the firm's own operations is vulnerable to certain factors that the company cannot control, such as price changes.* The firm's risk management programme should be designed to protect the company's supply of funds.

Within this framework the purpose of risk management is to ensure that the firm has cash available to make profitable investments. There are some bad outcomes that can disrupt a firm's cashflow so that the firm would not have enough money to make good investments. A company can protect itself against these outcomes by using derivatives.

MEASURING RISK: VALUE-AT-RISK

At the firm level, the most popular way to measure the risks that can impair a company's cashflow or endanger its solvency is to use a concept called *value-at-risk*. This is a useful way to summarise a firm's risk exposure in a single dollar figure.

We can illustrate VAR with a specific example. Suppose an investor owns a portfolio of common stocks. Roughly speaking, VAR provides an indication of how much money the portfolio can lose over a particular time period if things get really bad.

To make the definition more precise, the possibility of certain outcomes that may hurt the business actually occurring, are expressed in terms of probabilities. So, the VAR for one month for this portfolio might be US$50,000 at the 95% level. This means that the chances of the portfolios losses in one month being less than US$50,000 are 95%, or that we may expect that 19 times out of 20, such losses will be less than US$50,000. To put it another way, the chance of portfolio losses exceeding US$50,000 is 5%, or 1 chance in 20.

In the late 1990s, VAR became a popular tool for providing summary risk information. Barry Schachter maintains an informative website, which is entirely devoted to VAR.[2] The following description of VAR comes from this site:

> Folklore (if it is fair to attribute as folklore that which only dates back five years) tells us that VaR was developed to provide a single number which could encapsulate information about the risk in a portfolio, which could be calculated rapidly (by 4:15), and could communicate that information to non technical senior managers. Tall order, and not one that could be delivered upon without compromises.

Berry Schachter also provides the following amusing and irreverent description of VAR.

> A number invented by purveyors of panaceas for pecuniary peril intended to mislead senior management and regulators into false confidence that market risk is adequately understood and controlled.

Value-at-risk is now widely used as a risk management tool by major banks. For example, Citicorp used VAR figures in its December 1999 annual report to describe the potential losses in its trading portfolio.[3] Citicorp estimated the loss in market value based on a one-day-ahead time horizon and a 99% confidence level.

> For Citicorp's major trading centers, the aggregate pretax Value at Risk in the trading portfolios was $24 million at December 1999. Daily exposures at Citicorp averaged $18 million in 1999 and ranged from $14 million to $24 million.

Industrial corporations are also adopting VAR to measure and report risk. Microsoft, the company that we discuss next, is one example of this.

MICROSOFT

Microsoft illustrates how a large global corporation manages risk by using derivatives. It has almost 40,000 employees and US$23 billion in revenues. Microsoft conducts business all over the world and it is exposed to many different types of risks. These risks include financial and foreign exchange risks. Microsoft is a good example to discuss because it uses some innovative strategies to manage these risks. Our description is based on current information contained in Microsoft's financial statements and published accounts of Microsoft's hedging programmes.[4]

Microsoft employs VAR as a management tool to estimate its exposure to market risks and reports VAR figures in its annual report. Microsoft uses a longer time horizon – 20 days – than banks typically use in estimating its VAR. Furthermore, Microsoft uses a 97.5% confidence level rather than the 99% level often used by banks.

Microsoft's foreign currency risk

First, we will discuss how Microsoft manages its foreign currency risks. Microsoft is a US company and its home currency is US dollars. However, the company does business in many different countries throughout the world, which exposes it to potential foreign exchange risk.

Microsoft has two main approaches to this currency risk. In some regions it bills its customers in US dollars. At the time of writing, Microsoft tends to use this approach in Latin America, Eastern Europe and South-East Asia. We will see later that Microsoft is still exposed to some real economic risks if the domestic currencies of these countries were to weaken relative to the US dollar. We will also discuss how Microsoft attempts to hedge this risk.

In other parts of the world Microsoft conducts its business in the local currency (Microsoft's annual report for 2000 states: "Finished goods sales to international customers in Europe, Japan, Canada, and Australia are primarily billed in local currencies.")

The company has substantial expenses in Europe associated with its manufacturing, sales and service. These expenses are paid in the local currency. For example, Microsoft employees in Dublin receive their salaries in euros, not US dollars. The company's net revenue, which is the difference between its revenues and expenses, is calculated in terms of the local currency. This net revenue is exposed to the currency risk because, back in the US, the company's financial results are measured in terms of US dollars.

Every month Microsoft's profits (or losses) are converted into US dollars, based on the average exchange rate for the month. Because of this feature, it is the average exchange rate that matters for conversion and not the exchange rate prevailing at the end of the month. Hence, it makes more sense to use a hedging instrument that offers protection against adverse changes in the average rate. Consequently, Microsoft makes extensive use of average or Asian options to protect itself against this currency risk. We now give an example of how such an option works.[5]

Suppose a US-based company will receive 100 million euros from its European operations during the next month. The money is earned evenly over the month and the total amount for the month is to be converted into US dollars at the end of the month. The conversion rate will be based on the average of the exchange rate during the month and suppose that today, 1 euro is worth exactly US$1. If the value of the euro declines during the next month so that the average exchange rate is 1 euro per US$0.99, then the company will receive US$99 million for the 100 million euros. If the euro strengthens so that the average exchange rate is 1 euro per US$1.01 then the company will receive US$101 million at the end of the month. The currency risk faced by the company is that the average exchange rate will decline.

To protect itself against a fall in the value of the euro over this period, the company could buy a one-month average rate put option. Suppose that the company buys such an option with a strike price equal to the current exchange rate of 1 euro per US$1. For simplicity, assume that this option costs half a million US dollars. The payoff on the option will depend on the average exchange rate during the month. We consider three scenarios.

Suppose, first, that the euro weakens and the average rate works out to be 1 euro per US$0.99. In this instance, the payoff on the put option will be US$1 million because the *strike price* is US$100 million and the *asset value* is US$99 million. Hence the company will receive an amount of US$1 million from its put option. The put option has cost half a million dollars – the protection does not come for free.

Now consider what happens if the euro strengthens over the next month. Suppose that the average exchange rate is 1 euro per US$1.02. In this case, the average exchange rate exceeds the strike price so there is no payout on the put option. However, the rate used to repatriate the revenues is the average rate and so the total payment received by the company is US$102 million. So the company has benefited from the stronger euro.

The third case we consider is when the exchange rate remains fixed at 1 euro per US$1 during the next month. This means that the average exchange rate will also be 1 euro per US$1 and, should this happen, the option contract is worth zero at maturity. The company receives exactly US$100 million at the end of the month. However, under the third scenario, when the exchange rate did not budge, the company still had to pay half a million dollars for the option even though it did not receive any apparent benefit payment from the option. This last case illustrates the point that, under some outcomes, a firm would be better off finan-cially if it had not hedged. This example illustrates that hedging gives the company a measure of protection against certain detrimental events but that this protection comes at a cost.

We now explain why Microsoft is still exposed to a currency risk even if it bills its customers in US dollars. To see how this happens, suppose that a given currency experiences a severe crisis so that its value drops in terms of the dollar. Microsoft's distributors generally operate on tight margins and the crisis could cause them problems. The fall in the value of the home currency means that the amount of the local currency needed to buy US$1 rises, hence Microsoft's products expressed in terms of US dollars become more expensive. The increased price will mean that the demand for Microsoft's products will drop and there will be fewer sales. This puts pressure on the company's distributors who often operate on slim margins and, of course, the reduction in sales hurts Microsoft's profits.

Microsoft sometimes tries to soften the impact of a stronger dollar by entering a long forward contract to buy US dollars at a fixed exchange rate in terms of the local currency. For example, the forward contract might involve the purchase of US dollars in six months at the rate of R$2 per US dollar. If the Brazilian Real is devalued relative to the dollar, then Microsoft will make a profit on its forward position. Some of this profit can be passed on to the distributors to ease their pain. In 1999, Microsoft used this device to mitigate the impact of the devaluation of the Real. From Microsoft's perspective, the drawback of this approach is that if the local currency strengthens relative to the dollar, then Microsoft will lose money on its forward contract. The question then is whether Microsoft is willing to absorb this loss. The issues that arise under this type of hedging strategy have been summarised as follows (see Callinicos, 1999):

The most difficult issue to sell internally at Microsoft is the ramifications of hedging when the currency strengthens. Ideally, Microsoft would also like to pass on that risk symmetrically to distributors, so that they would have to pay us more to offset the cost of a hedge that is going against us if the foreign currency strengthens. Otherwise, the distributors potentially have the best of both worlds. This is a judgment call that Microsoft treasury works closely with the general managers of our subsidiaries to address.

Microsoft's interest rate risk

Even though Microsoft has no significant long-term debt, the company is still exposed to interest rate risk. This is because Microsoft owns a large portfolio of short-term and long-term bonds amounting to US$23.8 billion (mid-year 2000). If interest rates rise, the value of a bond portfolio will fall and the size of the fall depends on the amount of the increase. The company's annual report for the year 2000, summarises how Microsoft hedges this risk.

> The Company routinely hedges the portfolio with options in the event of a catastrophic increase in interest rates. The notional amount of the options outstanding was $4.0 billion and $3.6 billion at June 30, 1999 and 2000, June 30.

One of the tools that Microsoft uses to protect its bond portfolio against a dramatic rise in interest rates is a *swaption*. A swaption is an option to enter an interest rate swap in the future. We discussed interest rate swaps in Chapter 2, where we demonstrated how the Ontario Teachers' Pension Plan used interest rate swaps to change the nature of its assets. We now describe interest rate swaptions in more detail.

Interest rate swaptions

The owner of a payer swaption has a type of option whose value increases when interest rates increase. A payer swaption gives its owner the right to enter a swap to pay fixed-rate coupons in exchange for floating rates at some future date. If the swaption is European it can only be exercised when the swaption contract matures. At maturity, the owner of the swaption will check whether it is more profitable to exercise the swaption or let it expire.

An example will make this clearer. Suppose an investor owns a payer swaption, which is just about to mature and gives the investor the right to enter an interest rate swap, which will last for an additional 10 years. Suppose the strike price of the swaption is 7%, so that the owner has the right to pay 7% and receive the floating interest rate in exchange. The owner will compare the ruling market swap rate on a 10-year swap, with 7%. If the ruling rate is 8%, the owner should exercise the swaption. This is because it is cheaper to pay 7% per annum (pa) than 8% pa for the same floating rate series. In contrast, if the market swap rate for a new 10-year swap is 6%, it makes sense for the owner to pay the market rate of 6% rather than 7%. In this case the owner should let the swaption expire.

The owner of a payer swaption benefits if interest rates rise. Thus Microsoft can protect its fixed income portfolio against a sharp rise in interest rates by buying payer swaptions. We can show how this works using a numerical example. This example is highly simplified and is just intended to give the basic idea. Suppose that a fixed income portfolio consists of a stream of equal payments of US$100 pa for the next 10 years. If the initial interest rate is 5% pa, the initial market value of this portfolio is 772.17 but if interest rates rise to 6% pa then the value of the portfolio falls to 736.01. This constitutes a drop of about US$36 in the market value of the portfolio. We will discuss how interest rates affect bond prices more fully in Chapter 8. An investor who owns this portfolio will lose money when interest rates rise.

Suppose that the investor has purchased a 10-year payer swaption with a strike price of 5% and that, to make matters even more simple, the swaption is just about to mature. If interest rates are still 5%, when the swaption matures it is not worth anything and will expire worthless. However, if interest rates have risen to 6% then the swaption is worth something at maturity. More precisely, it is worth 1% of the notional amount of the swaption over a 10-year period. If the notional amount is US$500 then the value of the swaption is equal to an amount of US$5 pa (6% of 500 less 5% of 500) payable over the next 10 years. This payment stream will have a market value of US$36.8 and we see that this corresponds very closely to the loss of 36 on the basic portfolio. The increase in the value of the swaption offsets the decline in the value of the portfolio due to the rise in interest rates. This illustrates how the swaption protects a bond portfolio against a rise in interest rates.

Microsoft's equity price risk

Microsoft is exposed to equity price risk in two different ways. The first exposure arises because Microsoft owns a portfolio of common stocks of other companies. The second exposure arises from the price movements of Microsoft's own common shares.

Microsoft owns a very large equity-based portfolio whose value in mid-2000 was about US$18 billion. This is because the company makes strategic investments in high technology, cable and Internet-based stocks. At the time of writing, Microsoft had significant investments in a number of companies such as AT&T, Comcast, Nextel and Qwest. Technology stocks tend to be very volatile and Microsoft hedges the risk of a significant market drop in these stock prices using options. As noted in Microsoft's 2000 annual report:

> The Company hedges the risk of significant market declines on certain highly
> volatile equity securities with options. The options are recorded at market,
> consistent with the underlying equity securities. At June 30, 2000, the notional
> amount of the options outstanding was $4.0 billion.

Microsoft is also exposed to the price risk of its own stock thorough its
stock option plan. Stock options are granted to all employees. These
options give an employee the right to purchase shares in Microsoft after a
certain vesting period. Employee stock options are commonly used to pay
employees in the high technology sector. We will discuss them in more
detail in Chapter 7. Until January 2000, Microsoft had a policy of buying
back its own stock in the open market to meet these obligations. It
preferred this approach to the alternative of issuing more stock, which
would increase the number of shares outstanding and thus dilute the earnings per share.[6]

As part of its stock buy-back programme Microsoft also sold put
warrants, which are European puts where the strike price is set below the
level of Microsoft's current stock price. These warrants are attractive to
mutual funds that hold large positions in Microsoft because by buying put
warrants from Microsoft the fund is protected against a big drop in
Microsoft's share price. Microsoft collects a cash premium when it sells
these puts. The cash received from the sale of these puts helps Microsoft
defray the cost of buying back its shares in the open market. If Microsoft's
stock price has declined below the strike price of the put when the option
matures, then Microsoft has the option of settling the puts by handing over
Microsoft shares instead of cash.

This strategy works well as long as Microsoft's stock price keeps moving
up. As long as this happens, the cash from selling the put warrants
provides a handsome profit for the company. As long as the stock price
increases, Microsoft does not have to pay a cent when the put warrants
mature. However, if the price of Microsoft stock falls then the company
has to pay when the puts expire. Interestingly, after the company discon-
tinued the put warrant programme in January, 2000, the stock price
dropped by about 50% during the next 15 months in common with the
decline in the market prices of many "high tech" stocks. (It is quite
amazing how well Microsoft timed the discontinuation of the put warrant
programme.) At the time of writing, the company still has written a significant number of these put warrants with strike prices ranging from US$70
to US$78 and maturities extending to December 2002.

In summary, Microsoft has an elaborate risk management programme.
However, as with any company, there are sometimes other unforeseen
risks that can have a big impact on the company's fortunes. In an anti-trust
action, Microsoft was found guilty of monopoly practices in violation of
anti-trust legislation. Judge Thomas Penfield Jackson found that Microsoft

used its dominance in the computer industry to monopolise the Web browser market. At the time of writing, there is still a possibility that the company will be broken up. This risk is not usually considered within the framework of a traditional risk management programme; it is hard to imagine how a derivative could be structured to cover this risk.

HEDGING IN THE GOLD-MINING INDUSTRY

We now turn to a discussion of hedging in the gold-mining industry. There are several reasons to examine this industry:

❑ There is one single source of risk – the risk of a fall in the price of gold.
❑ There are liquid markets for derivatives based on gold and so there are hedging vehicles available to hedge the risk.
❑ Gold-mining firms provide detailed information on their hedging activities (more so than most other industries as they provide details of their hedging activities in their quarterly reports).
❑ Even though many gold producers hedge the price risk, some do not, leading to strongly opposing views among mining firms on the desirability of hedging. This controversy adds spice to the discussion.[7]
❑ Gold is a unique commodity and the factors that influence its price make for an interesting analysis of the advantages and disadvantages of hedging.
❑ Finally, the gold-mining industry provides a useful context for discussing the potential costs of hedging.

We mentioned earlier that there are potential costs associated with hedging and the gold mining industry provides ample illustration. In recent years, the price of gold has been low by historical standards. The existence of gold-price hedges may give an incentive for some high-cost producers to continue mining operations past the point where they should optimally close down. If the spot price is below the cost of production, the optimal decision may be to shut down the mine. The firm can buy gold on the spot market for less than its own cost of extraction. However, if the firm has hedged its production at a much higher price it can continue to make profits without shutting down operations. For example, if the price of gold is US$200 per ounce and if it costs US$270 to produce an ounce, then without any hedging it is unprofitable to operate the mine. However, if the firm has sold forward its production at a contract price of US$400 per ounce, then the firm can still make money by keeping the mine open. The firm would make more money if it shut down the mine and bought gold in the cash market for US$200, which it could deliver for US$400. This discussion is highly simplified as there are other factors we have not taken into account. In practice, there are costs associated with shutting down and opening the mine so that a full analysis of the optimal decision is much more complicated.

John Hathaway, an eloquent critic of hedging, echoes this sentiment:[8]

> In fact, the industry is downright sickly. We think that the industry is gutting its productive capacity by high grading, getting behind on development, squandering financial resources by keeping marginal properties afloat, and drastically reducing exploration expenditures. What prolongs these ill-advised practices long beyond what would be tolerated in any other industry is the unique ability to fix forward selling prices to guarantee (in theory) the spread over projected cash costs.

One argument against hedging by gold producers is that it is unnecessary. If a gold firm's shareholders want price protection they can do it themselves. There are plenty of different derivatives available for this. Furthermore, if a firm has a hedging programme in place, this can distort the price impact of gold price changes. There are situations where the firm's share price falls when the price of gold rises because of the nature of the hedging programme. This happened in 1999 to a number of gold firms that sold call options based on amounts in excess of their future production. As gold prices rose, their stock prices fell and almost pushed them into insolvency. We will provide further details of this later.

The actions of central banks are an important factor that affects the gold market. In many countries, central banks have substantial reserves of gold in their vaults. If the gold just sits there it earns no interest. By leasing out the gold at a rate known as the gold lease rate, the banks can make a profit on their gold. This rate has varied over time but is usually less than 2% pa. Usually the central banks are very careful about those to whom they lend their gold.[9] They restrict their lending to institutions such as large investment banks with strong credit ratings. The investment banks effectively use the gold loans to provide hedges for gold mining companies. Central banks are not usually allowed to deal directly with the mining companies, so the investment banks act as intermediaries and mitigate the credit risk by diversification and by contract design.

We can explain how this works with a simple example. Suppose the gold lease rate is 2% pa. The Sperrin Gold Mining Company wishes to lock in a price for next year's production. To do so, it enters a one-year forward contract with the Grendel investment bank to sell gold at a contract price of US$300 per ounce. The Grendel bank has agreed to buy gold at US$300 in one year from the mining company. Grendel, in turn, leases gold from the Swiss Central Bank in Zurich and agrees to pay the lease rate of 2% pa and repay the gold loan after one year. Grendel sells the gold it has leased and invests the proceeds for one year at the risk-free rate of say 6%. The proceeds of this investment will enable it to repay the interest on the gold loan and in addition cover the contract price on its forward contract with Sperrin. When the forward contract matures, Grendel buys the gold from the mining company, which is used to repay the gold loan to the central bank. If we ignore credit risk, there is no price risk for the Grendel bank in this transaction.

In 1999, a few gold producers ran into financial difficulties because of their hedging programmes. We give specific examples later but some background will help us appreciate why this occurred. The problems were related to the way in which gold prices moved in 1999. For some time it was known that the International Monetary Fund (IMF) was planning to sell some of its gold reserves to provide aid to a number of poorer nations. This debate intensified in early 1999 because a number of countries, including South Africa, opposed this move on the grounds that it would depress the price of gold and probably hurt some of the very nations it was supposed to help. The market had absorbed this information but it was taken by surprise when the UK announced on May 7, 1999 that it planned to sell off over half its reserves through public auctions. This caused an immediate drop in the price of gold. The price fell to US$253 an ounce, its lowest level in 20 years. The market was afraid that other central banks would increase their sales of gold.

Some gold-mining companies, worried by this development and fearful of further price falls, rearranged their hedging programmes. They sold large amounts of gold forward: in the first three quarters, gold producers stepped up their hedging sales by more than 400%, an increase equivalent to 10% of the total annual gold supply. Many industry observers suggested that this increase in forward sales accelerated the decline in gold prices.[10] Hedging may have caused the price of the underlying asset to change.

During the summer of 1999, there was intensive lobbying by gold producers and some affected countries to restrict central bank sales of gold. The producers' lobby group, the World Gold Council, produced a report that showed an apparent concern for the economic welfare of the heavily indebted poor countries that were gold producers.[11] The report argued:

> Many of the countries in this study have recently become more attractive to overseas investors. Exploration by mining companies of promising areas followed, sometimes resulting in mining developments. This trend is set to continue, though given the recent fall in the gold price, a question mark hangs over what might otherwise be a glittering future.

The suggestion that a recovery in the price of gold would provide these countries with a glittering future seems far fetched. There is evidence that other forms of political pressure were also applied. In September 1999, in response to this pressure, the major European central banks announced that they would cap sales and loans of gold for the next five years. Gold prices rose immediately. Several mining companies that had sold forward significant amounts of gold found that these positions were liabilities instead of assets. Firms were short large amounts of gold under these contracts and, as the prices rose, the value of the short position increased. If these gold producers had not overhedged they would have been in a position to deliver the amounts required from their own production. However, if the firms had to buy gold at the increased spot price, this would cause financial difficulties. The banks on the other side of these contracts were exposed to increased credit risk and were entitled to increased cash margins in these contracts. The two firms most mentioned in this connection were Cambior and Ashanti.

Cambior's hedges

Cambior is a mining company producing gold, copper, zinc and other base metals with operations throughout the Americas. In 1999, it produced 630,000 ounces of gold at an average direct mining cost of US$215 per ounce. Cambior had an active gold-price hedging programme that was, according to its 1998 annual report, "conducted to enhance revenues and to protect near to medium term cash flow". At the end of 1998, its prospects looked secure: Cambior had secured its 1999 gold production at an average price of US$358 per ounce. The five-year history of some key statistics is given in Table 6.1.

The price of gold moved steadily downwards over this period by about US$100 per ounce, from US$384 per ounce in 1995 to US$279 in 1999. Cambior appears to have countered this with lower production costs and increased production levels. Its effective selling prices were also significantly higher than the prevailing market prices. For example, in 1999 it

Table 6.1 Production and price statistics: Cambior 1995–9

Year	Production (ounces)	Cost per ounce (US$)	Realised price (US$)	Market price (US$)
1999	630,000	215	356	279
1998	638,000	233	389	294
1997	520,000	255	424	331
1996	502,000	257	423	388
1995	446,000	279	440	384

Source: http://www.cambior.com/english/3_investor/frfindat.htm

was able to realise an average price of US$356 per ounce, when the corresponding market price was US$279 per ounce. These figures suggest that 1999 should have been a good year for the company. In fact, it was a terrible year. The company almost became bankrupt because of its hedging operations. The hedges turned sour when gold prices rose after the central banks announced they would limit their gold sales.

At the end of the third quarter of 1999, Cambior reported that it had a total hedging position of 4.5 million ounces (made up of 1.9 million ounces in call options and 2.6 million ounces in forward contracts). This amount of gold corresponded to seven times the company's annual production and was close to the company's total reserves. The September 1999 quarterly report indicates that Cambior had sold 921,000 ounces of gold call options expiring before the end of 1999, with an average strike price of US$287. These call options covered about 150% of the firm's projected production for 1999. (Cambior's forecast production was 630,000 ounces). If these options were exercised, the company would be forced to sell gold that it was not producing. If gold prices were to rise, this would become a very risky position and by hedging more than it expected to produce, the company was taking a gamble.

On September 26, 1999, the European Central Bank announced that it would limit gold sales in the next five years. Gold prices shot upwards during the following week. In the week after the announcement the price rose from around US$275 an ounce to US$325 an ounce. With gold at US$325 an ounce, Cambior's call options were well in-the-money and it had sold more options than its production would cover. Often these options contain a provision that they can be renegotiated should they expire in-the-money.[12] In a market of gently rising prices, this strategy works. However, if there is a sharp upward spike (as in this case) it becomes far too costly to achieve the necessary restructuring of maturities. To meet its maturing options, Cambior would have to buy gold (at US$325 an ounce) on the cash market so that it could fulfil its option contracts that were struck at US$287 an ounce. This would mean a loss of US$38 per ounce, which is not the way hedging is supposed to work.

Another possibility would have been to buy back the options it had sold. However, Cambior had sold these options when gold prices were low and fairly stable. The volatility used to compute the option price was low. By early October 1999, two things had happened that made the options more valuable. First, the spot price had increased. Second, there was much more uncertainty in the gold market. Investors expected this uncertainty to be in the market for a while and the increase in uncertainty also served to increase option prices.[13] The options had become much more valuable and Cambior was short the options.

At this point the counterparties to Cambior's derivatives position became very concerned about credit risk. The increase in the market value of these contracts triggered margin calls. The purpose of a margin is to reduce the amount of loss on default. Ironically, insisting on the full margin amount can hasten default. For several years, gold prices had eased gently downwards so the possibility of margin calls must have seemed remote. However, on 6 October, following a press release disclosing its hedge position as of September 31, 1999, Cambior's shares fell by 40%.

Cambior entered discussions with its hedging counterparties to see if it could work out an arrangement to keep the company afloat. On October 27, 1999, Cambior reached a standstill agreement with its counterparties and creditors to buy some time. The agreement enabled Cambior to roll over its expiring positions into new contracts by extending the maturities. In turn, Cambior agreed to reduce its outstanding hedge positions with an immediate cost of US$33 million.

Cambior finalised an agreement with its counterparties and financial institutions on December 12, 1999. Under this agreement, Cambior agreed to sell assets to pay for a restructuring of its derivatives positions. Cambior's credit was extended to US$212 million. The interest rate on its debt was raised from Libor +0.75% to Libor +4%. In addition, Cambior undertook to pay US$75 million by June 2000 to cover hedging costs, interest expenses and partial repayment of its loans. The direct costs associated with the restructuring of the hedging programme were US$57 million. To obtain cash the company also sold some mining assets and when the 1999 results were announced, the company posted a net earnings loss of US$358 million.

We can see how Cambior's troubles began. It was speculating rather than hedging in some parts of its derivatives book. Its portfolio of derivatives was vulnerable to the gold price fluctuations that occurred in 1999. In this respect, Cambior was not alone. However, Cambior did not have the liquidity to weather the storm. Ashanti Goldfields, a major West African producer, was also in the same boat as Cambior and experienced similar difficulties.

These disasters raised questions about the future of hedging in the gold industry and a vigorous debate on the merits of hedging has followed.[14] Some producers contended that the practice of selling gold forward has depressed the price of gold and have announced reductions in their hedging operations. Newmont Mining Corporation affirmed its strategy of remaining largely unhedged in its 1999 annual report. On February 4, 2000, Placer Dome, the world's fifth largest producer, announced it was going to eliminate many of its hedged positions and not roll over others. Even Barrick, the most vocal supporter of hedging, announced that it was reducing and restructuring its hedge book.

The Cambior case provides an example where a hedging arrangement almost pushed a firm into bankruptcy. However, we emphasise that this is not a typical case. The gold market is not typical: the price gyrations in 1999 were highly unusual and in the vast majority of hedging programmes, derivatives reduce risk. For example, Géczy, Minton and Schrand (1997) provide evidence that that firms use currency derivatives to reduce risk, and not for speculation. Our next example concerns a case where a particular risk, which was so insignificant that it was ignored, later became so important that it threatened the solvency of some firms in the insurance industry.

THE RISK THAT KILLED EQUITABLE LIFE

The risk in question is a type of interest rate risk that originated from a seemingly innocuous provision that was included in many insurance polices written in the UK several years ago. The potential severity of this risk was not recognised at the time and its significance was not noted until the waning years of the 20th century. The risk lay quietly dormant for several years until it developed into an enormous liability.

These contracts were sold to individuals to provide money for their retirement and they would mature when the policyholder reached 65. Many of the policies contained a maturity guarantee that meant there was a guaranteed rate at which the money that had accumulated could be converted into a lifetime pension. We will see later that this type of guarantee meant that the policyholders were given a very long-term put option on interest rates. When this put option was granted in the 1970s, long-term interest rates were around 10% pa. The effective strike price of the put option varied between 5% and 6%. It was thought that there was virtually no possibility of interest rates falling to levels as low as these. The embedded option would only be valuable if the interest rates at retirement had fallen to these "impossibly" low levels. However, this in fact did happen. There were other factors that compounded the problem as we shall see.

The option embedded in these contracts is known as a guaranteed annuity option, where "annuity" refers to a set of regular annual payments. The monthly pension payments that a person receives from a pension plan correspond to a life annuity because the payments last as long as the person is alive. Insurance companies sell insurance products and life annuities. If a 60 year-old has an investment portfolio worth US$500,000, they can convert this into cash and use the proceeds to buy a life annuity. The annual amount of the annuity payment will depend on the prevailing long-term interest rates and it will also depend on what mortality assumptions the insurance company makes. If interest rates are high, the insurance company can invest the US$500,000 at these high rates and provide a higher annuity payment. If interest rates are low, the insurance company has to invest the US$500,000 at these low rates and provide a lower annuity payment. If the person is expected to live for a very long time, the payments will be lower than if the person is assumed to have a shorter life expectancy.

The reason for including the guaranteed annuity option was to make it easier to sell these policies. When the policies mature, the cash is available to buy an annuity. If the annuity is computed based on ruling market rates, then the amount of the annuity depends on the prevailing interest rate: the higher the interest rate the larger the payment. If interest rates are low when the policy matures, the annuity payment will also be correspondingly reduced. The existence of the guarantee means that there is protection for the policyholder against very low rates when he or she retires. The guarantee begins to take effect only when rates go below some threshold level. We now give more details of how the guarantee was arranged since this is relevant for our story.

We can illustrate the operation of the guarantee with a highly simplified example.[15] Suppose a 65 year-old, named Michael, has just inherited £100,000 under the terms of their aunt's will. He is planning to use this windfall to augment his pension as he has just retired. The current long-term interest rate is 8% and we will assume he will live for exactly 15 more years. On this basis, the yearly payment is £116.83 per 1,000. This is because the current value of 15 yearly payments of £116.83 is exactly 1,000, when we use 8% in the calculations. To restate this, if Michael invests £1,000 to earn 8% pa, he could withdraw exactly £116.83 at the end of each year for the next 15 years and there would be nothing left at the end.

If the prevailing interest rates are 6% instead of 8%, the corresponding yearly income is £102.96 per 1,000 initial investment. If the prevailing interest rate is 4%, the corresponding yearly amount is £89.94 per 1,000 initial investment. Table 6.2 shows how Michael's yearly income varies with interest rates.

Suppose Michael also owns an insurance policy and the insurance company has just informed him that the total proceeds are £100,000. Buried deep in the fine print in the policy is a guaranteed annuity clause, which states he is guaranteed a minimum yearly income of £100 per £1,000 of policy proceeds. This reflects an interest rate of just under 6%. If the prevailing market interest rate is actually 8%, Michael could do better by buying the annuity on the open market since he will then receive £116.83 pa in contrast to the £100 pa guaranteed in the policy. However, if the current rate is only 5% then the market annuity rate is just £96.34, which is below the guaranteed rate of £100. In this case, it is better for Michael to take the guaranteed amount of £100 per annum per 1,000 initial investment. From this example, we see that the insurance company has an additional liability when the guaranteed rate is below the market rate. If the prevailing market rate is only 5%, the extra amount corresponds to £3.66 per year for 15 years.[16]

The insurance company faces an additional liability whenever the

Table 6.2 Yearly income per 1,000 initial investments under different interest rates

Interest rate (percentage per annum assumed in calculation)	Yearly income per 1,000 for 15 years (£)
4	89.94
5	96.34
6	102.96
7	109.79
8	116.83
9	124.06
10	131.47

prevailing rate at maturity is below the guaranteed rate on the policy. If the market interest rates are below the fixed guaranteed rate then the insurance company has to make payment under guaranteed provision for all its maturing policies. Moreover, as interest rates drop, the liability imposed by the guarantee on all the outstanding contracts will increase. In recent years, interest rates have dropped and the size of these liabilities has grown (in 1999 the amount of these additional liabilities was estimated to be about £15 billion). An article in the December 1999 issue of *Risk* noted:

> With many policyholders retiring, or due to retire, some companies have faced insolvency as they struggle to meet their obligations. As a result the worst hit UK insurers, in particular Scottish Widows and National Provident Insurance (NPI) have succumbed to takeover bids in recent months.

There were other factors, in addition to the low interest rate environment, that made matters worse for the insurance companies that had granted these guarantees. Some of these factors were:

❏ the stock market performed well during the 1990s; and
❏ people are living longer.

We have a paradox here. Both of these items represent good news. How have they threatened the solvency of some UK insurance companies?
First, we explain why the strong stock market performance has

increased the liabilities under these guarantees. This is because the premiums from these policies are often invested in common stocks. United Kingdom insurance companies have a strong tradition of investing heavily in equities. Thus, the amount available when the policyholder retires is much larger if the stock market has performed well. Common stocks have provided high returns during the 1990s, so this has meant that the amounts subject to the guarantee have increased.

We now discuss why the increased life expectancy of retirees also made the guarantees more costly. The guarantee provides a fixed annual amount per £1,000 of proceeds. A common practice was to guarantee £111 pa per £1,000 initial amount. Under this approach the interest rate assumption and the mortality assumption are bundled together. If there is an improvement in mortality so that people are living longer this increases the value of the guarantee because retirees will be around for a longer time period to collect their pension. For example, suppose that the policyholders are expected to live for 17 years instead of 15 years (payments will then have to be made for an extra two years). This means that the guarantee will cost more.

The potential liability associated with these guarantees seems to have been ignored when these guarantees were included in the contracts. At that time there were no derivative instruments available that would have hedged the risk. The theoretical models that would help assess the size of such risk were just being developed in the late 1970s and early 1980s. It does seem surprising that the insurance companies missed the improvement in mortality and that they did not appear to have made any provision for the interest rate risk they were taking on. They gave away an option free: this is always a bad idea. They could have included features in the contract to limit the risk, such as restricting the application of the guarantee to a certain portion of the proceeds.

Instruments that can hedge this type of interest rate risk are now available and one derivative instrument that could currently be used by the insurance company to hedge against this type of risk solution is called a *receiver swaption*. This type of swaption gives the insurer the right to enter a swap in the future to receive a fixed payment corresponding to the strike price and pay the variable rate. When the swaption matures, it will be worthwhile for the insurance company to exercise it if the prevailing swap rate is lower than the strike price in the contract. For example, suppose that, when the swaption matures, the prevailing swap rate is 5% and the strike price corresponds to 6%. The insurance company has a benefit equal to 1% of the notional amount on the contract payable for the duration of the swap. To hedge its annuity risk the swaptions should be arranged to mature as the policyholders retire. The strike price on the swaption should correspond to the interest rate in the guaranteed annuity option and the term of the ultimate swap should match the life expectancy of the retirees.

There still remains the equity appreciation risk that we discussed. The insurers' liability under the guarantee increases in line with good equity performance. One possible solution is to buy a derivative whose payoff at maturity depends on the returns on the index and the level of interest rates. This is an option based on two assets. Dunbar (1999) describes one such derivative that is a hybrid swaption, where the actual payoff depends on the performance of the FTSE Index as well as the interest rate levels. It is difficult to find good hedging instruments for these options.

The liabilities arising from these guaranteed annuity options caused the fall of Equitable Life. The Equitable's liabilities under the guaranteed annuity options on 90,000 of its policies amounted to £1.5 billion. The insurance company proposed to meet the cost of the guarantee by reducing the bonuses payable on the policies covered by the guarantee. This proposal was exceedingly controversial. The Equitable had a large number of other policies that did not contain such a guarantee and their benefits would have had to be reduced to pay for the guarantee. The poli-cyholders who had the guaranteed annuity option argued that the Equi-table's proposal made a mockery of their guarantee and a long legal dispute followed. Ultimately, the House of Lords decided that the Equi-table had to honour its guarantees and that it could not reduce the bonuses on the policies with the guarantee. In December 2000, the Equitable closed its doors to new business and put itself up for sale. At the time of writing, there is a proposal from the Halifax Building Society to purchase the Equi-table. However, parts of the deal depend on the Equitable reaching an agreement with the 90,000 holders of its guaranteed annuity rate.

In summary, this once-neglected interest rate exposure grew so large that it brought down a venerable institution and threatened the solvency of several other insurers. The Equitable Life case shows that if certain risks are overlooked they can bring down an entire company.

1   See Froot, Scharfstein and Stein (1994).
2   See URL: http://www.gloriamundi.org.
3   See URL: http://www.citigroup.com/citigroup/fin/data/cci10-k99.pdf.
4   Microsoft Annual Report. See also Callinicos (1999).
5   Asian options were defined in Chapter 2. The payoff on an Asian option is based on the average of the asset price over a given period. In the case of an average strike Asian option the strike price of the option is equal to this average.
6   However, a stock buy-back is not a free lunch. The money used to buy back the stock comes from the firm's cash and thus depletes the assets available for the existing shareholders.
7   Some firms are avid hedgers while others are opposed to hedging. For example, Barrick Gold is an impassioned supporter of hedging the gold price risk. In contrast, Adriaan Steyn, the Treasurer of Gold Fields, has suggested that producer hedging of gold is spiralling out of control, leading to dangerous and unattractive instability in the market. See Steyn (2000).
8   See Hathaway (2000).
9   In 1990, the Central Bank of Portugal lost 17 tonnes of gold it had loaned to the investment banking firm of Drexel, Burnham, Lambert which went bankrupt.
10 Bank for International Settlements, 70th annual report, p. 100.

11 *A Glittering Future?* The World Gold Council, 1999.

12 If the options expire in-the-money, Cambior is obligated to make a payment to its counter-party. However, if Cambior issues more options to its counterparty rather than paying cash, we say that the position is *rolled forward*. Such a provision in an option contract relieves Cambior of coming up with cash if the options expire in-the-money.

13 We saw in the Appendix to Chapter 5 how an increase in the volatility leads to an increase in option prices.

14 See Falloon (2000).

15 The way that annuities are computed is more complicated than our short-cut method, which is intended only to give a general idea.

16 In the case of a life annuity there is the guarantee that the company will pay Michael as long as he lives, even if he lives to be 100. Our calculations assume a fixed lifetime. This is just to help make them simpler.

7

How Investors Use Derivatives

In Chapter 6, we discussed how firms use derivatives to hedge a variety of risks. When corporations buy derivatives, investors often take the opposite side of the transaction. Investors differ in their attitudes to risk and in the amounts of money they have but they share a common objective: they want their investments to make money and the more the better. High returns are associated with high risk and, because investors detest downside risk, they must find a balance between the two. Derivatives are powerful instruments for tailoring the risk-return profile of their investment portfolios.

The same considerations apply to institutional investors, which include mutual funds, insurance companies, pension plans, hedge funds, banks and endowment funds. These institutions each have different investment objectives and this is reflected in their investment philosophies and in their attitudes to risk. However, derivatives provide an efficient way to help institutional investors achieve their objectives. They can be used to reduce transaction costs, overcome investment restrictions and take advantage of accounting restrictions or tax laws. Institutional investors are subject to different types of regulations. These regulations may restrict the type of assets in which an institution can invest or limit the percentage of various kinds of assets that may be held in an institution's portfolio. For example, pension-plan laws in many countries limit the proportion of their portfolios that can be invested in foreign stocks. Derivatives provide a way to overcome restrictions of this nature.

This chapter will:

❑ discuss how investors use derivatives to achieve their goals;
❑ give examples both of cases where derivatives are used to reduce risk and of cases where they are used to take on more risk;
❑ describe a method known as *portfolio insurance* used to protect a portfolio from downside risk – an approach that was very popular until the stock market crash of 1987; and
❑ discuss equity indexed annuities and employee stock options and describe some of their unique features.

The first part of this chapter outlines different ways that investors use derivatives to achieve their investment objectives. We show how investors can use derivatives to express a particular view of the future. Next, we discuss how investors can use derivatives to protect their investment gains. We show how equity derivatives can be used to reduce an investor's exposure to a given stock. We also discuss how derivatives are used by institutions to streamline the asset allocation procedure. The creation of a common currency zone in Europe provides the context for a practical example. As a result of the common currency, the composition of pension plan assets was drastically revised since the definition of a domestic asset was extended to cover securities issued within the entire currency zone. After these changes, many European pension plans now had more freedom to invest their assets and we discuss how equity derivatives were used in the transition.

We next discuss portfolio insurance, which was introduced in the early 1980s and flourished until the 1987 stock market crash. The purpose of portfolio insurance was to provide a floor of protection for equity portfolios by synthetically creating a long-term put option. Portfolio insurers used a dynamic hedging strategy similar to that described in Chapter 4 to replicate the payoff of a put option and protect stock portfolios against downside risk. During the extreme market conditions of the crash of October 19, 1987, these dynamic hedging strategies were severely tested. We include a first-hand account, in Panel 1, of the crash from the perspective of someone who was actively involved in the market on that day. Then we discuss a popular insurance product that provides individual consumers with embedded options. These contracts have different names in different countries but in the United States they are called Equity Indexed Annuities. Finally, we discuss employee stock options and explain why they have become such a popular method of compensation. Employee stock options are superficially like standard call options but as will see, there are some important differences.

HOW INVESTORS USE DERIVATIVES TO EXPRESS A VIEW

If an investor has a particular view of the future, derivatives can be used to express this view. For example, if investors feel that a stock's price will rise, buying a call option enables them to make a profit if the price does increase. Similarly, if they think the price will fall, the purchase of a put option is one way to make money if their predictions come true. Even if the investor predicts the price movement correctly, the profit on these strategies depends on the cost of the options. In most cases, any information the investor has normally will be factored into the price of the options – but this does not stop investors from taking a view.

Suppose an investor thinks that a stock, currently trading at US$100, will be much higher in six months' time. One way to express this view would be to buy the shares and if, in six months, the share price is US$120, the investor makes a profit of US$20 on the initial investment of US$100.

This is a return of 20% over the six months. However, if the share price is still at US$100 at the end of six months then the return on buying the shares is zero. It costs much less for the investor to buy a call option than to buy the stock. If the option costs US$8, and if the stock price in six months is US$120, then the net profit will be US$12 on the initial stake of US$8. This translates into a six-month return of 150% – a much better return than the 20% that would have been obtained by buying the stock outright. However, if the stock price is unchanged at US$100 in six months' time, the payoff from the call option is zero. The option premium of US$8 is lost. The option strategy is therefore more risky because it magnifies both the returns on the upside and the losses on the downside. In other words the option provides leverage.

If the investor knew that the stock price would be at least 20% higher in six months' time, then the purchase of the call option would be preferable to buying the stock. In practice, investors will never have this sort of knowledge but suppose, for the sake of argument, that some do. As soon as they start to exploit this information then their actions will help bring the information into market prices. For example, if they start buying a lot of call options then this will tend to increase the price of call options. Indeed, the actions of market participants are one of the ways that information becomes impounded in market prices.

Prozac: patent protection and puts
We now give an actual example of a case where an investor could have made money by buying put options. The stock price of the drug company Eli Lilly fell by 31% on a single day in August 2000. A shrewd investor who had anticipated this drop could have bought put options and made a profit. The reason for the fall is related to Prozac, the widely used antidepressant drug manufactured by Eli Lilly. In 1999 it accounted for 30% of Lilly's sales. Lilly held a patent on the manufacture of Prozac that restricted competition from generic substitutes.

On August 9, 2000, Eli Lilly's period of patent protection for Prozac was drastically reduced by a court decision. The US Court of Appeals struck down Lilly's patent. Lilly's stock price dropped as soon as this news hit the market. Another drug firm, Barr Labs, won the challenge against Lilly's patent protection and its shares jumped by 50% on the news.

The Court's ruling surprised the market. It was not anticipated and it was not reflected in market prices. On 17 August, one week after the judgment, *Business Week* stated: "But even the savviest Wall Street investors didn't recognise how tenuous Prozac's patent protection was, nor did they expect a courtroom decision against Lilly." It is just possible that an astute investor who followed the case closely and monitored the judge's questions could have anticipated this result and bought put options on Lilly's stock. However, the price of Eli Lilly stock would have dropped in anticipation as this information became more widely known. The behaviour of investors acting on the information would cause the change in prices.

Derivatives can be created that will enable an investor to benefit from information about other types of future price behaviour. However, the same warning applies here: if the information is already reflected in the price then an investor will not – on average – make an excessively large profit from a transaction. If the information is not yet impounded in the price then the investor has to be the first, or one of the first, to acquire it. It is not easy to find such opportunities. There are many sophisticated investors on the constant lookout for such opportunities and it is their actions that help make the markets efficient and, ultimately, ensure that the market prices reflect the available information. Exotic options can be created to provide a payoff based on any possible set of possible future paths.

Protective puts

An event may be devastating to an investor even though that investor may not consider the event to be very likely. Derivatives provide a useful tool for dealing with these situations. An investor who has a retirement account consisting of common stocks is exposed to the risk of a fall in equity prices. Even though the investor might believe that the chance of such a fall is small, the consequences of a large drop would be very serious. History shows us that there have been some dramatic falls in the market within a short time span. For example, on October 19, 1987 (Black Monday), the market fell by over 20% in single day. If a portfolio is well diversified across a broad spectrum of stocks, its movements will correspond closely with a market index. In this case, the investor could eliminate most of the risk by buying an exchange-traded put option on the market index. There will still be some risk left, to the extent that the portfolio does not exactly mimic the market index, and this residual risk is known as basis risk.

HOW DERIVATIVES CAN BE USED IN ASSET ALLOCATION

The process of selecting which investments to hold in a portfolio is known as the *asset allocation* decision. It has been known for a very long time that one way to reduce risk is to diversify by buying different assets. The saying "don't put all your eggs in a single basket" neatly summarises this insight. Harry Markowitz, (1952) turned this intuition into a more formal set of rules in his landmark paper on portfolio selection. Markowitz demonstrated how an investor could compute the *correct* amounts of different stocks in the case of an equity portfolio. This was the first solid scientific approach but there are some real-world factors that make it difficult to follow Markowitz's prescription. These factors include transaction costs, taxes and other types of costs or restrictions. Derivatives are often ideally suited for handling these "frictions".

If a small investor wants to follow a portfolio diversification strategy it does not make sense to buy individual stocks. It would be very inefficient to do so because the amounts in each stock would be so small that transaction costs would eat up a large part of the investor's profit. It would also be very cumbersome to carry out the record keeping and administration for all the small holdings involved. Instead of investing directly in the stocks, the investor could invest in a mutual fund that is well diversified or in a mutual fund that replicates the market. Mutual funds charge a sizeable annual fee ranging from 1% to 2% of the invested assets. If the fund charges 1% and in a year the total fund return is 8% then the investor only receives 7%. An index fund that tracks the market has lower annual fees because any investment decisions can be made automatically. Derivative securities have been created that track the movements of some well-known indices. In the case of the S&P index, these securities are colloquially known as *Spiders*. The corresponding tracking stocks for the Dow Jones Industrial Average are known as *Diamonds*.

Derivatives are also useful in dealing with the asset allocation problem of individuals who have a lot of their wealth tied up in the fortunes of a single company. Derivatives can be used to reduce the risk of a heavy concentration in a particular stock. This method may not be directly available to the most senior executives of a corporation. For example, if the president or CEO of a company uses derivatives to reduce their exposure to the company's stock price, this is often interpreted as a bad sign by the market. Other investors will ask: "What do they know that we don't?" There is also a conflict of interest because the CEO and the board are often the first to know about the company's plans or an impending announcement. However, retired CEOs or individuals who have left the company no longer have a conflict of interest and can therefore diversify their holdings using derivatives. Start-up, high-tech firms that are short of cash, sometimes pay their lawyers using stock instead of cash and the law firm can use derivatives to reduce the price risk of this stock.

There are different ways to diversify the risk of a holding of common stock. The most direct approach, selling the stock, will normally trigger a tax liability. There is a tradeoff between diversification benefits and tax consequences. Derivatives can provide a method of reducing price risk as well as mitigating the tax consequences. One way to reduce the equity risk is to enter an equity swap with a counterparty. A so-called "equity collar" can be used to reduce the price risk of a stock position. In this case, the individual who owns the stock sells an out-of-the-money call and uses the money received to buy an out-of-the-money put.[1]

The equity collar does not involve any cash outlay because the strike prices on the call and put are chosen so that both options have the same initial price. The net effect of the collar is to limit the investor's exposure to the price risk. If the stock price drops they will receive price protection from the put in return for giving up some of the upside price appreciation. Once the collar is arranged the stock position is much less risky and the investor can use the stock as collateral to borrow from the bank. The put option means that the strike price on the put fixes a guaranteed floor for the price of the stock. The bank can safely lend an amount equal to the number of shares times the strike price on the put. The put option turns the risky stock into solid collateral and this type of loan is known as a *collared loan*.

How institutional investors use derivatives

Institutional investors use derivatives widely to attain their investment objectives. They often provide the cheapest and most efficient way for a portfolio manager to change the portfolio's investment mix. Derivatives can be used to alter a portfolio's exposure to a particular risk. For example, equity derivatives can be used to change exposure to the domestic equity market, a foreign market or the global equity market. If a portfolio manager enters a long position in a futures contract, this gives the same type of risk exposure as owning the underlying security. It may be cheaper and more efficient to use the futures contract than to buy the underlying security. Derivatives can also provide downside protection by buying put options or taking a short position in a futures contract.

Derivatives often provide a more efficient alternative than outright purchase in gaining exposure to emerging markets. Outright purchase of shares may be expensive not only in terms of transaction costs but also in terms of other obstacles. There may be legal restrictions on the holding of shares by foreigners. In addition, there can be withholding taxes when the shares are sold and it may take a while to sell the shares if they are thinly traded.

Many of these obstacles can be overcome by using derivatives based on a market index of the foreign stocks. Purchasing a derivative provides a much cleaner and simpler way to receive the same return as owning a portfolio of stocks in the foreign country. In this application, the derivative is used to mimic the return on the underlying portfolio.

Sometimes an institution may wish to retain ownership of an asset but does not want the return associated with the asset. For example, an investment fund might own a large block of a certain company's shares. Ownership of the shares confers voting rights, which might become valuable in certain situations – for instance, if the company becomes involved in a takeover or merger. However, from an optimal asset allocation perspective the fund might be overinvested in this particular company. The fund can reduce its exposure to this company and still retain ownership of the shares for voting purposes by using derivatives. One method would be to set up an equity swap in which the fund agrees to pay the return on the stock to a counterparty and receive fixed payments from the counterparty in return. The fund retains ownership of the shares under this arrangement.

Fund managers, like individual investors, can use derivatives to express a view and derivatives provide a flexible method of overcoming obstacles that stand in the way. Suppose the manager of an investment fund believes that over the next six months, silver prices will increase and gold prices will decrease. Further suppose that the fund is not allowed to trade directly in commodities or precious metals. This restriction rules out the direct approach of buying silver and selling gold. Another strategy might be to buy the shares in a silver-mining company and sell the shares in a gold-mining company. However, this strategy may not work because it might be hard to find a company that produces only one of these metals, as companies that produce gold often produce silver and perhaps other precious metals as well. Furthermore, the shares of a gold-mining company need not move in the same direction as the price of the metal. This divergence might be due to the firm's hedging activities. Recall from our discussion of Cambior Inc in Chapter 6 that the company's shares fell when gold prices rose and that this fall was due to the hedging programme.

Derivatives provide a more precise and reliable way to implement this strategy. The fund could purchase silver futures and simultaneously sell short gold futures. If silver prices rise and gold prices drop then this strategy will make a profit. Conversely, if silver prices fall and gold prices rise, then this strategy will result in lost money.

Equity derivatives in euroland

Institutions must often respond quickly to political and economic changes and derivatives are useful vehicles for making the required adjustments. The introduction of a common currency in Europe in 1999 provides a good example. The euro effectively eliminates exchange rate differences and interest rate differentials among the countries in the common currency block. In particular, it has changed the way in which European investors select their equity portfolios. Before the introduction of the euro, domestic investors tended to buy stocks in their home countries. Now there is no currency risk and it is much simpler to hold stocks from any country in the common currency zone.

The move to a common currency also had important implications for the investment of pension plan assets in the member countries, which are restricted to investing in "domestic assets". Domestic equities are now represented by equities originating from any country within the common currency zone, whereas before they were only the equities of the home country.

Moreover, investment laws for pension plans have been relaxed in several European countries to permit the funds to invest a higher proportion of their assets in stocks. For example, Denmark and Portugal changed their rules so that pension plans have more flexibility to invest in equities. Several funds have dramatically changed their common stock portfolios because of these changes. Derivatives played an important role in this restructuring, especially in the transition stages. Equity derivatives provided an efficient way for pension fund managers to reduce their exposure to their own country's stocks and increase their exposure to the equities of other European countries.

PORTFOLIO INSURANCE

Any investor who owns a portfolio of stocks is exposed to the risk of losing money. In the late 1970s, two Berkeley professors Hayne Leland and Mark Rubinstein, came up with an idea that would provide downside protection for equity portfolios.[2] The idea was to create a put option on the portfolio by following a dynamic hedging strategy similar to that described in Chapter 4. We saw that a call option's payoff could be replicated by rebalancing a portfolio of a long position in a stock and a short position in a bond. Likewise, a put option can be replicated by dynamically adjusting a long position in the bond and a short position in the stock. This is how a *synthetic put option* is created, whose payoff at maturity is equal to the payoff on the put. This concept lies at the very heart of modern option pricing.

Leland and Rubinstein foresaw a large potential market for this product and, together with John O'Brien, they formed Leland, O'Brien and Rubinstein Associates (LOR) to market portfolio insurance. It launched its first portfolio insurance product in 1982. The desired level of protection was achieved by a dynamic strategy that replicated a put option. In the first applications, the replicating portfolio was rebalanced by trading in the stocks in the portfolio. However, stock index futures were introduced in 1982 and provided a cheaper and more efficient method of adjusting the portfolio. Futures contracts were written on indices such as the S&P 500, which provided an elegant way to increase or reduce exposure to the equity market as a whole. There was no need to fiddle around with individual stocks as long as the composition of the portfolio to be insured was similar to the index. The return on the portfolio would approximately match that of the index. So instead of buying more stock, portfolio managers could achieve the same result by going long futures and rather than selling stocks they could go short futures.

Futures contracts, with their low transaction costs and price transparency, were well-suited for the investment strategies needed to implement *portfolio insurance*. Portfolio insurance provides downside protection for stock portfolios and was therefore appealing to large institutional investors such as pension funds. It allows investors to benefit from good stock market performance. The actual cost of the protection is not known at the outset because of the way the protection is provided – through a hedging strategy. The cost depends on what the market does over the life of the protection as this determines what transactions have to be made. If the market is volatile then there are more trades to rebalance the replicating portfolio and the cost goes up. Conversely, if the market remains fairly stable there is less trading and the cost goes down. In this respect, portfolio insurance differs from the purchase of a put option because, in the case of a put option, the cost of the protection *is* known at the outset. Another difference is that an exchange-traded option guarantees the payoff at maturity.

Portfolio insurance became very popular in the mid-1980s. Soon after LOR introduced it, Wells Fargo Investment Advisers (WFIA) and Aetna Life and Casualty began similar programmes. By October 1987, the volume of assets covered by such programmes was of the order of US$100 billion; Wells Fargo alone was managing US$13 billion by this time. The US stock market rose more or less steadily during the period from 1982 until October 1987 and institutional investors wanted a way to lock in their gains. Advertisements showed that if the programme had been in place for the 10-year period, ending in 1982, the insured equity portfolio would have outperformed either a fund fully invested in the S&P 500, or a fund fully invested in Treasury bills.[3] Portfolio insurance was attractive to pension portfolio managers because their performance is often evaluated on a relative basis. The managers' performance was ranked relative to other managers and if a manager could stay out of the lowest quartile then they kept the account.

The case for portfolio insurance for pension plans was made more attractive by a change in the accounting regulations in 1986. One result of this change was that large increases or decreases in the market value of a pension plan's assets had to be reported as income in a corporation's income statement. Before the change, a company's pension plan performance was not directly related to the company's earnings and, indeed, firms used the pension plan to smooth earnings. The Financial Accounting Standards Board (FASB) wanted to discourage this practice and, after the accounting change, a big fall in the value of a plan's assets would result in a big drop in a firm's earnings. One consequence of the change in the rules was that sponsoring firms became very interested in schemes that would reduce big drops in the market value of their pension assets. Portfolio insurance promised to provide exactly what the firms wanted.

Many in the investment community were quite euphoric about portfolio insurance but a few observers expressed reservations. Rendelman and McEnally (1987), argued that portfolio insurance generally did not perform as well as other plausible investment strategies under a wide range of assumptions. Bruce Jacobs (1999), author of a recent book on the topic, was a persistent critic of portfolio insurance. One of his criticisms was that if a large number of investors used portfolio insurance it could have a snowball effect that would destabilise prices. His logic was that during falling markets, these investors would all be selling and during rising markets they would all be buying.

The dramatic stock market crash of October 1987, brought a five-year period of strong market performance to an abrupt end and it had a devastating impact on portfolio insurance, which has never recovered. To this day, the causes of the crash are still controversial and the extent to which portfolio insurance contributed is still being debated. Some critics have argued that portfolio insurance caused the crash.

On "Black Monday", the Dow Jones Industrial Average lost 22.6% of its total value and the S&P 500 Index also fell by over 20% – the S&P 500 futures contract plunged even more dramatically – losing 28.6% on the day. On 19 October, the futures contracts that traded on the Chicago Mercantile Exchange were hit by a massive amount of selling when the market opened. The futures price became out of kilter with the prices on the underlying stocks and investors began to sell stocks on the New York Stock Exchange (NYSE). This wave of selling was so great that it clogged the system and the specialists who dealt in many of the stocks were unable to provide an orderly market. In these turbulent conditions, it became impossible to sell large amounts of stock or futures contracts at specific prices. Liquidity had evaporated.

However, it is precisely when there is a large market drop that the need is greatest for the portfolio insurer to adjust his portfolio. This is precisely the time when the insurer needs to sell the underlying stocks or go short on additional futures contracts. Under the turbulent conditions of 19 October it was very difficult to do this. The theory of dynamic replication assumes a liquid market where transactions can be executed at current prices with assurance. If there is a liquidity squeeze and the insurer cannot sell at the required prices, then the programme will break down. This is what happened. Portfolio insurance was designed for normal conditions and the crash was anything but normal.

This episode shows how critical an orderly liquid market is for the implementation of dynamic hedging. There has been a vigorous debate on the extent to which portfolio insurance contributed to the crash. Because dynamic hedging calls for sales in a falling market, it has been argued that the actions of portfolio insurers caused the crash.

During the crash, Jeremy Evnine was in charge of the hedging programme at Wells Fargo Investment Advisers, one of the largest providers of portfolio insurance. Panel 1 reproduces an eyewitness account written by Jeremy of this dramatic day.

After the crash came the predictable flood of reports by government agencies. They analysed its causes and searched for lessons to guide future policy. The Presidential Report on Market Mechanisms, otherwise known as the Brady Commission, put part of the blame on portfolio insurance and made several recommendations to prevent a recurrence. The Securities and Exchange Commission (SEC) reached similar conclusions and called for restrictions on speculation in the futures market. On the other hand, the Commodity Futures Trading Commission (CFTC) proclaimed the innocence of portfolio insurance and, in general, vindicated the role of futures. The NYSE suggested that futures were the culprits, whereas the General Accounting Office report blamed the breakdown of the computer systems on the NYSE. One thing seems clear: the conclusions of some of these reports fit rather too snugly with the interests of the organisations that commissioned them. Since then, the debate on the causes of the crash and the role of portfolio insurance has continued, with scholars lining up on each side of the issue.

The crash of October 1987, its causes and consequences, continues to hold a macabre fascination for students of financial markets. In some respects, the crash resembles the assassination of President John F. Kennedy some 24 years previously. Both events were subjected to a barrage of government reports and analyses but the controversies remain. In the Kennedy case, the conclusion of the official Warren report that Lee Harvey Oswald acted as a lone assassin contrasts with a raft of conspiracy theories. Despite all the investigations and analysis, the debate about who killed JFK rages on. There are similarities with the market crash. Most observers agree that the 1987 market crash caused the demise of portfolio insurance but the debate continues as to the degree to which portfolio insurance contributed to the crash. After the Kennedy assassination presidential security was improved and, so too, were changes introduced to make the markets work more efficiently after the '87 crash.

EQUITY INDEXED ANNUITIES

Many products that are sold to retail investors these days contain embedded options and the consumer buys the package as a complete contract. For example, many life-insurance and savings contracts contain embedded derivatives. In the US, so-called *equity indexed annuities* are a case in point.

These products include an option-like feature that permits the customer to benefit from good stock market performance. Typically, contracts will contain an embedded call option on an equity portfolio such as the S&P index and they also provide a basic guarantee that the customer will receive a minimum rate of return, regardless of how the stock market performs. The advantage for consumers is that they participate in the stock market when it does well and have the security of a guaranteed basic return when the market performs badly.

If an insurance company sells these contracts, then, it has sold call options on the underlying equity portfolio. The company is short the call

PANEL 1
MEMOIRS OF A PORTFOLIO INSURANCE MAN
Jeremy Evnine

I certainly won't forget October 19, 1987. At that time, I was co-manager of Hedging and Arbitrage at WFIA, along with my colleague Rolf Theisen. We were managing around US$13 billion in portfolio insurance strategies at that point. Almost all of it was long stock partially hedged with short stock index futures contracts, mostly S&P 500.

I remember a bit of tension over the weekend, wondering what Monday would bring, but nothing prepared us for what happened. My day started around 7:00 am with a telephone call from Nancy Feldkircher, who was operating the system at that time. We had a pretty nice system, quite automated for its day. As a rule, I didn't keep trading hours out in California, but Nancy knew she could call me at home any time.

I asked her what was going on. She replied "The market's down. Quite a bit actually. But the odd thing is that the system is telling me to unwind futures contracts." In other words, while we would expect to be reducing our exposure in a down market by going short even more futures, in order dynamically to replicate a protective put strategy, the system was telling us to do precisely the opposite, to unwind short futures positions, thereby increasing our hedge ratio. My first reaction was "there's a bug in the system". But I quickly reduced that to a low probability event. The system had been operating so well for so long.

I asked Nancy what else was going on. "Well," she replied, "the S&P 500 futures are at a 20-point discount to the spot price." Instantly, I could feel a rush of adrenaline and a slightly panicky feeling in the pit of my stomach. I knew something really big was happening. I also knew immediately why the system was telling us to increase our hedge ratio by unwinding futures positions. Since we were long stock, short futures, in a down market the portfolios were "poorer". However, by going to a 20-point discount, the futures were suddenly getting an enormous positive real-time mark-to-market, seeming to make the portfolios much richer. Ergo, increase the hedge ratios.

My mind was racing, but I couldn't quite put my finger on the issue at the instant. I told Nancy "Look, I'm going to drive my ten-year-old son to school. I need to think about this. I'll be home in about 20 minutes and I'll call you back. Do nothing till you hear from me" (as the old jazz song goes).

I think Ariel realised that his father was rather preoccupied on the way to school. Our usually talkative ride took place in silence as I examined the various options (no pun intended). When I got home, I called Nancy. "OK, here's my analysis of the situation. The futures aren't really at a 20-point discount to the spot. That's just an illusion. The real market prices of the futures and spot markets can never be very different, after adjusting for the basis. It only looks that way because the spot price you are seeing is doubtless really stale. You couldn't really trade it at that price and arbitrage the 20-point discount. Which is the real market? Clearly the futures market. It's a single, liquid contract, not 500 separate prices that have to be aggregated. So, what I want you to do is override the system and tell it that the price of the spot S&P 500 is the futures price. Forget the basis, it's second order at this. Now, what do you see?"

As soon as Nancy entered the futures price as the price of the spot S&P 500, all of the portfolios updated, looked much poorer, and the system recommended a massive reduction in the hedge ratios, ie, go short a lot more futures contracts. "Fine", I said to Nancy, "I'll be in in half an hour. Just keep doing that until I tell you otherwise".

And we did that all day. As prices tumbled we went short more and more futures contracts, always striving to keep the hedge ratios close to those required to replicate the protective put. WFIA was a big player in S&P 500 index/futures arbitrage in those days. However, on the day of the crash we did not execute a single arbitrage trade, certainly lending credence to the notion that the 20-point discount in the futures price was just an illusion of the price feed.

There were no circuit breakers back then. To the contrary, the circuit breakers, as well as intra-day marks-to-market, were put into effect as a result of the crash of '87. However, the CME did "ask" WFIA to ration its futures trades, and so it wasn't so easy to make the trades that the put replication required of us. We did have some accounts that did not hedge with futures, but adjusted their hedge ratio by buying and selling stock baskets. These accounts were able to sell stocks without limitation. Additionally, WFIA had one account for which it facilitated trades in response to directives from the client. In a commentary later, a journalist said something to the effect that "every time the market tried to rally, another wave of selling hit it". Likely that was us!

Late in the trading day, some of us began to wonder if we had really made the right decision, shorting so many futures at a seeming 20-point discount. Our colleagues at Leland O'Brien Rubinstein, the firm that created Portfolio Insurance as a commercial concept, were recommending that trading frequency be radically reduced. Their reasoning was that, if the futures were really selling so cheaply, then the transaction cost of the hedging vehicle were prohibitively high; the theory dictated that, in the presence of increasing transactions costs, optimal put replication should rebalance less frequently. This was contrary to the reasoning I had used early in the day. Patti Dunn, at that time the head of Portfolio Management, to her credit, backed up my original decision and said that we must continue to hedge, otherwise we risked failing to fulfil our obligations to our clients.

At the end of the day, Rolf and I phoned up each of our portfolio insurance clients. They were still in the office, as we were until 9:00 that night, or later; as indeed we were all week. We were able to inform almost all of them that they had hit their minima, and were fully hedged at the minimum required return. There were a few that were a couple of percent below their minimum return, but they and we felt that WFIA had delivered as advertised. They were uniformly overjoyed to hear that the protection that they had believed they were buying had indeed kicked in and kept them from sinking with the market.

I recall that we were all very nervous about the viability of the whole clearing system. At the end of the day, every futures trade has the Futures Clearing Corporation (FCC) as its counterparty. It wouldn't take many defaults for the FCC to be unable to meet all its obligations. Of course, in the end traders met their marks-to-market, and the system came through, but it wasn't obvious that it would on the evening of 19 October.

One of our clients had initiated a six-month, 0% minimum policy three months earlier. I'm sure he's still getting free drinks off that story. Personally, I felt a great sense of satisfaction that we had delivered on our commitments to our clients, that dynamic put replication had been shown to work as advertised, although, as we found out later that week, not all portfolio insurance managers had been able to "deliver the goods".

Rolf, Nancy and I have all been blamed since then for personally having caused the crash of '87, but I take this with a grain of salt. If demand for protective puts in the market greatly exceeds the supply, the equilibrium price will rise, causing implied volatilities to increase. We should not have been surprised when this translated into greater realised volatility.

Other portfolio insurance managers did not fare so well, however. As a result, the general notion of portfolio insurance was rather discredited, unfairly in my view. There is no doubt that many investors today decrease their exposure to risky assets as they get poorer and increase them as they get richer. They just don't call it portfolio insurance.

options and one way it can cover this risk is to buy a similar option from an investment bank. The risk has been passed on to the bank and it can either hedge the risk using a dynamic hedging strategy or buy similar call options in the market or from another institution. In the OTC market, hedge funds have been natural buyers of these long-dated equity options and we will see in Chapter 8 that Long-Term Capital Management was active in this market.[4]

EMPLOYEE STOCK OPTIONS

We now turn to a discussion of employee stock options. We saw that these options are an important form of remuneration when we discussed Microsoft's hedging programme. In this section, we describe these options in more detail and explain why they have become so popular. We will also discuss why the reporting of the cost of these contracts in firms' financial statements has generated so much controversy.

Employee stock options are like standard options as they give the employee the right to buy, at a fixed price, shares of the firm that employs them. They are attractive to the issuing company because they can be issued without paying any cash. They are thus especially attractive to cash-strapped start-up companies. In principle, these options provide an incentive for the employee to work hard to increase the company's share price and thus they align their interests with the outside shareholders. They also provide an incentive for the employee to stay with the same firm because the options can only be exercised after a certain period, known as the *vesting period*, has elapsed.[5]

Stock options now represent the largest single component of compensation for top executives in the US. Some 97% of the S&P corporations granted executive stock options to their top executives in 1998 and these options represented approximately 40% of the executives' total compensation package. Business practices in the US are often copied elsewhere and this method of compensation is increasing in popularity in other countries. Stock options are also widely used as part of the compensation for rank-and-file workers. Indeed, Cisco Systems grants stock options to its summer interns to encourage them to return to Cisco when they graduate. The options only remain in force if the intern comes back and stays with Cisco for a certain period.

On the surface, these options resemble standard call options because they give the employee the right to buy shares of the corporation at a fixed price at the end of a pre-specified term. However, they differ from standard call options in several important ways. The executive is restricted from trading in the option or selling it because one of the aims of the option is to align their interest with that of the firm's shareholders. If they use capital markets transactions to unravel these options, this would diminish the options' incentive feature.

Another difference is that when a standard option is exercised, there is no impact on the underlying company because a standard option contract is between two independent parties and the stock price is merely used as a reference to determine the option's value. When an employee stock option is exercised, the employee has the right to buy shares from the company. The company has to deliver shares to the employee and if it issues more shares then the number of outstanding shares increases. This effect is known as *dilution* and it means that the proportional stake in the company of outside shareholders is reduced. For example, suppose a company has 100 shares and it issues another 100 executive stock options. When the options are exercised the company issues another 100 shares. An outside shareholder, who owned two shares of the company would now find that his ownership percentage would be diluted from 2% to 1% by the issuance of the new shares. In this respect, employee stock options resemble warrants. However, warrants are held by outside investors and employee stock options are held by people who work for the company.

Reporting stock options

The consequence of current reporting practice is that an employer can pay employees without recording any salary expense when the stock options are awarded. The employee is also able to postpone paying any tax on this benefit until the options are exercised. When the option is exercised, the corporation receives a tax deduction. Under traditional practice, the issuing firm must recognise a cost equal to the difference between the stock price and the exercise price at the date of issue. Most of these options are issued with the exercise price (strike price) equal to the current stock price, so this results in a zero cost. Hence, the firms' income is not reduced when such options are granted to the executive. Most observers would agree that these options have a positive value at inception. However by not including any cost, issuing these options has no impact on a firm's earnings.

There has been a heated debate on how to account for these options. The FASB issued an exposure draft in June 1993, concluding that executive stock options are compensation and should be recognised in the income statement. The draft generated so much opposition that the US Congress considered legislation to reverse the exposure draft's requirement that earnings be charged when options are granted. Additional opposition came from the SEC, the major accounting firms, and most chief executive officers.

Several arguments were marshalled against a change in the accounting standards and we will mention three:

❑ it was claimed that the Black–Scholes formula significantly overstated the value of these options to corporate executives;
❑ it was claimed that the users of financial statements did not want this information and that information on these options should be disclosed in the footnotes; and
❑ it was claimed that the inclusion of the cost of these options in the income would lower share prices and increase the cost of raising money. According to those opposed to the draft, this would induce firms to cut

back on the use of executive stock options, which would in turn reduce their competitiveness in getting the best people.

So loud were the howls of protest that the exposure draft was modified in December 1994, giving firms discretion on whether to charge the executive stock options to earnings or continue to disclose them in footnotes.

The debate over the right number to put in the income statement continues but it is hard to defend the practice of entering zero. Warren Buffet summed up the situation in his 1998 Annual Letter to Berkshire Hathaway shareholders as follows:[6]

> Whatever the merits of options may be, their accounting treatment is outrageous. Think for a moment of that $190 million we are going to spend for advertising at GEICO this year. Suppose that instead of paying cash for our ads, we paid the media in ten-year, at-the-market Berkshire options. Would anyone then care to argue that Berkshire had not borne a cost for advertising, or should not be charged this cost on its books?
>
> Perhaps Bishop Berkeley – you may remember him as the philosopher who mused about trees falling in a forest when no one was around – would believe that an expense unseen by an accountant does not exist. Charlie and I, however, have trouble being philosophical about unrecorded costs. When we consider investing in an option-issuing company, we make an appropriate downward adjustment to reported earnings, simply subtracting an amount equal to what the company could have realized by publicly selling options of like quantity and structure. Similarly, if we contemplate an acquisition, we include in our evaluation the cost of replacing any option plan. Then, if we make a deal, we promptly take that cost out of hiding.
>
> Readers who disagree with me about options will by this time be mentally quarreling with my equating the cost of options issued to employees with those that might theoretically be sold and traded publicly. It is true, to state one of these arguments, that employee options are sometimes forfeited – that lessens the damage done to shareholders – whereas publicly offered options would not be. It is true, also, that companies receive a tax deduction when employee options are exercised; publicly traded options deliver no such benefit. But there's an offset to these points: options issued to employees are often repriced, a transformation that makes them much more costly than the public variety.
>
> It's sometimes argued that a non-transferable option given to an employee is less valuable to him than would be a publicly traded option that he could freely sell. That fact, however, does not reduce the *cost* of the non-transferable option. Giving an employee a company car that can only be used for certain purposes diminishes its value to the employee, but does not in the least diminish its cost to the employer.
>
> The earning revisions that Charlie and I have made for options in recent years have frequently cut the reported per-share figures by 5%, with 10% not all that uncommon. On occasion, the downward adjustment has been so great that it has affected our portfolio decisions, causing us either to make a sale or to pass on a stock purchase we might otherwise have made.
>
> A few years ago we asked three questions in these pages to which we have

not yet received an answer: "If options aren't a form of compensation, what are they? If compensation isn't an expense, what is it? And, if expenses shouldn't go into the calculation of earnings, where in the world should they go?"

Moral hazard

We have already noted that one of the features of employee stock options is that they are supposed to align the interests of the corporation's managers with those of its shareholders. If the stock price rises, both parties benefit. This helps reduce the so-called moral hazard that arises when a principal hires an agent to perform a task and the principal cannot monitor what the agent does. Moral hazard occurs when the agent takes (private) actions to benefit himself at the expense of the principal. In these situations, Bengt Holmstrom (1979) has shown that a compensation plan that gives the agent a share of the profits and forces him to bear some of the risk, is a more efficient contract than a contract that pays the agent a fixed fee. In the case of a corporation, the outside shareholders correspond to the principal and the managers correspond to the agent(s), so a performance-based compensation plan captures the desired features. However, even manager stock options cannot eliminate all the sources of moral hazard. They can still arise because management can still manipulate the value of the option-based compensation to some extent.

It is not easy to pin down this effect for the following reason. If a company introduces an incentive-based compensation plan and the firm performs well subsequently, it could be that the good performance derives from the hard work and good decisions of the managers. This is the way things are supposed to work. A more cynical view is that managers have some advance knowledge of how the stock price will behave and influence the terms of the compensation package to their own advantage. David Yermack, (1997) of New York University decided to distinguish between these two hypotheses. He analysed the stock option awards to CEOs in cases where there was discretion as to the timing of the award. He discovered that the awards tend to be granted just before the release of favourable news about the company.

Suppose, however, that the grant date has been settled well in advance. Might this not get rid of opportunistic behaviour by management? Senior managers will still have some discretion over when news is released to the public and this news can increase or decrease the stock price. If the CEO knows there is impending bad news, it may be possible to release it before the option grant date and this reduces the strike price of the option. If there is good news, it may be possible to delay it until after the options have been granted. A CEO who acted in this way would be maximising his own welfare at the expense of the shareholders. David Aboody and Ron Kasznick (2000) analysed cases where the grant date was already fixed. They studied stock price patterns of 572 firms that awarded options on the same dates year after year to their CEOs. They found evidence that firms were more likely to disclose bad news just before the award date and more likely to defer good news until after the award date. Their conclusions are:

> Overall, our findings provide evidence that CEO's of firms with scheduled awards make opportunistic voluntary disclosures that maximize the value of their stock option compensation.

In summary, employee stock options are an important component of the compensation, not only for senior executives but also for lesser mortals. These options are much more complicated than exchange-traded options and this adds to their fascination.

1 A call option is said to be out-of-the-money if the strike price is above the current asset price. A put option is said to be out-of-the-money if the current asset price is above the put option's strike price.
2 Peter Bernstein (1992) provides a very readable account of the genesis of portfolio insurance. Bruce Jacobs (1999) has written a more critical account of portfolio insurance.
3 This analysis is discussed in Jacobs (1999). He notes that this particular decade was atypical and explains why portfolio insurance would have worked so well under these conditions. One unusual aspect of the decade was that Treasury bills outperformed a fully invested equity portfolio based on the S&P 500.
4 Indeed, the price of these options rose dramatically in the aftermath of the September 1998 hedge fund crisis. Hedge funds can often play a useful role as suppliers of liquidity.
5 It is only after the options vest that they can be exercised. The vesting period typically lasts four to five years, with 20% or 25% of the options vesting after the employee has been with the company for one year.
6 The website for the Annual Letter is URL:http://www.berkshirehathaway.com/letters/1998htm.html.

8

Disasters: Divine Results Racked by Human Recklessness

This chapter describes three highly publicised disasters: Orange County's investment fund, Barings Bank and Long-Term Capital Management (LTCM). We analyse the reasons for these three failures and show that they share some common features.

David Emanuel (1996) has given a perceptive diagnosis of this type of phenomenon. He observed that:

> Collapses are not caused by lax oversight or regulation. Those deficiencies are
> symptoms of our willingness to be seduced by the impressive track records
> of apparently invincible traders. Oversight and regulation fall down because
> everyone is afraid to bother the "producer" and nobody with clout has the
> energy and knowledge to defuse the problem.

Emanuel noted that there is a common pattern associated with derivatives disasters. In these cases an individual (or a group of individuals) who has achieved spectacular investment results in the past, comes to be regarded as being invincible. The usual regulations and standard oversights are relaxed and it becomes increasingly difficult to challenge their actions. Because of their past successes they are given more freedom and more funds to invest. Their past results may have been due to their superior skill or good luck or a mixture of both. They become more confident and, buoyed by their past success, they take on more risk. There may be some particular outcomes that would be devastating to their portfolios if they occurred but that possibility is not even considered or, is viewed as being too remote to worry about. Of course sometimes one of the "impossible" events does occur. This event is a big disaster for the portfolio, which loses lots of money.

Recent derivatives disasters illustrate the "star performer" syndrome. For example, Long-Term Capital Management started life with an aura of stardom; its band of top academics and traders was described as the "dream team"; Spiro, (1994). The main reason why the fund was able to attract so much initial capital, without giving any details of its investment strategies, was due to the reputation and previous record of the fund's principals (see Lowenstein, 2000). Nick Leeson who played a key role in the fall of Barings was the bank's star trader. In the Orange County debacle, the county was bankrupted by a US$1.7 billion loss on its investments. The county's treasurer, Robert Citron, was hailed as a financial genius because he had obtained good investment results in the past.

We shall see that in these three cases, the principals who had the halo of stardom were given considerable freedom and their investments were not subject to prudent checks and balances. As long as the investors or citizens who have hired these managers see that their investments are producing high returns there are few complaints or warnings. After all, these people are generating lots of money for the portfolio. It is much easier to count the profits at the end of the year than to assess the risks that were taken in order to obtain them. If the investment team has a stellar reputation it is doubly hard to argue against its strategies. The presumption is that it knows what it is doing and there is the evidence to prove it.

However, if a big disaster occurs, much hand wringing and calls for more stringent controls to prevent further occurrences inevitably follow. The disaster receives wide coverage in the news media. Commissions and boards of inquiry are set up to review what happened and make recommendations to prevent such occurrences in the future. There is a search for the causes of the disaster. The disaster often stimulates changes in industry practices. For example, many banks became much more serious about the risk management of their portfolios in the aftermath of the collapse of Barings Bank. Derivatives disasters have provided the impetus for increased regulation and self-regulation of financial institutions.

ORANGE COUNTY

In 1994, Orange County, which is one of wealthiest counties in California, declared bankruptcy. It was the largest municipal failure in US history. The central character in this case was Mr Robert Citron, the then 69 year-old treasurer of Orange County. Orange County lies between Los Angeles and San Diego and votes Republican. The government of the county provides a variety of services and funds them with grants from the federal and state governments, property taxes and other taxes. The county's funds are managed by the Treasurer's office. Robert Citron, a Democrat, had held this post since he was first elected in 1972. In 1994, he was re-elected for the seventh time.

The financial pressures on Orange County were strongly affected by the change in the California property tax law in 1978. This change resulted from the passing of the famous Proposition 13 in the state of California. The legislation severely reduced the property tax revenues that could be collected and the resulting drop in revenues put severe financial pressure on many municipalities in the state. This pressure intensified with the recession of the early 1990s, when the decline in economic activity further reduced the amount of taxes that were available. The state of California passed on a bigger share of the responsibility for social programmes to the local governments. The state government also decided to allocate a greater proportion of the property tax revenues to the school districts and less to the city and county governments. This also made things worse for Orange County.

To meet its cash needs, Orange County began to rely increasingly on income from its investment portfolio, which was managed by Robert Citron. Citron had acquired the reputation of being an investment genius because the portfolio had done so well under his stewardship. Under Citron, the fund often outperformed comparable funds by as much as 2% per year. When he was first elected there were much stricter guidelines on the allowable investments for municipal funds. Citron lobbied success-fully to relax these restrictions so that he could invest in more exotic instru-ments. Citron was so highly regarded that, even as a Democrat, he was consistently re-elected as treasurer in this Republican stronghold. His accomplishments were particularly welcome during a time of increased demand on public services with declining tax revenues. As Philippe Jorion (1995) notes:

> In Orange County [Citron] could do no wrong; in a militantly tax averse political environment, he produced enormous revenues "painlessly" thus allowing government to function and expand.

How Citron made money and the risks he took

The essence of Robert Citron's investment strategy involved a bet on the direction of interest rates. To explain how this worked, we need to review the connection between interest rates and bond prices. We can do this using an analogy with a seesaw. If an adult sits on one end of the seesaw and a child on the other, the child will shoot up into the air, hanging tight to the wood. If we look at the portion of the plank on the child's side, a point that is two feet from the fulcrum will not move up as far as a point that is six feet from the fulcrum. Just as when one side of the seesaw goes up the other side goes down, so the bond prices go up when interest rates go down. However, bonds of different maturities go up by differing amounts just as the different parts of the seesaw rise by differing amounts. If interest rates fall, the prices of long-term bonds increase more than the prices of short-term bonds, just as the points that are further from the fulcrum increase more than points that are closer to the fulcrum.

We now illustrate the connection between interest rates and bond prices with a numerical example. Suppose all interest rates are 6%, then the price of a two-year 6% coupon bond is US$100. This bond pays six units at the end of the first year and 106 units at the end of the second year. The price of a 10-year, 6% coupon bond will also be US$100 if all rates are 6%. The 10-year bond pays six units at the end of each of the next nine years and 106 units at the end of the tenth year. If all interest rates now drop to 5%

the price of the two-year bond rises to US$101.86 but the price of the 10-year bond rises to US$107.72. Thus, the same 1% drop in interest rates generates a rise of US$7.72 in the price of the 10-year bond and an increase of only US$1.86 in the price of the two-year bond. The rise in the price of the 10-year bond is over four times as large as the rise in the price of the two-year bond. This is true in general: the prices of long bonds are more sensitive to interest rate changes than the prices of short-term bonds.

Citron's strategy involved buying long-term bonds or taking positions that had the same exposure to interest changes. He also levered up the portfolio. One method of levering the portfolio was to borrow at the short-term rate and invest in long-dated bonds. We can use the results of the last paragraph to illustrate how this works. Suppose interest rates are all now 6%. If Citron simultaneously sells short (borrows) the two-year bond and buys the 10-year bond, he receives US$100 for the two-year bond, which is immediately invested in the 10-year bond. If interest rates fall to 5%, the 10-year bond is worth US$107.72 and the fund owes US$101.86 on the short position (the price of the two-year bond is US$101.86 after the interest rate drop). The profit on this strategy is US$5.86 (107.72 – 101.86). This strategy always makes money *provided interest rates continue to fall*. Notice that Citron could increase the leverage of his portfolio using this strategy and in 1994 the fund was levered up from an asset base of US$7.6 billion to US$20.5 billion. This represented a leverage factor of 2.7.

Citron also used interest rate derivatives to achieve this leverage. These derivatives also involve a gamble that interest rates would continue to fall. Citron's use of derivatives in his portfolio made it easier for him to assume riskier positions. It was because he made an incorrect call on the direction of interest rate movements that he lost money. Citron also purchased large volumes of so-called inverse floaters. An inverse floater is a derivative instrument whose payments fall as interest rates rise. Typically, the payments are expressed as the difference between a fixed interest rate (say 10%) and a floating short-term interest rate, such as Libor.[1] Figure 8.1 illustrates how the payment stream from an inverse floater varies with the level of short-term interest rates.

An inverse floater becomes more valuable as interest rates fall. This happens for two reasons. First, the cashflow payable increases because it is equal to a fixed rate (eg, 10%) minus the floating rate. If the floating rate is 5.5% then the rate received from the inverse floater is 4.5% (10 – 5.5). If the floating rate drops to 4.0% the rate received on the inverse floater is 6.0% (10 – 4.0). Second, the market value of the inverse floater increases when interest rates fall. This is because we can think of the inverse floater as a receiver swap plus a stream of fixed payments. Both these components become more valuable as interest rates fall. Inverse floaters are very sensitive to interest rate changes and provide high returns in a regime of falling interest rates.

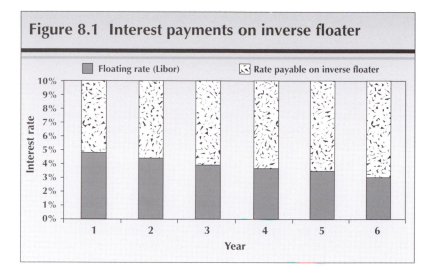

Figure 8.1 Interest payments on inverse floater

■ Floating rate (Libor)   ▨ Rate payable on inverse floater

The essence of Robert Citron's investment strategy was to borrow short term and invest long term. This strategy promised good results as long as interest rates kept falling. This plan had worked well for Citron in the past as interest rates had fallen from their peak in the early 1980s until 1994. Figure 8.2 shows how the five-year bond rate had varied over this time. On the same graph, we also plot the three-month rate (the bold line). We see from the graph that over much of the period, the five-year rate was higher than the three-month rate. When long-term interest rates are higher than short-term rates we say that the yield curve is rising. The combination of a rising yield curve accompanied by a downward trend in the overall level of interest is especially favourable to a strategy of borrowing short term and investing long term.

Citron had obtained an impressive record for the County's investments because the decline in interest rates provided the perfect conditions for his strategy. His investment record was so impressive that the fund attracted money from six cities and four agencies outside the County. Indeed, several Orange County school districts issued bonds to raise funds to invest in the investment portfolio managed by Citron, in the expectation of earning high returns. The Orange County Board of Supervisors gave him a free hand – no one wanted to disturb the goose that laid golden eggs.[2] One of the few discordant voices was raised during the 1994 election campaign belonged to John Moorlach. Moorlach, an accountant who ran for the Treasurer's post against Citron and who was to eventually win this position, stated:

> Mr Citron believes he can accurately anticipate the market all the time and also outperform everyone. That's impossible. The incumbent has structured the portfolio on the premise that interest rates would continue to decline.

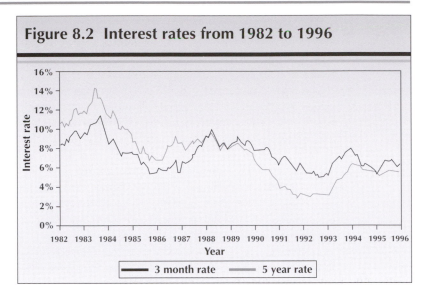

Figure 8.2 Interest rates from 1982 to 1996

Moorlach's warnings were ignored and he lost the election to Citron even though he had diagnosed the risks accurately. If interest rates were to rise, Citron's investment strategies would lose money. In February 1994, there was a dramatic change in US interest rates triggered by the action of the US Federal Reserve. Interest rates rose steadily throughout 1994. This rise in interest rates in 1994 can be seen in Figure 8.2. (The dot on the horizontal axis corresponds to the end of the year in question. The graph shows that rates were rising during the calendar year 1994.) This rise in interest rates devastated the Orange County portfolio. In December 1994, Orange County shocked the financial world with the announcement that its investment pool had suffered a loss of US$1.6 billion and declared bankruptcy shortly afterwards.

As a result of the disaster, Orange County instituted new policies for its investment pools.[3] These policies put tighter restrictions on the type of allowable investments and introduced stringent reporting requirements and internal controls. The main investment objective is now stated as:

> It is the policy of the Orange County Treasurer to invest public funds in a manner which will provide the maximum security of principal invested with secondary emphasis on achieving the highest yield.

It is clear that this is a reaction to the disaster. The fund now prohibits strategies that increase leverage and there is an outright ban on derivatives.

BARINGS BANK

Barings Bank was established in 1762 and, until its demise, was the oldest merchant bank in London. Barings financed British armies during the American Revolution and the Napoleonic wars. It collapsed in 1995 with a loss of US$1.4 billion. Many commentators put the blame for the failure on Nick Leeson, the then 28 year-old head trader in the bank's Singapore office. While Leeson certainly played an important role, it is naïve to saddle him with all the blame. Leeson's activities were amazingly free from supervision and control. His trading activities went undetected as a consequence of the failure of management and the failure of internal controls.

Leeson was able to create a special account numbered 88888 in the bank's computer system to hide the bank's losses.[4] This account was set up in 1992 as a client account. As we show below, the amounts concealed in this way increased dramatically.

In 1994, the bank's financial reports indicated that Leeson's own trading activities produced £28.5 million profit. This accounted for 71% of the total profits of the bank group within Barings. Of course, this did not represent an accurate view of the situation because Leeson was hiding huge losses in account 88888.

Leeson was able to conceal these losses because in addition to trading he was also in charge of carrying out the paperwork to settle his trades. This was very bad risk management. The paperwork should be dealt with by someone completely independent of the trading function to verify that the trades took place and to prevent unauthorised trading. Barings' internal auditors had recommended in August 1994 that these functions should be segregated. They pointed out that Leeson had too much power and that there was a clear conflict of interest. Barings failed to implement this recommendation.

The availability of derivatives no doubt enabled Leeson to take on riskier positions than might have been the case in other markets. However, it was his freedom from supervision and control that ultimately brought down the bank. The incentive effects of his bonus arrangement seem to have been a factor as well. Leeson, and indeed the senior members of the bank's management team, were paid mainly by bonuses. In the Barings

Table 8.1 Account number 88888 (£ millions)

Year	1992	1993	1994	1995
Loss for the year	2	21	185	619
Cumulative loss	2	23	208	827

Group about 50% of pre-tax profits were earmarked for bonuses. In 1994 Leeson's proposed bonus was half a million pounds. Four other members of the Bank were allocated higher bonuses of two to three times that of Leeson. The Bank of England report on the Barings affair noted that his income was related to the level of profits but ducks the incentive issue (Bank of England, 1995): "As to Leeson himself, the bonus system meant that he stood to benefit materially from the false level of profits reported by him but we are unable to conclude that this was his only or main motivation." It is unclear why the report baulked at making this obvious connection. Leeson's own account shows clearly that his bonus was a very important factor (see Leeson, (1996)).

The securities that Leeson employed were fairly basic as far as derivatives go. It is instructive to examine the strategy he used because, like Mr Citron, of Orange County, Nick Leeson took big bets. Leeson's bets were on the Japanese market and he was able to use Barings' capital to finance these bets. Leeson assumed that the Japanese market would rise. He invested in futures contracts based on the level of the Japanese stock market. One of the distinguishing features of futures contracts is that an investor can take large positions with very little capital. The Japanese market fell by 13.5% during the first two months of 1995. Part of the fall was due to the Kobe earthquake, which occurred on January 17, 1995. To try to recoup some of his losses, Leeson took on additional risky positions.

One of Leeson's strategies involved taking positions on the Nikkei 225.[5] He sold straddles (took short positions in straddles) on a Japanese index known as the Nikkei 225. In this case, he stood to make money if the level of the Japanese market remained fairly constant and, of course, he would lose money if the market moved violently either upwards or downwards. The payoff on a short straddle is shown in Chapter 2 in Figure 2.9.

Nick Leeson sold straddles short in large numbers throughout 1994. This strategy was very vulnerable to any large movement (either increase or decrease) in the level of the Japanese market. The position was also vulnerable to any increase in the so-called volatility of the market. We can think of volatility as a measure of the market's uncertainty about the future. After the Kobe earthquake, the market became more uncertain about the future of Japanese stocks and this was reflected by an increase in option prices.[6] However, Leeson had sold options to construct the straddles and, when the prices of these options increased, he lost money. Like Citron, Leeson was taking reckless, big bets and he lost. His position suffered very heavy losses and eventually brought down the entire bank. On Sunday, February 26, 1995, the Bank of England announced that Barings was insolvent.

The UK government regulators were very embarrassed by this failure. The Chancellor of the Exchequer, Mr Kenneth Clarke, set up an enquiry the next day with these words (Hansard, February 27, 1995):

> The House will be rightly concerned about how such huge unauthorised exposures could be allowed to happen and build up so quickly without the knowledge of the company, the exchanges or the regulators. I am determined to address that question rigorously and to review the regulatory system thoroughly in the light of this collapse. However, before we come to any firm conclusions, it will be necessary to establish in detail the facts of the case.

The final report was submitted to the House of Commons on July 18, 1995. The main conclusions of the report were that Nick Leeson's unauthorised trading had caused the losses and that management had not exercised proper controls. The report presents its main conclusions on p. 232 as:

❑ the losses were incurred by reason of the unauthorised and concealed trading activities within BFS (Barings Futures Singapore);
❑ the true position was not noticed earlier by reason of a serious failure of controls and management confusion within Barings; and
❑ the true position had not been detected prior to the collapse by the external auditors supervisors and regulators.

The Singapore Finance Ministry also commissioned the accounting firm Price Waterhouse to prepare a report on the Barings collapse. The Singapore report was more critical of the Barings management than the Bank of England report. It noted that, in the first three weeks of February, Barings in London sent almost US$1 billion to BFS (despite an earlier order for Leeson to reduce his positions). Peter Norris, Barings CEO told the Singapore investigators that the bank continued to send money because it believed that Leeson's trading activities produced high returns while posing little or no risk. The Singapore report finds this explanation unconvincing. "This explanation is absurd, because the suggestion that a low-risk trading strategy can consistently yield high returns is implausible."

The Singapore report suggests that senior management connived to conceal the losses. The conclusions of the two reports differ. The UK Banking Supervisory Report blames Leeson and the failure of some of the senior management to institute a sound risk management system. The UK report does not find evidence of deliberate wrong doing by Barings. The report is remarkably restrained in assigning any blame to the Bank of England itself. On p. 244 it states:

> However, we consider that the Bank [of England] reasonably placed reliance on local regulators of the overseas operations; and it was also entitled to place reliance on the explanations given by management to the profitability of these operations and on other information provided by Barings.

This suggests a very passive and trusting approach to regulation. In a recent book Augar (2000), suggests that the Barings failure was symptomatic of the general decline of British merchant banking in the 1980s and

'90s. Augar argues that the British banks were totally unprepared for the increased competition, technological advances and globalisation that took place during this time. He points out that other banks also made serious strategic errors and that the Bank of England adopted a very *laissez faire* approach to regulation.

LONG-TERM CAPITAL MANAGEMENT

We discussed the role of speculation in the fall of Long-Term Capital Management in Chapter 1. Here we describe in more detail the stellar growth and spectacular fall of this hedge fund: the most infamous hedge fund in the world. We start by describing the main features of hedge funds and explain why they have been permitted to operate with minimal regulation.

Hedge funds

Hedge funds are investment vehicles for wealthy investors (wealthy individuals or other institutions). In comparison with other financial institutions such as pension funds and mutual funds they are largely unregulated. Their investors are presumed to be sophisticated enough not to require the same protection as the average investor. Hedge funds can invest in anything that is legal and have no limits on the amount of risk they can take on. The fees charged are high and managers of a successful fund are very well paid. However, the principals normally invest a substantial amount of their own wealth in their fund and this helps to align incentives. The thinking is that the managers' incentives are better aligned with those of the fund's investors if the managers have a big chunk of their own money in the fund.

The first hedge fund was set up in 1949 by Alfred Winslow Jones. He used a strategy of selling short stocks that he considered to be overvalued and using the proceeds to buy stocks that he thought were cheap. A portfolio constructed in this manner would not be adversely affected by broad market movements because losses on one side would be offset by profits on the other. In this way, the portfolio would be protected or hedged, hence the name "hedge fund". The President's Working Group on Financial Markets (1999) reports that there were about 3,000 hedge funds operating by mid-1998. In terms of total assets under management, hedge funds are much smaller than mutual funds, commercial banks, pension plans and insurance companies.

Hedge funds operate without much publicity. They are private institutions and so their activities are not usually reported in the financial press. The only time they are in the news is when a large fund is involved in something dramatic. In general, hedge funds engage in more active trading than, for example, pension plans. Hedge funds often use leverage and make extensive use of derivatives. It is often difficult to know what risk a fund is assuming because of the limited disclosure that is required but this may change in the aftermath of the LTCM fiasco.

Most hedge funds are small enterprises with less than US$100 million in capital. In general any investment restrictions are self imposed. Studies show that hedge funds provide both higher returns and higher risks than broadly based stock market indices such as the S&P 500 (Brown Goetzman and Ibbotson, 1997). This is not surprising as common sense tells us that above-average returns are associated with higher-than-average risk. Hedge fund returns do not always move exactly the same way as those of the market as a whole and this feature can be attractive to investors seeking additional diversification.

Given the adverse publicity surrounding the LTCM collapse, it is useful to point out that hedge funds also provide benefits to the financial system. Hedge funds are in the business of taking on risk and they can absorb the risk that other market participants wish to shed. In this way, they assist in making the markets more efficient and more liquid. If an anomaly is observed in market prices hedge fund managers are in an excellent position to exploit it and, by so doing, remove it. Eichengreen and Mathieson (1999) note that hedge funds can also have a stabilising effect: "When big moves are under way, the data show that hedge funds often act as contrarians, leaning against the wind, and therefore often serve as stabilizing speculators."

Paradoxically, the very features of hedge funds that are beneficial to the system can be dangerous if taken to excess. The LTCM saga shows that a large hedge fund can quietly build up an enormous highly leveraged portfolio that is so vulnerable to unusual market movements that the stability of the entire financial system is threatened.

There are three reasons why investment vehicles such as hedge funds may be regulated. The first is to protect investors in hedge funds who, as we noted earlier, are assumed to be able to take care of themselves. The second reason is to protect the integrity of the market. This is why a number of countries collect information on the positions taken in exchange traded derivatives, certain securities and major currencies. This information is useful in preventing market manipulation as hedge funds are required to report their positions in these securities. The third reason for regulation of investment funds is to protect the financial system as a whole from systemic risks. The financial sector is interested in preventing systemic risk and so financial institutions have adopted a number of prudent risk management practices to reduce systemic risk. These include the management of credit risk, ongoing monitoring of the risk of counterparties and updating the market values of their portfolios. At the regulatory level, the implementation of legislation to prevent systemic risk is uneven both across institutions and across jurisdictions. It is often difficult to regulate an investment vehicle that operates on a global basis and some large hedge funds fall into this category.

The growth of LTCM

Long-Term Capital Management was founded by John Meriwether and started operations in 1994. Meriwether was already a Wall Street legend. When he was at Salomon Brothers, Meriwether had put together an outstanding team of traders and analysts with strong academic credentials. He convinced the key members of this group to join him when he set up LTCM. In addition, he persuaded both Robert Merton and Myron Scholes to join the team. In late 1994, David Mullins, who was vice chairman of the US Federal Reserve, joined LTCM. Mullins had helped write the Brady report, which had investigated the 1987 stock market crash.

The stellar reputations of the firm's principals made it much easier for it to raise money than if it was just another hedge fund.[7] In the US, the partners raised money from rich individual investors and institutions. In Europe and Japan, the fund raised funds from commercial banks and institutions. LTCM was able to obtain cash from quasi-governmental agencies and even the central bank of Italy invested US$250 million; LTCM had a target of raising US$2.5 billion in initial capital. The firm was able to raise US$1.25 billion, which was an unprecedented investment in a new hedge fund.

Hedge fund fees are based on performance as well as asset size. One component is based directly on how well the fund does. Normally, this incentive component is 20% of the fund's profits. The other component is normally 1% of the net assets of the fund. The fees of LTCM exceeded both industry norms. It was able to charge higher fees than the average hedge fund because of the reputation of its principals. In the case of LTCM, the incentive component was 25% of the yearly increase in the fund's net asset value. This incentive fee was subject to a *high water mark provision*, which meant that if the fund suffered a big loss in one year it would first have to recoup the loss before any incentive fee could be levied. The base fee was an annual amount of 2% of the fund's net asset value.

During the fund's marketing campaign investors were told that the annual returns after expenses could be as high as 30% (Lowenstein, 2000). For the first three years of its operations the fund lived up to this promise. Its returns net of fees and management charges were around 40% for the two years 1995 and 1996 and slightly less than 20% in 1997. The fund's basic strategy was to find situations where there were temporary price discrepancies and exploit these opportunities to make profits. For example, if the fund found two bonds that were mispriced relative to each other, it would buy the cheap one and sell the dear one until the prices came back into line. One of its early trades involved two US Treasury bonds with very similar maturities whose prices were slightly out of line.[8] The fund bought US$1 billion of the cheaper bond and sold US$1 billion of the same amount of the dearer bond.

Investment strategies

This Treasury-bond transaction is known as a *convergence trade* and was one of the strategies widely employed by LTCM. In a convergence trade there is a fixed future date when the two securities values will converge. The fund buys the cheaper of the two securities and sells the dearer of the two and holds these positions until the prices come back into line. Another related strategy was known as a *relative value trade*. In a relative value trade there is a strong expectation but no absolute guarantee that the prices of two related securities will converge. As we will see later, LTCM set up a trade of this type based on the shares of two oil companies – Shell (listed in London) and Royal Dutch Petroleum (listed on the Amsterdam exchange) – on the assumption that the prices would converge. LTCM also engaged in *directional trades* where it would take a position based on its view of the future. For example, when the value of index stock options increased reflecting a higher degree of uncertainty about the future than normal, LTCM took positions in index options.

LTCM invested not only in the US but also in markets all over the world to exploit its investment strategies. It was an active investor in bonds and interest rate derivatives in Canada, France, Germany, Italy, Japan and the UK (the G-7 countries). The fund also invested in equities and corporate bonds as well as in emerging markets. It made extensive use of both exchange-traded derivatives and over-the-counter derivatives because this afforded a cheap way to gain exposure to different markets and increase leverage. In particular, it took significant positions in equity index futures and interest rate futures in a number of countries.

It was also extremely active in the OTC derivatives markets and had a very large portfolio of swaps with a number of different counterparties. For example, the gross notional amount of swaps in August 1998 was over US$750 billion. There is ample evidence that LTCM's counterparties and lenders, who were often major Wall Street banks, tended to give the fund special treatment and did not always adhere to the best risk management practices as far as the fund's trades were concerned.[9] Once again, this special treatment was given because of the reputation of the fund's partners.

LTCM used its models and trading expertise to take calculated risks that were very profitable in the fund's first few years. For example, LTCM began life in early 1994 during a period of turmoil that existed in the bond markets. As we have noted earlier, there was a rise in interest rates in early 1994 that took the market by surprise (it was this rise in interest rates that had devastated Mr Citron's portfolio in Orange County). At that time, many of the existing hedge funds had placed very large bets that interest rates would continue to fall not only in the US but around the world. These hedge funds had ramped up their exposure to interest rates through derivatives that would increase in value if they were right and rates fell, but would lose money if they were wrong and rates rose. However, the bond market interpreted the initial hike in US short-term rates by Alan Greenspan, the first in five years, as posing a real danger of inflation. Long-term rates jumped. This caused a drop in bond prices and the derivative portfolios of the hedge funds that reacted by dumping bonds on the market and this put further pressure on interest rates. These funds lost heavily, as interest rates continued to rise and they were forced to sell bonds and other securities to cover margin calls, which put further pressure on interest rates that made bond prices fall even further.

LTCM was just entering the market flush with cash at this stage and was in a position to buy securities that everyone else wanted to sell and thus supply liquidity to the market. In these turbulent conditions, LTCM was able to identify and exploit even small price discrepancies between bonds of differing maturities or bonds of different types. For example, if LTCM noticed that the spread between the yields on corporate bonds and Treasury bonds was higher than the historical spread, it would buy the corporate bonds and sell Treasury bonds in the hope that the spread would return to its normal levels. If the spread returned to its historical level LTCM would make money but if the spread persisted or if it widened, then the trade would lose money. It involves a strong expectation that certain price differences that seem to be temporarily out of kilter will return to their normal level.

Another LTCM strategy was to identify and exploit price discrepancies between cash markets and the derivatives market. European bond markets proved a fertile hunting ground for opportunities of this type and the fund was able to profit from discrepancies between the bond markets and their associated futures markets.

The fund's initial successes were due to its astute trades in bonds and their associated securities and derivatives. LTCM would identify securities that were either overpriced or underpriced relative to similar securities. Then the fund would swoop in with a large leveraged position and scoop out the profit when the prices went back to normal. In 1996, the fund made very profitable trades on Japanese convertible bonds, junk bonds (described in Chapter 9), interest rate swaps and Italian bonds. It was also able to exploit a spread between French bonds and German bonds that seemed unsustainable. There were a couple of reasons why the interest rate area appealed to LTCM. Meriwether and his band of star traders had honed their skills in the interest rate area as members of Salomon's Arbitrage Group. In addition, interest rates could be modelled with much more precision than equities and LTCM had some of the best quantitative modellers in the world.

By the end of 1996, the opportunities for profitable trades in this area were diminishing. This was partly because of competition from other institutions such as the proprietary desks of investment banks and other hedge funds. Indeed the main reason why LTCM was so secretive about its operations was to protect its trading strategies. In the investment business imitation may not be the highest form of flattery but it is certainly the most sincere. Eric Rosenfield, one of the fund's partners, is quoted as saying:

"Everyone else started catching up on us. We'd go to put on a trade, but when we started the opportunity would vanish" (Lewis, 1999).

At the firm's 1997 annual meeting, the partners indicated that they were concerned about the declining spreads (profits) on the bond arbitrage business, which had been so profitable (Lowenstein, 2000). It was revealed at the same meeting that LTCM was becoming more involved in equity trades and there was also a rumour that the firm was becoming more involved in risk arbitrage.

One of its equity trading strategies involved a paired share trade. The idea is to find a stock that is listed on two exchanges or a pair of stocks that represent roughly the same claim on a firm's assets. In theory, the prices of the pair should be equal but for institutional reasons price discrepancies can open up and persist. One of LTCM's paired trades involved the oil companies Royal Dutch Petroleum and Shell Transport. These two companies derived their income from the same asset, which they jointly owned. Historically, the shares of the English company traded below those of the Dutch company. Victor Haghani, an LTCM partner, reasoned that the spread would contract as European markets became more integrated and proceeded to go long Shell and short Royal Dutch Petroleum with a position of at least a billion dollars in each stock. This was a riskier strategy than some of the earlier bond plays because the convergence of the prices was less assured. The sheer size of the trade meant that LTCM's positions in these two stocks could not be unwound quickly at their current market prices.

LTCM also began to try to anticipate and profit from merger and takeover activity, which represented a more speculative form of activity. This involved buying stocks of companies that were potential takeover targets and profit from the price rise that would occur when the takeover was announced. This trade is a form of *risk arbitrage* that requires considerable research to be profitable as so many imponderables are involved. One such trade involved the stocks of a communication company based in Chicago, called Tellabs, which had planned to acquire another telecommunications company called Ciena Corporation. Ciena had expertise in producing technology that was used in the increasingly important area of optical networks. This trade was very controversial within the partnership: "A lot of people felt we shouldn't be in the risk arb business because it was so information sensitive and we weren't trying to trade in an information sensitive way".[10]

The acquisition was announced on June 3, 1998. On August 21, 1998, AT&T unexpectedly announced it would not go ahead with a large purchase of equipment from Ciena, effectively torpedoing the merger. This announcement caused Ciena's stock price to drop dramatically and LTCM lost US$150 million.

Another of LTCM's strategies was to take a position based on the premise that equity options were overpriced given reasonable estimates of volatility. Recall that volatility is a measure of uncertainty and it is one of the parameters in the Black–Scholes–Merton option-pricing model. The higher the volatility in the market the higher the option prices. LTCM took the view that when the implied volatility in the market reached 20%, it would eventually revert to more normal levels of 13–15%.

In 1997, LTCM began to sell five-year options on the S&P 500 Index. The table below shows how the price of a typical five-year call option depends on the volatility. Note that when the volatility is 20% the price is US$17.7 whereas if the volatility is 19%, the option price is US$16.8. So, if a hedge fund sells short a five-year option based on a 20% volatility it receives US$17.7 and if the volatility then drops to 19% the option is worth US$16.8. This represents a profit of US$1.1 (17.7–16.8) on the strategy. This was LTCM's plan but implied volatility remained high throughout 1998, which resulted in losing money.

These investments, as well as other directional trades, represented a shift in the riskiness of some of the fund's trades. Because of competition, the fund had to work harder to gain high returns and this involved taking on more risk. The fund was straying well beyond its proven range of expertise. A number of partners including Robert Merton, David Mullins, James McEntee and especially Myron Scholes, were very concerned with the risks the fund was now taking on and protested about the size of the firm's various positions (Lowenstein, 2000). The warnings were ignored.

Lowenstein (2000), notes that the direction of the firm was becoming increasingly dominated by its two senior partners: Larry Hilderbrand and Victor Haghani.

The fall

We have seen that the hedge fund was moving to more risky investment strategies in 1997. However, during this period there were important international economic events that would affect the hedge fund in a major way. The reason was that these events increased investors' perceptions of risk and adversely affected some of LTCM's positions. One of these events was the Asian economic crisis of 1997.

During most of the mid-1990s, the economies of the so-called Asian

Table 8.2 Relation between volatility and option prices

Volatility used to compute call price (%)	Call option price
15	13.3
16	14.2
17	15.1
18	15.9
19	16.8
20	17.7

tigers were booming. These countries included the Philippines, South Korea and the "MIT" economies of Malaysia, Indonesia and Thailand (see Krugman, 1998). Western banks and investors provided funds during the economic boom times with apparently little monitoring of their usage. Until the recent crisis, Asia attracted almost half of the total capital inflows to developing countries: nearly US$100 billion in 1996 (see Fischer, 1998). The crisis took the financial world by surprise. Krugman notes that based on many of the conventional indicators, things looked just fine: "On the eve of the crisis all of the governments were more or less in fiscal balance: nor were they engaged in irresponsible credit creation or runaway monetary expansion. Their inflation rates, in particular were quite low."

In mid-1997, signs of impending trouble began to appear when the Thai baht fell by 20% triggering a fall in other currencies in the area. The level of economic activity in the Asian tigers began to fall swiftly.

During the boom times, a generous supply of credit was available to the domestic banks in these countries to finance economic activity. These banks had a strong incentive to take on high-risk ventures because they stood to benefit if the investments did well. There was an implicit guarantee that their governments would protect them if things went wrong. These conditions led to excessive risk taking and investment in speculative ventures, which drove up the prices of domestic assets. When asset prices began to fall it threatened the solvency of the banks and triggered further falls in asset prices. Once the crisis had started, the foreign banks that had financed the expansion began to withdraw these funds, which served to exacerbate the situation. The Asian crisis also affected global equity markets, culminating in a severe fall in October 1997. Investors became more frightened and the levels of implied volatility in equities increased. Seeing an opportunity to make money, LTCM began to take on large option positions based on the assumption that implied volatility levels would fall.

In this new environment, it was becoming increasingly difficult to make money with the type of strategies that LTCM had been using. The risk arbitrage group at Salomon, Meriwether's former group, had been using some of the same types of strategy as LTCM and was also facing the same sorts of difficulties. In 1998, Salomon's risk arbitrage group began to scale back its operations and decrease its leverage. In June 1998, the Travelers Group, which had acquired Salomon in 1997, made a decision to close down its risk arbitrage operations. In September, Travelers reported that Salomon lost US$360 million in July and August because of "extreme volatility" in global markets. The swap positions that Salomon and other firms were unwinding at this time were similar to those held by LTCM, and so as these trades came to the market this put downward pressure on the market prices. If you own a lot of apples and everyone wants to sell apples and nobody wants to buy apples, then the market price of apples will fall and the market value of your holding will also fall.

There were a number of factors that lead to the near collapse of the hedge fund in 1998. Long-Term Capital Management's financial position was very sensitive to market movements because of its highly leveraged positions. On August 17, 1998, Russia declared a moratorium on its domestic dollar debt and this triggered a flight to US government debt, which meant that the price of US bonds rose. LTCM was long Russian debt and it was also short US bonds. The hedge fund lost money on both these positions. On 21 August, LTCM lost US$553 million. Many of the hedge funds' trades were losing heavily at this time and the counterparties on the other side of these transactions were requiring cash payments from LTCM to protect their own.

During the last week of August, the firm's partners tried in vain to raise the US$1.5 billion in additional capital needed to keep the fund afloat. This proved to be impossible and by mid-September, a collapse was inevitable. As we discussed in Chapter 1, LTCM was rescued by a consortium of Wall Street banks with an investment of US$3.6 billion.

The aftermath
The fall of LTCM was highly publicised and it was subsequently analysed in a number of reports. The near collapse of the huge hedge fund renewed fears about the vulnerability of the entire financial system to system-wide risk or systemic risk.[11] Questions were raised concerning the role of hedge funds in the economy and the extent to which the trading practices of LTCM contributed to the crisis. In the aftermath of the fall, questions were raised about the risk management practices of LTCM but also the risk

management practices of the institutions that had lent it so much money. Some observers called for better hedge fund disclosure so that external parties could have more information on the risks that hedge funds were taking on.

Others argue against this requirement claiming that no useful public policy objective is served by mandatory disclosure of hedge fund portfolios. For example, the Report of the Financial Economists Roundtable (1999) supports this view: "The law already requires that hedge fund investors be wealthy and sophisticated investors and hedge fund creditors are typically large financial institutions which are already highly regulated. All of these parties have a strong incentive to protect themselves from excessive risk." However these safeguards did not appear to function properly in the case of LTCM. For example, Governor Laurence H. Meyer noted in his testimony on March 24, 1999, that LTCM received special treatment.

> Investigations of the management of the LTCM account at several institutions found that an over-reliance on the collateralization of the current market value of derivatives positions and the stature of LTCM's managers led to compromises in several key elements of the credit risk management process.

These counterparties were often large institutions with sophisticated risk management programmes, so this lapse seems surprising. The market discipline failed in this case because of the reputation of LTCM's principals, the outstanding investment performance and the opportunity to profit from the relationship with LTCM.

CONCLUSION

This discussion brings us back to the theme that seems to run through many derivatives disasters. If a trader or a firm acquires the status of a superstar then there is a strong temptation to abandon caution and give this trader (or firm) more money to invest and relax the usual prudent controls. We saw this same process at work in the cases of Orange County and Barings bank. Although the details of all the cases differ there is a clear common thread. The individuals and institutions that could have reduced the risk exposure were either mesmerised by the stars or not powerful enough to challenge them. While the lessons from these disasters have helped to improve risk management practices, the lesson to be learned from indulging the superstars seems to be harder to learn.

1   LIBOR stands for London Interbank Offer Rate and is a reference rate used in the financial markets for loans in international markets.
2   The Orange County Board of Supervisors (the "Board") is the body that controls the financial affairs of the County. The Board may delegate some of its duties to County officers and employees but it is ultimately responsible for the execution of these duties. In 1985, the

Board formally delegated its authority to invest County funds to its Treasurer, Robert Citron.

3   These policies were instituted by the new Treasurer, John Moorlach and are available on the website. URL: http://www.oc.ca.gov/treas/ips2000.pdf.

4   When asked by David Frost in a BBC interview why he picked these numbers, Leeson responded "It's a lucky number or considered to be a lucky number by Chinese people. I think it means – it actually means prosperity".

5   For a discussion of Leeson's trading strategies see the case study by Lillian Chew (1996).

6   We explained in the Appendix to chapter 5 how the price of an option increases and the volatility of the underlying asset increases.

7   Lowenstein (2000) gives details of the investors in Long-Term Capital Management. Among the institutions that invested in the fund were Paine Webber, the Black & Decker Pension Fund, Continental Insurance of New York, St Johns University, and Yeshiva University. Some senior executives of a few prominent Wall Street firms also invested their own money in the fund. Other investors included Sumitomo Bank of Japan, Dresdner Bank of Germany, the Government of Singapore Investment Corporation and the Bank of Taiwan.

8   One bond had a maturity of 29.5 years whereas the other had a maturity of 30 years. The yields on the two bonds should have been the same but in 1994, LTCM noticed that the shorter term bond had a yield of 7.24% and the longer term bond had a yield of 7.36%.

9   See Lowenstein (2000), President's Working Group on Financial Markets (1999).

10 As quoted by Eric Rosenfield in Michael Lewis's (1999) *New York Times Magazine* article.

11 Writing before the LTCM near collapse Thomson (1998) foresaw the impact of a huge hedge fund disaster on financial markets: "If a big hedge fund collapsed the effects could be daunting. It would probably happen in the midst of some major market upheaval such as the bond market collapse of 1994. Its assets would probably be liquidated in a panic creating further market disruption. To make matters worse, the effects would almost certainly feed through the banking system because hedge funds use huge amounts of bank credit as their major sources of leverage. The fact is that two of the largest groups of speculators in the world – the hedge funds and the banks – are connected like Siamese twins".

9

Credit Risk

Credit risk is as pervasive in business as snow in the Canadian winter and has existed since humans first began to trade. It is *the risk that one party in a transaction is unable to or unwilling to fulfil the terms of a contract*. The development of a standard legal system with appropriate remedies for non-performance helped the growth of commercial trade and business activities, and reduced some of the risks. However, key business risks remain because the future is uncertain. The promise of favourable outcomes persuades investors to take these risks. In financial markets the lower the expected return the lower the risk tends to be and, generally, the higher the expected return the higher is the risk.

INTRODUCTION

We begin our discussion of credit risk at the individual level because the issues are more familiar here. People are good credit risks if they are in good financial shape. Suppose Jill is a tenured professor at a leading university and dean of the business school. She also owns a very valuable art collection and does not have any liabilities. A bank will happily lend her money and give her high limits on its credit cards. On the other hand, if Jack's income is precarious and he has few assets he will be viewed as a poor credit risk. Jack's position will be even worse if he has fixed debts such as alimony payments. The credit risk of individuals is evaluated by estimating the security of their future income as well as their other assets.

In the same way, a corporation's credit rating is based on the security of the firm's future net income and its assets. Suppose that the LTX steel company, which borrowed US$100 million from the Grendel bank five years ago, now has trouble meeting its interest payments on the loan because the price of steel has dropped so much. When the loan was arranged, LTX promised to pay a fixed interest amount of US$7 million per year to the bank while the loan is outstanding and to repay the full amount of the loan in 10 years. In these circumstances, LTX may have trouble making its promised interest payments and if conditions in the steel market deteriorate even further, the company might not be able to repay the loan. The bank loan is exposed to credit risk, which increases in the event of an adverse change in the creditworthiness of the borrower.

Banks have always been aware of credit risk and have traditionally used different ways to deal with it. The interest rate charged on the loan should reflect the risks that the bank is taking on. The bank can reduce its exposure by prudent lending practices. In theory, the bank could reduce its risk exposure by spreading its loans across different types of borrowers. In practice a bank may operate within a specific area and its loans may be concentrated in a few industries; regional banks often enjoy a strong relationship with a few large customers. However, only having one or two big clients exposes the bank to a heavy concentration of credit risk as the bank itself will be in trouble should one of these clients experience financial distress. The nature of this relationship is summed up neatly in the following piece of banking folklore: "a bank's best customer is its worst customer".[1]

Credit derivatives[2] can reduce the bank's exposure to this type of credit risk. The bank can purchase a credit derivative from a third party so that the third party pays money if a certain credit event affects its main customer.[3] Credit derivatives enable this type of risk to be unbundled and transferred. Credit derivatives took off in the mid-1990s, to reach a point where – during the period from 1995 until 2000 – the volume of credit derivatives grew at an astonishing rate of 74% per annum.[4] The notional value of credit derivatives in 2000 is estimated to be $US893 billion. The initial impetus for this growth came from banks through their efforts to reduce the concentration of credit risk in their loan portfolios and bond portfolios. They were the natural buyers, as were insurance companies, for which credit derivatives represented an insurance-type business and an opportunity to diversify both product and risk.

The Asian crisis of 1997 and the Russian crisis of August 1998, highlighted the value of credit derivatives, but the Russian crisis also highlighted the problems of credit derivatives.

In the case of Russia, the central issue was: what constitutes default in the case of a sovereign country? Both buyers and sellers of certain derivatives were unclear about whether their individual contracts covered the unfolding events. Worse still, it was unclear for a long time whether Russia had defaulted. As a result of the Russian crisis, the definition of sovereign risks was tightened and a distinction between domestic (local currency) debt and foreign currency debt was made. Nevertheless, the experience of the Russian crisis demonstrated the benefits of credit derivatives to potential players who were watching the credit derivatives market develop from the sidelines. Incidentally, Russia defaulted on and rescheduled certain domestic currency debt, while maintaining payments on its foreign currency debt.

As in the case of other derivatives markets, advances in information technology have facilitated the growth of the credit derivatives market. Intellectual breakthroughs in the modelling and pricing of credit risk have provided the foundations for pricing and hedging these new securities.

WHY FIRMS FAIL

To understand credit risk and credit derivatives we need to analyse the nature of credit risk, which we will do in the next section. Here we shall explain how credit risk arises and why it is an integral component of business activities.

The types of risk that can cause financial distress are many and varied and are extremely hard to predict. Adverse macroeconomic conditions such as a depression or recession can lead to an increase in the number of bankruptcies and financially distressed firms. One of the most dramatic examples of this occurred during the Great Depression of the early 1930s when there was a large number of business failures. Sometimes a particular industry can experience a very dramatic increase in business failures, as in the case of the savings and loan industry in the US during the 1980s. Ironically, one of the main causes for this disaster lay in government regulations.

During the Reagan administration the investment restrictions for these institutions were liberalised so that they could invest in very risky assets. However the existence of a government-sponsored deposit insurance scheme meant that the deposits of individual customers were insured by the federal government in case of default. These conditions provided incentives for the owners of savings and loans to use their depositors' funds to make very risky investments. If the returns on these investments were high, the owners would make a fat profit and if the investments went sour then Uncle Sam would cover the losses suffered by the policyholders. Because their deposits were insured by the federal government, depositors did not have to worry about the financial health of the savings and loan banks. This meant that customers did not have any incentive to monitor the banks, which in turn permitted the banks to indulge in excessive risk taking.

When a large financial institution fails, it sends a chilling effect throughout the economy because of the special role played by these organisations. Governments often take a special interest in maintaining the solvency of these financial institutions and, when one of them fails, there is no shortage of culprits. Confederation Life Insurance, which failed in August 1994, is a case in point. At the time of its demise, it was the fourth largest life insurance company in Canada with assets of C$19 billion. MacQueen, in his analysis of the disaster, pulls no punches.[5]

> Confed went under because there was not a single director, officer, regulator, auditor, politician, or industry honcho who completely fulfilled his or her job.

> Directors did not hold management sufficiently accountable; officers acted irresponsibly and with reckless disregard; regulators were tardy to react, they threatened with a stick too small; auditors peered at the books but missed the big picture; weak-willed politicians had neither courage nor conviction; and rather than help, the industry leaders were reduced to a mere dither.

Confederation Life's major objective was growth of business rather than profitability. It also concentrated too heavily on one asset class: real estate. By 1990, Confederation Life had about 75% of its assets in real estate, which included investments such as mortgage loans. Furthemore, in its drive for growth the company took on some very high-risk loans because it accepted business that other lenders had turned down. Starting with the recession in 1990, the real estate market in Toronto began to collapse and the market value of Confederation's assets plummeted. Ultimately, this brought down the entire company.

Several Japanese financial institutions experienced severe financial distress in the 1990s because of bad real-estate loans, also called non-performing loans. In the mid-1980s Japan's economy was booming, there was a huge upsurge in stock prices and real estate prices. Demand for real estate was especially high in Tokyo and interest rates were at very low levels. Japanese banks expanded their real-estate lending business and prices shot up even higher. In the early 1990s the so-called bubble burst and both stock prices and real estate prices came tumbling down. (Real estate prices fell by 50% from 1991 until 1995.) The 1990s seemed as if it would be a decade of economic stagnation in Japan. Many of the companies that had borrowed the money to fund real-estate development were also in trouble and could not cover their interest payments. This left the financial institutions with a large concentration of bad loans that, in turn, threatened their own financial solvency.

The prolonged recession in Japan has had a devastating impact on the solvency of the Japanese life-insurance industry.[6] Japan has the largest life-insurance market in the world and, on a per-capita basis, the Japanese buy more insurance than citizens of any other country. Many popular Japanese insurance contracts guarantee a certain rate of return on their policy-holders' deposits. During the late 1990s it was impossible to obtain this rate in the Japanese market because both the stock market and real-estate returns were dismal, and the Bank of Japan implemented a zero rate of interest policy that lasted 18 months. In the half-century following the Second World War, no Japanese life insurer had failed. In contrast, there were six failures from 1997 to 2000.[7]

Product liability suits arising from class actions can also cause financial distress and increase credit risk. For example, Owens Corning filed for bankruptcy in October, 2000 because of the liabilities it faced as the result of selling a pipe insulation product called Kaylo that contained asbestos.

The firm sold this product from the 1940s until the early 1970s. Similarly, Dow Corning filed for bankruptcy protection in 1995 because of the claims it faced as result of silicone breast implants. There is now widespread evidence that tobacco smoking causes lung cancer and tobacco firms have been the subject of a number of legal suits on this issue.

Who gets paid when firms fail

If a firm becomes insolvent and is declared bankrupt there are rules on how the assets that are left are to be divided between the firm's claimants. These claimants include employees, tax authorities, the firm's unpaid suppliers and other creditors, as well as the holders of the firm's financial securities; legal fees also have to be paid. Suppose the financial securities issued by the company only consist of stocks and bonds. The bondholders have loaned money to the firm and have first priority. They are entitled to the residual value of the firm. This will normally be less than the total amount they have lent. For example, if the total remaining amount available is US$45 million and the total amount owing to the bond holders is US$100 million, then each bondholder will be paid at the rate of 45 cents on the dollar. Even though these rules exist, it is often not clear in advance how much a particular set of security holders will receive if a firm goes under.

In the last example, there is nothing left for the stockholders and their securities are worthless. These are the rules of the game and the stockholders knew this ahead of time. Of course, if the firm had done spectacularly well the stockholders would have made a killing. Consequently, the stockholders do better than the bondholders if the firm does well and fare worse than the bondholders if the firm performs badly. The returns to stockholders will be more variable than those of bondholders. It is also worth noting that because of limited liability the total amount that the stockholders can lose is the amount they invested in the firm to buy its shares. If the common shares did not have limited liability they could be liable for all the unpaid debts of the failed corporation. For example, the amounts owing under a product liability suit could exceed all the assets of the corporation and, were it not for limited liability, the courts could go after all the assets of common stockholders.

These differences between stockholders and bondholders explain the origin of some basic conflicts of interest that arise between them in certain situations. Suppose a firm gets into serious financial distress and unless it takes some action it will surely fail. Suppose also that the firm has the opportunity to invest in either one of two investment opportunities.[8] The first project has little risk and will produce a secure but low return. If the firm takes on this project the chances are that it will survive and be able to repay its bondholders; the second project is extremely risky but there is a chance it will generate enormous profits. However, the most likely outcome is that the second project will fail and bring down the firm. We see that the bondholders would prefer to undertake the first project since it increases the value of their investments. The stockholders would prefer to undertake the second project since they have nothing to lose and it gives them a chance of a making a large profit. Since the stockholders usually dictate matters, safeguards have evolved to reduce this conflict of interest.[9]

THE RATING GAME

Bond investors are thus very interested in the creditworthiness of the firm that issues the bonds. They can obtain information on this from the firm's financial statements. In addition there are different rating agencies that provide an arm's length assessment of the firm's financial health. These agencies grade the bonds using a system of letter grades like that used by some universities to measure performance in academic courses. The three main rating agencies are Moody's, Standard & and Poor's and Fitch's. They all use similar rating classes for bonds: Moody's uses Aaa to denote the most credit worthy bonds followed by Aa, A, Baa, Ba, B and so on to denote bonds of decreasing credit quality. The other two agencies use AAA, AA, A, BBB, BB, B and so on for the same purpose. Triple A bonds are of the very highest credit quality. Bonds in the top four categories, AAA, AA, A and BBB are rated as investment grade bonds and bonds of grade BB and lower are rated as speculative grade bonds. Speculative grade bonds are often known as "junk bonds".

John Moody[10] was the first person to develop and publish a bond-rating scheme. Moody was a financial analyst and entrepreneur with literary aspirations.[11] He spent 10 years with the Wall Street firm of Spencer Trask gaining wide exposure to investment banking. In 1900, he started the firm of John Moody & Company to publish statistics on the stocks and bonds of financial institutions and government agencies. At first, the company prospered but eventually floundered during the stock market crash of 1907. Moody faced huge debts and, with creditors breathing down his neck, he hit upon a new idea. He realised there would be a demand for an independent rating of securities. In 1909 he started a service to rate the bonds of railroad companies. This was the forerunner of the firm that bears his name today. It is interesting to note that a few years previously, A M Best had introduced a similar service that provided an objective rating of insurance companies on the basis of their financial strength. Perhaps John Moody picked up the idea of using letter grades from A M Best.

The firm established by John Moody has analysed the default experience of long-term bonds from 1920 until the present.[12] Bond defaults vary in tandem with economic conditions. The highest default rate for corporate bonds was during the Great Depression, reaching an all-time high during 1932 when, in one year, the default rate was 9.2% implying that nearly one bond in 10 defaulted. The incidence of default declined more or less steadily until the end of the Second World War. For the next 25 years, default rates were relatively low and stable. The rate increased in 1970 with the collapse of the Penn Central Railway but remained fairly low until the recession in the early 1980s. During the final 20 years of the 20th century, default rates moved steadily higher and by 2000 they had reached relatively high levels again.

The rating of a bond is a good indicator of how likely it is to default in the future. The rating agency assigns the bond to a risk class in the same way that an insurance underwriter classifies risk: the better the credit rating the lower the chance of default. Speculative grade bonds are more likely to experience default than investment grade bonds although both experience more defaults during a severe depression. For example, based on the 1983–99 experience, the estimated default rate on a triple A-rated bond was zero after one year. This means that if we bought 100 triple bonds and held them for one year, none of the bonds would have defaulted. The corresponding rate for investment grade bonds was 0.46% and for speculative grade bonds it was 3.68%. However, the longer the period during which we hold a bond, the higher the chance of something going wrong. Based on the 1983–99 experience, a portfolio of 100 newly issued *speculative* grade bonds will experience about 20 times as many defaults in eight years that a portfolio of 100 newly issued *investment* grade bonds, during the same period.[13]

If a bond starts the year in a particular class the chances are it will still be in this class one year later. Historical studies show that if there are 100 triple A bonds at the start of the year the vast majority (92%) will retain this rating at the end of the year. For B-rated bonds 85% retain the same rating one year later. In the case of the 100 triple A-rated bonds, seven of the eight rating changes are to double A-rated bonds and one to single A. This movement from one rating class to another is known as rating migration. There is a simple connection between rating migration and default. When a firm that starts out with a strong credit rating becomes financially distressed, it does not normally happen overnight but on a more gradual basis. Thus, if a bond that starts out its life as a double A-rating defaults after eight years, the bond's credit rating will normally be downgraded a few times before the firm defaults. Historical data show that rating changes, if they occur, tend to be from one rating class to the next rating class and so changes tend to occur one step at a time.

Fallen angels

Fallen angels are bonds that were issued as investment grade bonds but were downgraded when the issuer fell on bad times. These fallen angels may sometimes be good buys if the market values them at less than what they are worth. For example, suppose a company is teetering on the edge of bankruptcy and its junk bonds are trading at US$25 per US$100 face value. Suppose that six months later, after the firm goes under, the assets are parcelled out and the bonds receive US$55 per US$100 face value, they will have yielded a tidy one-year profit. On the other hand, if the payout on dissolution is only US$15 per US$100 this investment will have lost money.

Fallen angels (junk bonds) are therefore highly risky investments for two reasons:

❑ there is higher risk of default; and
❑ if default occurs there may be little left for the investor because the other parties who are ahead of them in the queue receive most of the firm's assets.

Alternatively, an investor may achieve a reasonable or even a high return from investing in junk bonds if the firm recovers or even if the firm goes bankrupt and the junk bondholders receive more than the market expects them to receive. The return to the investor depends on the price for which the bonds are purchased and what happens afterwards. Warren Buffet of Berkshire Hathaway describes his rationale for buying junk bonds in some circumstances:[14]

> Just as buying into the banking business is unusual for us, so is the purchase of below-investment-grade bonds. But opportunities that interest us and that are also large enough to have a worthwhile impact on Berkshire's results are rare. Therefore, we will look at any category of investment, so long as we understand the business we're buying into and believe that price and value may differ significantly.

As an example, in 1983 and 1984, Berkshire Hathaway bought about US$140 million of Washington Public Power Supply System bonds, the price of which had slumped when the power authority defaulted on some of its existing bonds.

The Washington Public Power Supply System was set up in 1957 as a municipal corporation to supply nuclear power. The name was shortened to WPSSS or the unfortunate acronym WHOOPS. It estimated that the demand for electricity in the North West would double every 10 years beyond the capacity of hydropower. Five major nuclear power plants were planned to meet this projected demand. Even in the best of cases it takes a long time to build a nuclear power plant. In this case, construction was further delayed and due to inflation and poor project management the cost rose to several times the original estimate. WHOOPS became a classic example of how not to run a public works project. During the 1970s, there was an increased awareness of the environmental hazards associated with nuclear power plants and public support for the project waned. The Seattle City Council voted not to participate in two of the projects, Projects 4 and

5, and in January, 1982, construction on these projects was stopped. At that time the estimate for the total cost of all the proposed plants was US$24 billion and WHOOPS was forced to default on US$2.25 billion of bonds that were issued to finance the construction of the two abandoned projects.

In his 1984 chairman's letter, Buffet describes his purchases of these bonds and his appreciation of the credit risks involved.

> From October, 1983 through June, 1984 Berkshire's insurance subsidiaries continuously purchased large quantities of bonds of Projects 1, 2, and 3 of Washington Public Power Supply System ("WPPSS"). This is the same entity that, on July 1, 1983, defaulted on $2.2 billion of bonds issued to finance partial construction of the now-abandoned Projects 4 and 5. While there are material differences in the obligors, promises, and properties underlying the two categories of bonds, the problems of Projects 4 and 5 have cast a major cloud over Projects 1, 2, and 3, and might possibly cause serious problems for the latter issues. In addition, there have been a multitude of problems related directly to Projects 1, 2, and 3 that could weaken or destroy an otherwise strong credit position arising from guarantees by Bonneville Power Administration. Despite these important negatives, Charlie and I judged the risks at the time we purchased the bonds and at the prices Berkshire paid (much lower than present prices) to be considerably more than compensated for by prospects of profit.[15]

He goes on to specify more clearly the risks and the rewards associated with this investment:[16]

> However, in the case of WPPSS, there is what we view to be a very slight risk that the "business" could be worth nothing within a year or two. There also is the risk that interest payments might be interrupted for a considerable period of time. Furthermore, the most that the "business" could be worth is about the $205 million face value of the bonds that we own, an amount only 48% higher than the price we paid.

These bonds turned out to be a good deal for Berkshire Hathaway. By the end of 1988, they were rated by Standard and Poor as AA.[17] Buffet made a handsome profit on his risky investment.

CREDIT DERIVATIVES AND INSURANCE
The most popular type of credit derivative is known as a credit default swap. A credit default swap is a contract that provides a payment if a particular event occurs. The party that buys the protection pays a fee or premium to the party that sells the protection. If the credit event occurs within the term of the contract a payment is made from the seller to the buyer. If the credit event does not occur within the term of the contract the buyer receives no monetary payment but the buyer has benefited from the protection during the tenure of the contract. A credit default swap is similar to a life-insurance contract, which makes payment if the life

insured ends within the term of the contract. The death of the person whose life is insured corresponds to the credit event.

Life insurance

This insurance analogy is helpful in discussing credit derivatives, so we now recall some basic features of a term life insurance contract. Under this contract the individual, who pays the premiums to the insurance company is normally the life insured.[18] The premiums are paid on a regular basis, either monthly or annually, and the sum insured is set out in the policy document. If the person insured dies within the term of the policy, the insurance company pays out this amount specified in the policy once it is convinced that the event has occurred. The event triggering the payment is very clearly defined and the insurance company will pay over the funds to the deceased's estate or beneficiary when it receives the death certificate. There is usually no dispute on the event that triggers the payment.[19] There is a legal expectation that the life insured will disclose items of information that are material such as age, occupation and whether or not he or she smokes. Insurance contracts have been around for centuries and so the documentation has become standardised and the terms in the conditions have been interpreted thoroughly by the courts. Disputes are relatively rare.

The life insured need not be the same person as the person who pays the premium. In the 18th century it was common in England for citizens to take out insurance on the lives of prominent public figures. This practice was eventually prohibited because it provided an incentive for unscrupulous agents to hasten the demise of the life insured.[20] This is an example of moral hazard whereby the very existence of a contract alters the incentives of one of the parties to increase the risk. However, there are a number of business and personal situations where it is perfectly legitimate for one person or corporation to take out an insurance policy on the life (or health) of another. For example, a sport franchise has a large insurable interest in its star players; a bank has an insurable interest in someone to whom it has loaned US$10 million. Spouses are deemed to have an unlimited insurance interest in each other's lives.

The risk, in these cases, is covered by a distinct third party: the insurance company that sells the insurance. For example, Santa Claus has a strong insurable interest in the survival of his chief elf. Santa can take out an insurance policy on the chief elf's life with the North Pole Insurance Company. Santa is buying the protection and the insurance company is selling the protection. The event that will trigger the payment of the sum insured is the death of the chief elf. Santa has sometimes wondered what would happen if the North Pole Insurance Company itself were to go bankrupt but he is comforted by the fact that the insurer enjoys a triple A-rating as a wholly owned subsidiary of the Grendel Investment Bank.

Credit default swaps

A credit default swap is very like a term insurance contract. The protection seller in the case of the default swap corresponds to the insurance company. The triggering event is the death of the life insured in one case and the occurrence of the credit event in the other. We saw that, in the insurance example, we can have three parties involved; the life insured, the owner of the policy and the insurance company. In the case of the default swap, the entity that pays the fee for the protection corresponds to the owner of the policy. The entity that provides the protection corresponds to the insurance company. The underlying security whose credit is the focus of the credit default swap corresponds to the life insured. In a term insurance contract the premium payments cease when either the life insured dies, or the contract expires. The payment of the fee in a credit default swap stops when the credit event occurs or at the expiration of the contract, whichever occurs first. In both cases, protection can be purchased by paying a single fee or premium up front.

With a life insurance contract there is just one way to settle a claim; by paying cash. There are two ways to settle a claim under a credit default swap. The first way involves a pure cash payment; the second involves both a cash payment and a transfer of the defaulted security. For example, suppose the underlying security is a 10-year bond with a face value of US$100. If the credit event occurs and the market value of the bond drops to US$35, the cash settlement will be US$65 and the protection seller hands over this amount to the protection buyer. One of the problems of this approach is that it is difficult to determine the market value of the defaulted security. One solution is to base the market value on the average of prices quoted by leading dealers. Despite these difficulties cash settlement is much less common than the second method.

The second method, which involves the exchange of both cash and a security, is known as physical settlement. In this case, if the credit event occurs the protection seller will pay the buyer the full notional amount (US$100) and receives in return the defaulted security.[21] This procedure neatly solves the problem of determining a fair market price for the defaulted securities. There is no need to establish a market value for the troubled security. Under physical settlement, the protection writer (seller) now owns the underlying security. If the writer holds on to the security it has a powerful incentive to ensure that the security receives a good deal in any bankruptcy negotiations. Typically the writer would sell the defaulted debt in the market. This eliminates its exposure to the risk of a future decline in price or actual recovery levels. It is in the writer's best interests to obtain as much as possible for the distressed security in these negotiations.

There is no analogy with physical settlement in the case of life insurance but there is in other branches of insurance. Property insurance is one example. In some contracts the insurance company pays the claim and takes possession of the damaged asset. It has an incentive to sell this asset for the best price it can get. Consider physical damage coverage under an automobile insurance contract. If the owner wrecks his car in an accident and the damage is so severe that it is written off as a total loss, the insurance company will take ownership of the car and obtain the highest price it can.

Salvage recovery provisions can have a huge impact on the contract as the next example shows. The Scotch whisky firm of Bells offered a £1 million reward for the capture of the Loch Ness monster.[22] This mythical creature is supposed to live in the depths of Loch Ness in Scotland. The idea was a marketing ploy but the whisky firm decided to insure the risk with Lloyd's of London to cover the risk that the monster would be captured.[23] Lloyd's underwrote the risk and threw in a clause that stated that, in the event of capture, Lloyd's would own the monster. Presumably this was a very good deal for Lloyd's, assuming it could enforce the contract. Even if the monster were caught, Lloyd's would own a very valuable asset. The salvage value under the contract would be very high.

The terms and definitions under a credit default swap have become more standardised through the efforts of the International Swaps and Derivatives Association (ISDA).[24] This improved standardisation allows the parties to specify the precise terms of the transaction from a menu of clearly defined alternatives. In the early stages of the credit derivatives market there was considerable legal uncertainty, which impeded the growth of the market. As the terms become standardised the parties know what the terms in the contract mean and how they are to be interpreted. This helps the market to grow because it reduces legal risk thereby attracting more investors and improving market liquidity.

At this stage it is useful to summarise and briefly explain some of the key contract terms in a credit default swaps agreement.

❏ The *reference entity* is the firm or organisation that issues the security and whose credit risk is the subject of the credit default swap. For example, the reference entity might be a large public company and the reference asset might be just one of its bond issues, because the firm may well have several debt issues. The credit event can be triggered by what happens to any one of the other bond issues.

❏ The *credit quality* of all a firm's bonds will be adversely affected if the firm experiences financial difficulties and it makes sense to allow for this in the contract specification. For example, when WHOOPS defaulted on the bonds that were issued to finance Projects 4 and 5 the prices of its other bonds also fell. When Southern California Edison declared on 16 January, 2001, that it could not make available the US$596 million due to its bondholders and power suppliers, Standard & Poor's downgraded the debt of its parent Edison International from investment grade to speculative grade (junk bond).

❑ A *credit event* is the credit-related occurrence that triggers the payment on a credit default swap. Unlike death, which is very well defined, there can be a number of credit events with various meanings. These include bankruptcy, a rating downgrade, repudiation, failure to pay and cross-default. Bankruptcy includes insolvency, a judgement to wind up the reference entity or the appointment of a receiver. Failure to pay means that the firm issuing the security cannot scrape enough cash to make an interest payment on a bond, as happened with Southern California Edison.

❑ A *cross-default clause* on a bond means that that any default on another security of the issuing firm will also be considered as a default on the bond in question. Cross-default clauses are part of bond and loan documentation. Often a credit default swap refers to a class of debt. Any bond, loan, or default on borrowed money will typically trigger default because of the cross-default clauses in the debt documentation. The rationale here is to protect those who hold the bond, because the firm might otherwise use up all its assets to pay the claims of the other securities and there would be nothing left.

Credit variations

In addition to credit default swaps there are a number of other credit-based derivatives. A credit-linked note consists of a basic security plus an embedded credit default swap. The contract defines the reference entity and the triggering event. The triggering event usually refers to a class of debt. The contract also specifies what can be delivered in the case of default. This provides a useful way of stripping and repackaging credit risk. Suppose the reference entity is a Detroit car company. An investment bank can transfer the credit risk in the car-maker's debt to an investor by issuing a credit-linked note to the investor. The investor receives a higher interest rate to cover the default risk in the car-makers's bonds. If the car maker defaults within five years then the investor receives an amount equal to the recovery price on the deliverable debt. If there is no default the investor receives the full face value. This package provides a way for the investment bank to transfer the credit risk associated with the car maker.

Another innovation in the credit derivatives market is the combining of credit risks of different instruments in a portfolio. This portfolio is then divided and repackaged as several new securities. The new securities are backed by the portfolio of bonds. By combining bonds from different industries and possibly, from different countries, the benefits of diversification are achieved. New securities are created by dividing the cashflow from the portfolio up into tranches and assigning them to the different securities. The new securities are designed to have different credit risk features by construction. Suppose the cashflows from the underlying portfolio of bonds (or loans) are used to create three securities:

❑ A bond with a fixed coupon rate. This is the most senior security and its coupons are paid first. It is termed senior debt and this senior piece might carry an AAA-rating.
❑ A bond whose coupons are paid as long as there is enough left after the payments on the senior debt are made. This bond might carry a BB or B-rating and it is often known as the mezzanine piece or mezzanine tranche.
❑ A claim on the residual cashflows from the original portfolio after the two senior claims have been paid. This third tranche might be a high-yield speculative bond or it might be considered as an equity claim.

By repackaging in this way, the original portfolio of bonds has been used to create new securities whose credit risks are quite different from one another. Such a structure is called a *collateralised debt obligation* (CDO). Banks with large portfolios of loans often use such structures. The bank keeps the loans – and keeps the client relationship – but will sell the senior and mezzanine tranches (typically keeping the small – about 3% – equity piece) and achieve a big reduction in its capital solvency charge.

USES OF CREDIT DERIVATIVES
We have already noted that credit derivatives enable institutions to transfer the credit risk in their portfolios. By using credit derivatives an institution can separate interest rate risk from credit risk. This means that an institution can reduce or take on more credit exposure to a given firm or industry or country without dealing directly in the underlying physical assets. Credit derivatives can be used under a cloak of anonymity. A bank might not want to publicise that it was buying credit protection on its largest customer and credit derivatives can accomplish this objective.[25]

A credit default swap provides an efficient way for a bank to reduce or increase its exposures to a particular credit risk. By the very nature of their businesses, banks tend to hold a high concentration of their loans in particular areas or industries. For example, an Australian bank may have a very high concentration of loans to firms in the mining industry. A Texan bank may have heavy exposure to the oil industry in the South Western United States.

By the same token, banks can take on additional credit exposure by selling credit protection. For example, an Australian-based bank could sell a credit default swap to a Detroit bank where the reference credit is one of the big US car makers. Credit derivatives permit a bank to replace an unbalanced credit exposure with a credit exposure that is diversified by industry and by country. Note that the net cost of this realignment may be quite low as the premiums will offset one another. This diversification can be attained without any transactions in the underlying loans. Indeed, loan documentation sometimes forbids the sale or assignment of the loan.

There are both economic and business motives for using credit derivatives; the regulations that govern banks provide a powerful reason for using credit derivatives. The aim of these regulations is to ensure that banks have enough capital available to protect themselves against credit losses. The group that grapples with this question is the Basle Committee on Banking Supervision, which attempts to harmonise the banking regulations of the G-10 industrialised countries. In 1998, the Basle committee established specific capital charges for different types of risk.[26] The risk categories were very broad and tended to lump together, for credit assessment purposes, securities that had different underlying credit risk exposure. These regulations gave rise to a substantial gap between the market's estimate of the amount of capital needed to cover a particular credit risk and the amount required by the Basle committee. This differential provides considerable opportunities for banks to engage in regulatory arbitrage using credit derivatives.

To see how this works, suppose that the regulatory capital requirement for a particular corporate loan is 8%. This means that if the Grendel Bank makes such a loan and the amount is US$100 million, the bank must hold US$8 million in capital against the loan. This capital is set aside to cover the credit loss if the loan defaults. However, the bank can obtain protection against this credit risk by buying a credit default swap. At first glance it might appear that the bank has eliminated all the credit risk associated with the loan, however there is still the possibility that the protection seller itself might default. The regulations include an adjustment to cover this possibility. For example, if the protection seller is an OECD bank then the regulatory capital required is reduced from US$8 million to US$1.6 million by applying a 20% factor to the original capital charge. If Grendel buys the credit default swap this action releases an amount of US$6.4 million which can be invested elsewhere.[27] Of course, the Grendel Bank has to pay the required fee for the credit default swap but the release of regulatory capital may more than compensate for the reduction in net income.

Although the initial impetus for the growth of credit derivatives arose from the banking sector it is anticipated that corporate applications will become more important in the future as long-term contracts with producers and suppliers expose a firm to substantial credit risk.

MODELLING CREDIT RISK
The successful development of the market for credit derivatives is due in part to the availability of a theoretical framework for modelling credit risk. This framework was developed by a number of individuals, both academics and practitioners. It provides the basis for procedures that are now

used to model credit risk and develop pricing formulae. Just as the Black–Scholes–Merton (BSM) approach laid the foundations for the pricing, hedging and risk management of the early financial derivatives, the credit risk models are the intellectual lifeblood for activity in credit risk. This activity includes an entirely new approach to the measurement and risk management of credit risk by banks and other corporations.

We saw earlier in this chapter that the causes of financial distress are wide ranging. Models of credit risk cannot hope to include all of the possible factors that could cause financial distress. It is necessary to make drastic simplifications: otherwise the model will be too big and, like the Spruce Goose, will have trouble leaving the ground.[28]

The Merton model

The first major credit model is based on an important paper by Robert Merton that was published in 1974, a year after the publication of the BSM option pricing model.[29] Black and Scholes had noted that the option pricing framework could be used to value the stock and debt of a firm and Merton's paper fleshes out this notion. Consider that a firm's securities consist only of common stock and bonds, which mature in five years. In five years' time, the bondholders will be repaid, assuming the firm does not experience financial difficulties within this time. If the firm is unable to repay the bondholders then the bondholders are entitled to receive what is left of the firm in settlement of their claim. The stockholders of the firm are the residual claimants and are entitled to whatever is left after the bondholders are paid.

We have noted earlier that the stockholders' claim is like a call option because, if the firm performs well over that period, the common stockholders will own the firm in five years after the bonds have been repaid. The stockholders own a call option to buy the firm from the bondholders when the debt matures. Merton noted that the bondholders' claim can also be viewed in option terms. The current market value of the firm is equal to the sum of the current market values of the stock and the bonds, so the value of the bonds is equal to the value of the firm minus the value of the stock. This is more than an empty accounting statement because we can price the equity (common stock) as a call option. Merton used the recently developed stock options model to price the bonds.

We can reframe Merton's result using an important option result known as put-call parity. Put-call parity states that if we have a call option and a put option with identical strike prices and the same maturities on the same asset, there is a simple relation among the prices of the underlying asset, the call, the put and a risk-free bond.[30] This risk-free bond matures at the same time as both options and is a zero coupon bond. The put-call parity relation is:

Price of Asset – price of bond = price of call option – price of put option

Merton noted that this put-call parity relationship could be used at company level. In this case, the face value of the firm's debt corresponds to the strike price. He noted that when the debt matures, the stockholders own the entire amount of the firm minus the face value of the debt, as long as the firm's assets are sufficient to pay the entire debt. By the same token, the stockholders' claim is worth zero when the debt matures, if the assets are insufficient to pay the entire debt. Thus, the stockholders' claim resembles a call option to buy the entire firm, where the strike price is equal to the maturity value of the firm's debt. Therefore, the put-call parity result in this case becomes:

$$\text{Firm value} - \text{risk-free bond} = \text{stock value} - \text{put option}$$

However, we have seen that the value of the risky debt is equal to the value of the firm minus the value of its common stock. Hence the market value of the risky debt is given by

$$\text{Risky debt} = \text{firm value} - \text{stock value} = \text{risk-free debt} - \text{put option}$$

This put option is, in fact, a credit derivative that is similar to a credit default swap. The only difference is that, if the firm defaults before the bonds mature, the payment under the put option is made at the maturity of the debt and not when default occurs, as would be the case with a credit default swap. The last relationship indicates that the market value of the risky debt is equal to the market value of the risk-free bond minus a put option (credit derivative).

Merton's model gives sensible predictions. We saw in the Appendix to Chapter 5 that the value of an option increases with the volatility (riskiness) of the underlying asset. In this case the firm is the underlying asset and as the firm becomes riskier the put option becomes more valuable and so the firm's debt is worth less. This makes intuitive sense: the riskier the firm the more likely it is to default and the less valuable will be its bonds. Merton's model also predicts that, other things being equal, firms with higher amounts of debt are more likely to default and the yield in their debt will be higher to compensate for the higher probability of default. This finding is very consistent with our intuition.

The advantage of Merton's approach is that it provides a possible conceptual framework for quantifying credit risk and relating it to other economic variables. In Merton's model the key determinants of credit risk are the riskiness of the underlying firm and the amount of debt in the firm's capital structure. We can illustrate this with a simple example. Suppose we have a firm that has current assets worth US$120 and its liabilities consist of stock and bonds. The market value of its liabilities is also US$120. We assume the bonds mature in five years with a maturity value of US$100 and do not pay any coupons. In the same way, assume the stock pays no dividends over the next five years. The risk-free rate is assumed to be 6%. If we assume that the volatility of the firms assets is 25% per annum we can use Merton's model to find the market value of debt and equity and thus the yield on the risky debt.

We find:[31]

Value of stock	=	US$51.45
Value of risky debt	=	US$68.55
Yield on risky debt	=	7.55%

Note that the value of the stock plus the value of the debt is US$120: the total value of the firm. The yield on the firm's debt is 7.55%, which is 155 basis points higher than the risk-free rate of 6%. This yield is computed as the interest rate at which the current market value of the debt (US$68.55) accumulates to its face value (US$100) in five years.

Merton's model enables us to calculate how the yield on the debt changes as we change some of the inputs. Suppose we increase the face amount of the debt from US$100 to US$200 but maintain everything else as before, including the firm value at the same level. In this case, the yield on the debt increases from 7.55% to 13.36%, reflecting a much higher probability of default. Merton's model can be used to show how an increase in the riskiness of the firm translates into an additional yield on the firm's debt. If we increase the volatility of the firm's assets from 25% pa to 35% pa, keeping the other inputs the same as in the first example, the yield on the risky debt increases from 7.55% to 9.42% respectively.

Further extensions

Merton's model has been extended in a number of ways. For example, the original version assumed that the debt could only default at maturity and that there was only one issue of debt. In 1995, Francis Longstaff and Eduardo Schwartz proposed an extension of Merton's model that allowed for interest rates to be stochastic.[32] In the original Merton model, it was assumed that the firm kept the total amount of debt outstanding constant over the life of the bonds. In practice, if a firm prospers it tends to add more debt. Firms seem to work towards maintaining a target level of debt in their capital structure. If a firm's debt level rises very high it seeks ways to add equity and if its debt level sinks too low it tends to take on more debt. Recent work by Pierre Colin Deufresne and Robert Goldstein extends the Merton model to accommodate a dynamic capital structure.[33] In this framework, they find that the credit spreads on junk bonds increase with maturity, consistent with observations in the market place.[34]

Another approach that has been used in the modelling of credit risk is the one most commonly used to price credit derivatives. Under this approach the process that governs default is modelled directly. In this respect, the method resembles the way actuaries model mortality to estimate life insurance premiums and reserves. From an analysis of historical mortality statistics, actuaries can develop a model that can predict how many individuals of a certain age will die in the next year. These models can also factor in relevant information such as whether or not the individual is a smoker or a racing car driver. Armed with this knowledge, the actuary can estimate how much an insurance company should charge for a term insurance policy. In the same way, researchers have modelled the process that governs default. In the case of default the task is much more challenging.

Indeed, Benjamin Graham wrote that it would be impossible to develop a quantitative approach to model credit risk along these lines. He flatly states: "It may be pointed out further that the supposed actuarial computation of investment risk is out of the question theoretically as well as in practice".[35]

Graham goes on to give some reasons why such an approach would not work:

> But the relationship between different kinds of investments and the risk of loss is entirely too indefinite and too variable with changing conditions, to permit of sound mathematical formulation. This is particularly true because investment losses are not distributed fairly evenly but tend to be concentrated at intervals, i.e. during periods of general depression.

Graham's scepticism was quite understandable given the difficulty of the task but in the last few years considerable progress has been made in overcoming these difficulties.

Several researchers have made important contributions to the modelling of credit risk. Philippe Artzner and Freddy Delbaen (1990) were among the first to grasp the subtleties of some of the mathematical issues involved. Dick Rendelman (1992) was one of the first to study the valuation of swaps subject to credit risk and demonstrated that they could be valued in a recursive fashion. Bob Jarrow, Stuart Turnbull and David Lando (1995 & 1997), in a series of important papers, constructed a rigorous framework for modelling credit risk by building on the no-arbitrage models for pricing risk-free securities. Darrel Duffie and his co-authors have also made a number of significant contributions to the credit risk area. See Duffie and Huang (1996), Duffie and Singleton (1999) and Duffie, Schroder and Skiadas (1996). Along with his colleague Ken Singleton, he developed an elegant and intuitive formula to price a bond that is subject to default risk.

We now give a very simple example that captures the flavour of their result. Consider a default-free bond that pays US$100 in one year and that is currently worth US$95. The interest rate is therefore 5% (approximately).[36] Now suppose that we have an insurance contract that pays US$100 in one year, if the insured is living then and zero if the insured dies during the year. This contract is called a pure endowment. Assume the life insured has a 2% chance of dying during the year and hence a 98% chance of surviving the year. In this case, the single premium for the insurance contract will be 98% of US$95, which is US$93.1. In fact, there is a strong similarity between the interest rate and the mortality rate. Together the interest rate and the death rate add up to $7 = (5 + 2)$. The current price of the pure endowment is thus obtained by discounting US$100 for one year at 7%.[37]

Now we amend the insurance contract so that there is death benefit if the insured dies during the term of the contract. Let us assume that the death benefit is half of the maturity payment (that is US$50). We make this assumption to parallel the risky debt case where the recovery is usually some fraction of the bond value. To price this new contract consider an insurance contract similar to the first one except that the death rate is half of the previous death rate. In other words, under the new assumptions the chance of dying in one year is only 1%. A pure endowment based on this reduced death rate will cost US$94 by the same reasoning as above. However, this pure endowment costs the same as a one-year insurance contract that pays US$100 on maturity and US$50 on death within the year; under the first mortality assumption (when the death rate is 2% pa). The price in each case will be obtained by discounting at 6%, this rate corresponds to sum of the risk-free rate (5) and half the death rate.

We now indicate how the ideas from this example apply in the case of risky debt. Suppose we have a risky bond and we assume that the recovery rate is 50%. We define the loss rate as 1 minus the recovery rate. If the recovery rate is 50% the loss rate is also 50%. Corresponding to our insurance example, the rate used in the pricing of risky debt is the sum of the risk- free rate and the product of the default rate and the loss rate. For example, suppose the risk-free rate is 6% and the default rate is 3%; this would result in the interest rate corresponding to the risky debt being 7.5% (six plus half of three). In a very simplified way this example conveys the intuition behind the Duffie–Singleton result.

CONCLUSION

The development of an active market for credit derivatives is a remarkable achievement, especially given that there are many and varied factors that can cause financial distress. As a result, modelling credit risk is a formidable task and we noted that Ben Graham said it could not be done. When the first credit derivatives were arranged, the definition of a credit event was imprecise. The market did not really begin to grow until an accepted set of definitions and procedures were developed.

The new approaches that have been developed mean that banks and other firms now have more precise ways to measure their exposure to credit risk and they also have scientific methods for managing credit risk. We mentioned at the start of this chapter, that credit risk is as pervasive as snow in the Canadian winter and although we cannot eliminate this snow we can move it to a less inconvenient place. Credit derivatives can be used in the same way to transfer credit risk – they are powerful tools for changing how we deal with business risk.

1   Quotation from David Lawrence, Citibank during a coffee break conversation with the author at a Risk Training Seminar in London , 29 March, 2000.
2   In fact a precursor of the modern credit derivative has been used by banks for many years under other names. The traditional form is called a "guarantee" or "bank guarantee". It differs from a modern credit derivative only in detailed terms and conditions and the documentation it is written under. Another major difference is pricing: modern credit derivatives tend to be priced scientifically; guarantees and other traditional bank derivatives tend to be priced based on experience or guesswork.
3   Naturally, it is important to state clearly at the outset what will constitute this credit event.
4   Estimates from "Credit Derivatives and Structured Credit", Deutsche Bank Global Markets Research, 30 August, 2000.
5   See MacQueen (1996).
6   See *Japan Financial Review* (3), October, 2000, Japan Center for Economic Research. Website, http://www.jcer.or.jp/eng/
7   In 1997, Nissan Mutual Life Insurance, Japan's 16th largest insurer, failed with debts of ¥300 billion. In June, 1999, Toho Mutual Life Insurance failed and it was taken over by a subsidiary of General Electric. There were four failures in 2000: Daihyaku Mutual Life Insurance, Taisho Life Insurance, Chiyoda Mutual Life Insurance and Kyoei Life Insurance. At the time of its demise, Kyoei Life Insurance had debts of ¥4.5 trillion (US$42 billion) – it was one of Japan's largest ever corporate failures.
8   We assume the two projects are mutually exclusive.
9   One arrangement is to empower the bondholders to appoint one or more directors when the firm experiences financial difficulty. Another solution is to include an embedded call option in the bonds under which the bondholder can covert the bond into the firm's common stock. This feature helps align the interests of the stockholders and bondholders.
10 See Moody (1933).
11 Moody wrote several short stories, his autobiography, *The Long Road Home*, (see Note 8) and a biography of John Henry Newman (1946, *John Henry Newman*, London: Sheed & Ward).
12 Moody's defines default as missing or delaying a coupon payment, bankruptcy, receivership or any exchange of debt resulting from financial distress.
13 We obtain these estimates from the website: http://www.moodysqra.com/research/defrate.asp, Exhibit 31, p. 27 of *Historical Default Rates of Corporate bond Issuers, 1920–1999*, (Moody's Investors Service). We see that a portfolio of investment grade bonds would experience, in total, 1.46% defaults after eight years. A corresponding portfolio of 100 speculative grade bonds would experience a total of 28.73% defaults after eight years.
14 Berkshire Hathaway, 1990, chairman's letter.
15 Berkshire Hathaway, 1984, chairman's letter, *http://www.berkshirehathaway.com/letters/1984.html*.
16 Berkshire Hathaway, 1984, chairman's letter, *http://www.berkshirehathaway.com/letters/1984.html*.
17 Berkshire Hathaway, 1988, chairman's letter, *http://www.berkshirehathaway.com/letters/1988.html*.
18 We discuss later situations when someone other than the life insured, pays the premium.
19 In some very rare cases, the evidence may be hard to come by. For example in the 2000 film *CastAway*, an update of the Robinson Crusoe story, Chuck Nolan (Tom Hanks) is presumed

dead in an airplane crash. In reality, he miraculously escapes safely from the crash and makes it to a small island in the South Pacific. Chuck survives for four years before he is rescued. The film does not raise the life insurance issue. However, if his girlfriend Kelley (Helen Hunt) was the beneficiary of Chuck's life insurance, it seems clear that the insurance company would have paid a claim despite the absence of a death certificate.

20 In 1774, the English Life Assurance Act (commonly known as the Gambling Act) was passed to prevent an individual taking out a life insurance contract on the life of someone where there was no insurable interest.

21 In practice, the securities delivered (the so called "deliverable obligations") may be bonds of the defaulted firm that rank equally in terms of seniority with the underlying security. The writer often doesn't know what debt will be delivered until the buyer issues a credit event notice to the seller after the occurrence of the credit event. Here the buyer has to specify the debt he will deliver.

22 See Borch (1976).

23 Indeed some cynical folks have suggested that the Loch Ness Monster is itself a powerful marketing ploy.

24 The ISDA is the global self-regulating body that represents the leading players in the OTC derivatives markets.

25 Such an approach is sometimes called a relationship-friendly approach.

26 At the time of writing, these regulations were being revised and new regulations were being proposed that discriminate more finely among different risk classes than the 1988 regulations.

27 A credit-linked note will release the entire US$8 million.

28 A legendary huge airplane designed by the eccentric billionaire Howard Hughes. The Spruce Goose had a wingspan of over 300 feet and was powered by eight engines. Howard Hughes flew the plane on its first flight on 2 November, 1947. The Goose's first flight was also its last as the plane was too heavy.

29 See Merton (1974).

30 This risk-free bond pays an amount equal to the strike price of the option at the maturity date.

31 These number were obtained using the BSM formula, which was discussed in the Appendix to Chapter 5. In terms of the notation used there, the input variables are:

$$S = 120, K = 100, \sigma = 0.25, T = 5, r = 0.06.$$

If we insert these values into the BSM formula, we find that the call option value is equal to US$51.45. In the present context, this means that the current market value of the firm's stock is equal to US$51.45. Hence, the market value of the firm's debt is US$68.55 (120 – 50.45).

32 See Longstaff and Schwartz (1995).

33 See Dufresne and Goldstein (2000).

34 See Opler and Titman (1997).

35 See Graham and Dodd (1934).

36 The interest rate is actually 5.26%.

37 This is approximately true. We are not focusing on exact arithmetic; rather the intuition.

10

Financial Engineering: Some Tools of the Trade

The expansion of derivatives markets has given birth to the new profession of financial engineering. Financial engineers are the specialists who deal with the quantitative aspects of the derivatives business and in this chapter we discuss the evolution of this profession. We describe some of the basic numerical tools that are used by financial engineers to price derivatives and in risk management. We also discuss two challenging problems that financial engineers have worked on and have now solved: the valuation of Asian options and the pricing of complex American style options using Monte Carlo simulation.

We saw in Chapters 6 and 7 that the increased use of derivatives has caused profound changes in financial practice. There has been an expanded use of derivatives both by financial and non-financial corporations. Derivative instruments have become more complicated and more sophisticated. The technology has been extended to new areas of application such as credit, power and weather. In Chapter 6 we saw that modern risk management often involves complex derivative strategies. The overall management of risk is now of central importance to financial institutions and non-financial corporations. These developments have, in turn, created a demand for individuals with strong analytical and quantitative skills who can handle the technical aspects of derivatives and risk management.

Individuals who work in this area have backgrounds in quantitative disciplines such as mathematics, engineering, physics or economics. In particular, the employment opportunities in this field are often attractive to physicists. As many physicists made the transition to Wall Street, the term "rocket scientists" was coined in the 1980s to describe them. This term has now become somewhat *passé* and the more prosaic job title of quantitative analyst ("quant" for short) is now widely used. Less flattering terms such as "derivatives geek" are also used. The term "financial engineer" is now the most popular to describe individuals who work as quantitative analysts in the derivatives and risk management fields.

Initially the demand for strong quantitative skills came mainly from Wall Street investment banks. Traders needed advice on how to price and hedge different types of derivatives. Nowadays, financial engineers work in many different types of organisations across the world and their tasks can range from constructing models of electricity markets to implementing a risk management system for a pension fund. They could also give advice to accountants who may not otherwise be capable of auditing a derivatives book. In recent years, financial engineers have been involved increasingly in risk management, building the underlying models and creating the necessary software.

Financial engineers use a wide range of computational tools in their trade. These methods were already well known to the scientific community before they were first used in financial applications because finance has only emerged as a quantitative discipline within the last 50 years. These tools have become very important in financial engineering as the applications have become more complex and, because of increased computer power, they can now solve very large-scale problems.

In this chapter, we describe some very basic numerical approaches that are used in pricing derivatives and in risk management. These approaches were initially used to obtain prices for simple contracts that were extensions of the basic European call and put contracts but now they have much broader applications. The spread of option pricing was greatly facilitated by the introduction of a number of numerical methods. These methods not only made it easier to understand the basic model: they also made it easier to value non-standard options and compute the items required to set up the replicating portfolio. The stimuli for the development of numerical methods in finance were the Black, Scholes and Merton papers. When these papers were published in 1973, they were inaccessible to most practitioners and finance professors, who did not have the mathematical background to understand them or use the results. In this connection, the binomial method played a valuable role in translating the esoteric mysteries of the Itô calculus into a simple and intuitive numerical method that could be understood by traders and implemented by MBA students. It provides a flexible method of obtaining prices for some basic derivatives contracts.

THE BINOMIAL METHOD

The idea of approximating a continuous distribution with a simpler discrete distribution has a long history in physics and mathematics and was used by Bachelier (1900) in his thesis. The first person to suggest using the binomial model as a method to price options seems to have been Bill Sharpe. He had the idea of using this model to capture both the stock price movements as well as the essence of the hedging argument.[1] The binomial method was developed more fully by John Cox, Steve Ross and Mark Rubinstein and published in 1979. Rubinstein summarised the method as follows:[2]

It showed in a very simple way the basic economics that underlay option-pricing theory in a mathematically unadorned fashion.

The binomial method became much better known to the financial community through the publication of an influential book by Cox and Rubinstein (1985).

We introduced the binomial method in Chapter 4 and can summarise it as follows. We divide the time period into discrete steps and assume that in a single step the asset price can move either up or down. The size of the up movement and the down movement remains fixed. This framework enables us to model the uncertainty in the underlying asset's price in a convenient way. At any vertex there are just two possibilities: the asset price either goes up or down. We saw that if we had another asset that was risk-free, then at each step we could match the value of a derivative security to that of a portfolio, which had the right investments in the underlying asset and the risk-free bond. As we then have a portfolio that replicates the derivative's value one time step ahead, we can use the no-arbitrage principle (from Chapter 3) to find the current price of the derivative. Under the binomial approach we work backwards, one step at a time, until we obtain the price of the derivative at the current time.

The binomial method has a number of advantages:

❑ It is a very useful way to obtain the price of a number of common derivative contracts. For example, it can be used to price an American option because the early exercise feature can be modelled at each time step by testing if it is better to exercise the option or hold on to it.

❑ It has the simplicity and visual clarity of a spreadsheet: one can see directly how the method works and, just as with a spreadsheet, it is very easy to handle on a computer.

❑ It has an elegant economic interpretation because the construction of the replicating portfolio, which is an economic concept, ties in directly with the structure of the binomial tree.

It is common in science for the same discovery to be made almost simultaneously by different people and the binomial tree model for the pricing of stock options is a case in point. Within weeks of the publication of the Cox–Ross–Rubinstein paper, Richard Rendleman and Brit Bartter published a paper on the very same topic. The Cox–Ross–Rubinstein paper was the lead paper in the September 1979 issue of the *Journal of Financial Economics*[3] and the Rendleman–Bartter paper was the lead paper in the December, 1979 issue of the *Journal of Finance*. Bartter and Rendleman collaborated on this project when both were on the faculty at Northwestern University in the late 1970s.

We next turn to a discussion of two other methods that are also widely used to obtain prices of options and other derivatives. Both these methods were first applied to price derivatives in the early 1970s.

The Canadian connection

We start at the University of British Columbia (UBC) in Canada. This university became an important centre for option research in the 1970s. In particular, it became an active research centre for option pricing. Michael Brennan and Eduardo Schwartz (a doctoral student of Brennan's) made pioneering contributions to derivatives research. David Emanuel invented the Asian option while he was an assistant professor of finance at UBC. Another faculty member, Phelim Boyle, wrote the first paper that applied the Monte Carlo method to finance problems. Other academics who would later make contributions to the field also spent time at UBC. These included Stuart Turnbull, who later worked with Robert Jarrow on the development of credit risk models, and John Hull (1999), who was active in the options area in mid-1980s and wrote a well-known textbook, was also a visiting professor at UBC.

Under Brennan's guidance, Schwartz became interested in the problem of valuing American warrants in the Black–Scholes–Merton (BSM) framework. American warrants pay dividends and their exercise prices can change but their price still obeys the BSM differential equation. At this time, the Cox–Ross binomial method had not been published so there was no simple way to price them.

THE FINITE DIFFERENCE METHOD

We mentioned in Chapter 5 that the Black–Scholes equation for the price of an option is a differential equation. Merton had shown that any type of derivative contract written on a stock satisfied a similar type of equation. The contractual provisions could be translated into mathematical conditions known as boundary conditions. Until the advent of the BSM model such equations were not widely used in finance. However, they had been used for a long time in mathematics, physics, engineering and chemistry. In a few exceptional cases these equations have closed-form solutions. Otherwise they can be solved using *finite difference methods*.

Merton had set out the problem as a partial differential equation so it was natural to use methods from this field. To get warrant prices this equation would have to be solved numerically. Schwartz discussed this problem with Phelim Boyle, who put Schwartz in touch with Alvin Fowler. Fowler had a background in nuclear engineering and was an expert in computer programming.[4] He was well used to solving partial differential equations and had employed them before in physics and fluid dynamics. With Fowler's help, Schwartz wrote a Fortran program that was able to provide numerical solutions to the BSM equation for American options. This method was the finite difference method and we now describe the basic idea.

The idea behind the finite difference method is to start at maturity where the solution is known and then find the solution at regular time intervals all the way back to the present. The future is mapped into a regular grid of stock prices and times to maturity. Figure 10.1 illustrates this method. The vertical lines correspond to a fixed time and the horizontal lines correspond to fixed stock prices. At maturity, we know the value of the call option for each stock price so we can fill in all the maturity option prices. We know how the call price evolves according to the BSM equation. By using this equation to handle discrete time steps we can connect the call values at two successive time points. (Wilmott, Dewynne and Howison (1995) explain in detail how to use the finite approach to value derivatives.) This gives a large set of equations for the call prices one period earlier for each stock price on the grid. These equations can be solved on a computer to give the individual option prices at each grid point one small time step from maturity. We then repeat the process moving backwards, one step at a time, until eventually we arrive at the current time. Special features like dividend payments can be accommodated in the program and it can also be modified to handle the early exercise feature of American options.

Eduardo Schwartz used the finite difference method in two different applications: the valuation of AT&T warrants, which were more complicated than standard options, and the valuation of the guarantees embedded in certain types of life insurance contracts.

Under these insurance contracts, the premiums were invested in a stock portfolio and when the policy matured the policyholder would receive the

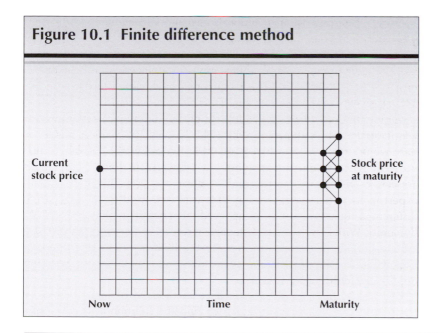

Figure 10.1 Finite difference method

Current stock price

Stock price at maturity

Now   Time   Maturity

market value of the portfolio. However, there was also a guaranteed minimum floor in case the stock market did poorly. These guarantees were popular in the UK and the market fall in 1974 provided a vivid reminder of their value. Traditional actuarial methods were not really suitable for dealing with financial guarantees of this nature. Michael Brennan noted that these guarantees corresponded to long-term put options on equity portfolios. In his thesis, Schwartz used the finite difference method to obtain prices for these guarantees and also AT&T warrants. In subsequent work, Brennan and Schwartz wielded this weapon with considerable success.

Brennan (1999) has noted the importance of this numerical approach in the introduction to a volume of his collected papers:

> Armed with numerical skills, we discovered that the solution to a whole range of problems was within our reach. We valued American put options using over the counter data from Myron Scholes and found that before the Black–Scholes era there were big differences between the Black–Scholes prices and the market prices. Contemporaneously with Oldrich Vasicek, we began to apply the same principles to interest rate contingent claims. (Brennan and Schwartz (1977)); our inspiration was the humble savings bond which gave the investor the right to redeem early and which at that time played a major role in Canadian government finance.

The finite difference approach continues to be a useful tool for the computation of numerical values of the prices of derivatives. This approach can handle the early exercise feature of American options. However, if the derivative is based on the value of several assets or variables it is generally more efficient to use another method called the Monte Carlo method.

THE MONTE CARLO METHOD

We start with the story of how the Monte Carlo method was first used to value options. While Eduardo Schwartz was testing his first programs to value the European put options embedded in the insurance contracts, he had frequent discussions with Phelim Boyle. Boyle wanted a quick way to obtain values that would verify Schwartz's numbers. He was motivated by reading a working paper by Cox and Ross (1976), which showed how an option could be valued by pretending that the stock's average return was equal to the risk-free return and discounting the expected value of the option payoff under this assumption. The Monte Carlo method provides a simple way to compute an average, so Boyle used this method and was able to verify Schwartz's results.

The name "Monte Carlo" comes from the city of the same name in Monaco because the method is based on the use of so-called *random* numbers, which can be generated by a roulette wheel. The first large-scale applications of the Monte Carlo method were in physics and arose from work on the Manhattan Project in the 1940s. Truly random numbers are unpredictable. For example, if you throw a six-sided die then it will land on any one of the numbers from one to six; this is one way of generating a random number between one and six.

Here is an example that illustrates how the Monte Carlo method can be used to value a security using random numbers to compute the average value. Suppose there is a security that will pay either 10, 20, 30, 40, 50 or 60 and that each of the six possible payoffs is equally likely. We could simulate the situation by throwing a die. If the die shows a one, the security pays 10; if the die shows a 2 the security pays 20 and so on. To estimate the average payoff of the security using the Monte Carlo method, we would throw the die a large number of times and find the average value of the payoff. Instead of throwing the die, we can generate the outcomes on a computer. The technical term used to describe the generation of a possible outcome on the computer is a *simulation trial*. For example, we used 100 simulation trials and found that the average payoff was 36.6. If we increase the number of throws, we will obtain a more accurate estimate. For example, based on 100,000 simulation trials we obtained an estimate of 35.06.

For this example, we can compute the accurate value by other methods and it works out to be 35. The Monte Carlo method has the property that, as we increase the number of simulation trials, the estimate will converge to the true value (35 in this case). The estimate that we obtain, however, contains some error. Nonetheless, our estimate of the average value itself has a distribution around the true value. In fact, it will have a normal distribution and we can estimate our error because we can estimate the standard deviation of this distribution. This means that when we use the Monte Carlo method we obtain not only an estimate of the answer but information on how accurate the results are.

The Monte Carlo method can be used to value derivatives and we illustrate the procedure for the case of a standard European call option. First, we generate a possible stock price at the maturity of the option. This can be easily carried out on a computer by selecting a random outcome from the stock price distribution. In the BSM case, this distribution is lognormal and we only require its expected value and the standard deviation to generate its distribution. Second, we compute the option payoff by comparing this stock price with the option's strike price. If the stock price exceeds the strike price, the call payoff will be equal to the difference. If the stock price is below the strike price the call payoff will be zero. Third, we repeat this process many times thus obtaining the values of the call option at maturity for the different stock prices. Fourth, we compute the average of these option payoffs. Finally, we convert this average payoff at option maturity to its current value using the risk-free interest rate. This provides an estimate of the price of the call option.

We now give an example that will help to explain the method. Assume we want to value a European call option on a stock whose current price is US$100; the strike price of the option is also US$100 and it will mature in one month. We assume that this stock does not pay any dividend during the next three months. The standard deviation of the return on the stock is 25% and the risk-free interest rate is 6% per annum. Table 10.1 shows the steps in the Monte Carlo method, assuming we just use 10 trials.

In the first trial, the computer generated a stock price at maturity of US$126.81 and in this case the payoff on the call option was US$26.11. In the third trial, the computer generated a stock price at maturity of US$93.88 and the payoff on the call option was zero. The average of the 10 possible payoffs in the third column is 6.96. To obtain an estimate of the current option price, we discount it for three months at 6% obtaining 6.86. The Monte Carlo estimate of the call price is US$6.86. The accurate price in this case, from the BSM formula, is 5.73. The Monte Carlo price differs considerably from the accurate price because we just used 10 simulation trials. If we had used more trials the Monte Carlo estimate would have been closer to the accurate value. The accuracy of the Monte Carlo method is proportional to the square root of the number of simulation trials. This

Table 10.1

Trial number	Stock price at maturity (US$)	Option payoff (US$)
1	126.81	26.81
2	122.77	22.77
3	93.88	0
4	96.57	0
5	88.66	0
6	92.28	0
7	89.47	0
8	115.94	15.94
9	104.11	4.11
10	92.26	0

means that if you want to increase the accuracy by a factor of 10, you have to increase the number of trials by a factor of 100.

The Monte Carlo method is well suited for complicated valuation problems. For example, it can be used to find the price of an equity derivative whose payoff depends on several underlying stock prices.

Another example of the application of the Monte Carlo method would be the valuation of the Asian option that we introduced in Chapter 2. The payoff on the Asian option depends on the average of the asset prices over some time. Using the Monte Carlo method we use the computer to simulate one possible price path. Along each path, we can simulate the asset price path so that we obtain a value for the asset price at each point on the path where it is needed. For instance, the contract might define the average based on prices at the end of each day, or at the end of each week. We can compute the average price of the asset along this path from these prices and this average is used to compute the option's payoff for this particular path. Then we repeat this process and obtain the Asian option's payoff for each path. We take the average value of these payoffs over all the paths. The final step is to convert this average payoff at option maturity to its current value using the risk-free interest rate. This provides an estimate of the price of the Asian call option.

The Monte Carlo method is now widely used in risk management applications. A common problem involves the estimation of the distribution of the profit-and-loss statement of a portfolio at some future date. This information may be required as an input for a value-at-risk (VAR) calculation (see Chapter 6). The future value of the portfolio can be estimated from the price movements of each of its component securities. The Monte Carlo method can be used to estimate the future value of the portfolio by estimating the market values of its individual parts.

The Monte Carlo method has two main drawbacks. For large-scale problems, a naive application of the method can waste a lot of computation time. Indeed it has been described as "The most brutish of the brute force methods".[5] However, there are tricks that can be used to make the method more efficient. The second drawback concerns the valuation of American options by Monte Carlo. This has proved to be a challenging numerical problem and, at one time, it was believed that American options could not be valued using this method. As we will see below, financial engineers have made considerable progress in solving this problem.

ASIAN OPTIONS: THE QUEST FOR SOLUTIONS

Asian options, or average options, have their payoffs computed with reference to the average price of the underlying asset or commodity. They are widely used for hedging commodity price risk and currency risk. This averaging feature means that Asian options are more difficult to value than standard options because the payoff depends on the asset price at many different times, not just at the time when the option contract matures. Financial engineers have developed a number of different ways to handle this problem. In this section, we start with a brief review of the development of Asian options and then discuss some of the approaches that have been developed to value them.

The idea of basing a contract on the average value of some variable has been around for many years. For example, in some pension plans the pension benefit is based on the plan member's average yearly salary taken over the five years prior to retirement. To our knowledge, David Emanuel was the first person to propose an option based on the average when he was an assistant professor at UBC in 1979. Emanuel also noted that if the option payoff is based on the geometric average rather than the arithmetic average, then there would be a simple expression for the price of the option.[6]

Angelien Kemna and Ton Vorst independently discovered this result in 1987. Kemna and Vorst's research was motivated by a commodity-linked bond issued in 1985 by the Dutch venture capital company Oranje Nassau. Each bond contained an embedded call option to purchase 10.5 barrels of North Sea oil. An investor who bought the bond was entitled to the appreciation (if any) in oil prices over the strike price. To pay for this feature, Oranje Nassau was able to pay a lower coupon rate on the bond than if the bond did not have the option feature. In order to protect itself against possible price manipulation just prior to the option maturity, Oranje Nassau based the settlement price of the option on the average of oil prices over the previous year. Kemna and Vorst (1990) showed how this feature of the contract could be valued.

The term Asian options was first coined by financial engineers and traders working for Bankers Trust who independently invented this concept. Bill Falloon (1995), describes the story of how they came up with the idea. The geographical associations can be confusing. Most Asian options can only be exercised at maturity and hence they are of the European type. However some Asian option contracts can be exercised early. There is no standard name for such contracts but the meaning of the terms Asian American or American Asian is already firmly established in the language.

We now turn to a discussion of a few of the different approaches that have been developed by financial engineers to value Asian options. More precisely, we will discuss options where the payoff is based on the arithmetic average of the price of the asset and which can only be exercised at maturity. As we have mentioned earlier, this problem can be solved numerically using Monte Carlo simulation.

There is a clever trick that can be used in this case to speed up the computation time if we are using Monte Carlo simulation to solve the problem. The trick involves using information from a related problem for which we know the exact solution. In the case of the Asian option, the related problem is an option based on the geometric average. In terms of simulation, the technique is known as the *control variate procedure* and the option based on the geometric average of the prices is the control variate in our case.

We first note that the arithmetic average of a set of stock prices will be strongly correlated with the corresponding geometric average. If the arithmetic average is large, so is the geometric average and if the arithmetic average is small, so too will be the geometric average.

There is a very simple formula for the price of the option based on the geometric average used. We use the Monte Carlo method to estimate the price of the option based on the arithmetic average and the corresponding option based on the geometric average taking care to use the *same random numbers* for both calculations. Then we compare the estimate of the geometric average option from our simulations with the accurate price from the formula. This comparison tells us how biased the estimate of the geometric average option price is. It is reasonable to suppose that the estimate of options based on the arithmetic average suffers from a similar bias because it was generated using the very same random numbers. We can use this information to remove the bias from our Monte Carlo estimate of the arithmetic average option. This procedure gives excellent numerical options for short to medium-term options (up to five years).

Binomial trees

The binomial method is a very inefficient tool for pricing Asian options because it quickly leads to an enormous number of computations. For a standard option, the binomial method is fine because the number of terminal asset prices increases at the same rate as the number of time steps. In a one-period tree we have two possible final asset prices. In a two-period tree, we have three possible final asset prices. (The figures in Chapter 4 illustrate this.) In a three-period tree, there are four final asset prices. In general, when the number of periods is equal to N the number of final asset prices is $(N + 1)$. We describe this pace of growth as being "linear".

To use the binomial method to price an option based on the average, we need to store information on all the different possible paths through the tree. This is because we need to compute the average asset price for all the possible price paths. The number of paths quickly becomes very large and this is the source of the problem. In a one-period tree, there are just two paths, in a two-period tree there are four paths and in a three-period tree the number of different paths through the tree is eight. For a general N-period tree, the number of different paths through the tree is 2^N. The number of paths is equal to 1,024 for a ten-period tree, over a million for a 20-period tree and over 33.5 million for a 25-period tree. If we have a one-year option with 50 weekly averaging points, then the number of different paths through the 50-period tree is $(1.125)10^{15}$ (a number with 16 digits). This number of paths is much too large to deal with on a computer, which is why the binomial method is not suitable for pricing Asian options.

It turns out that there is a closed-form solution for the price of an Asian option, which is based on the arithmetic average. This solution is based on fairly sophisticated mathematics.

At this point, it may be useful to explain why financial engineers find the quest for closed-form solutions so fascinating. Recall that the towering example of closed form solution in this field is the BSM formula for a standard European option. We described this formula in the Appendix to Chapter 5 and saw that the price of a standard call can be written in terms of five input variables. Closed-form solutions are often simpler and more intuitive than numerical solutions. They can lead to fresh insights and sometimes have an intrinsic beauty of their own. Sometimes, as in the case of the American put option, the closed-form solution does not appear to exist. In other cases such as the arithmetic Asian option case, it was not known if a solution existed or not. The intellectual challenge was therefore to find it if does exist.

The closed form solution to the Asian option involves some elegant but complicated mathematical expressions. To the best of our knowledge the first person to solve this problem was Eric Reiner while he was a doctoral student in chemical engineering. Unfortunately Reiner's solution has not been published. Independently, Marc Yor and Hélyette Geman (Yor, 1993; Geman and Yor, 1993) also developed a closed-form solution for the price of an Asian option based on the arithmetic average. This closed-form solution deepens our knowledge about the theoretical structure of Asian options. The formula is elegant from a mathematical perspective but it is hard work to obtain numerical solutions from it in practice. Other approaches such as finite difference methods and Monte Carlo methods are normally used.

VALUATION OF AMERICAN OPTIONS USING MONTE CARLO

American options are harder to value than European options because they can be exercised at any time. For some basic contracts such as an American option on one underlying asset, either the binomial tree or the finite difference approach provides a practical and efficient method of finding the price. For certain more complicated American-style derivatives, such as those based on several underlying assets, both these methods become inefficient. Normally, the numerical weapon of choice when there are many variables would be the Monte Carlo simulation.

It turns out that the valuation of an American style derivative using Monte Carlo simulation is a very hard problem to solve. Indeed, until Tilley published a paper in 1993, it was generally believed that American options could not be valued using the Monte Carlo approach. We now explain why the problem is so challenging.

The price of an American option is based on the assumption that the holder of the option exercises it optimally. The valuation procedure has to incorporate this decision problem. At each step, the decision is whether to exercise the option or continue to hold it. Usually the best way to tackle this problem is by working backwards from the option's maturity. However, in the Monte Carlo approach the future asset prices are generated from the current asset price and so we are marching along the price path. At any point on the price path, the early exercise decision requires some information about the future and, in the standard Monte Carlo approach, all we know is the price path up to this point; the future is still to unravel. This forward marching approach is in direct conflict with the requirements for the valuation of an American option because we have to use information based on the future to decide whether we should exercise the option or hold on to it.

Tilley's key insight was to adjust the Monte Carlo method to capture some of the aspects of a binomial tree. He had the idea of sorting the stock price at each time step into ordered bundles, so that the stock prices in a given bundle were close to one another. He then assumed that all the stock prices in a bundle had the same *holding value*. The holding value is the value of the option if it is not exercised. Tilley computed the holding value for each bundle by discounting the expected value of the option prices associated with the successor stock prices of the bundle one step ahead. In his own words:

> The goal of this paper is to dispel the prevailing belief that American-style options cannot be valued efficiently in a simulation model, and thus remove what has been considered a major impediment to the use of simulation models for valuing financial instruments. We present a general algorithm for estimating the value of American options on an underlying instrument or index for which the arbitrage-free probability distribution of paths through time can be simulated. The general algorithm is tested by an example for which the exact option premium can be determined.

Since Tilley's paper, other authors have developed more generalised and efficient methods to value American options by simulation, but Tilley's paper was of great importance because it showed that the problem could be solved.

CONCLUSION

In this chapter, we have discussed some of the methods used by financial engineers. We concentrated on the basic numerical methods for pricing derivatives and provided some historical context. Nowadays the most challenging numerical problems arise in the context of portfolios and risk measurement. The field of financial engineering is attracting some very gifted graduates who are well-equipped to surmount these challenges.

1 Mark Rubinstein describes discussions with Bill Sharpe on this topic at a 1975 conference in Israel. For details see Rubinstein (1999).
2 *Derivatives Strategy*, March 2000. Interview with Mark Rubinstein.
3 See Cox, Ross and Rubinstein (1979).
4 Alvin Fowler passed away on February 8, 1999. A summary of his accomplishments is contained in the website: URL: http://www.itservices.ubc.ca/newscentre/into_it/spr99/memoriam.shtmlA.
5 Oren Cheyette (1997), website: URL: http://www.barra.com/Newsletter/nl164/TNCNL164.asp
6 The simplest way to explain the geometric average is by example. The geometric average of any two numbers is the square root of their product. For example, the geometric average of 1 and 4 is 2. The arithmetic average in this case is 2.5. In the case of three numbers, the geometric average is the cube root of their product, eg, the geometric average of 1, 3 and 9 is the cube root of 27, which is 3. The arithmetic average of these last three numbers is 4.33.

Further Reading

For readers who wish to learn more about derivatives, we have prepared a brief summary of some additional sources. We have kept the list short and we have focused on introductory texts.

For a scholarly yet readable discussion of the history of speculation in financial markets, we recommend Edward Chancellor's *Devil take the Hindmost: A History of Financial Speculation*. Robert Shiller provides a perceptive analysis of the remarkable growth in the US stock market during the Clinton era.

Peter Bernstein's book, Capital Ideas, provides a wide-ranging discussion of the evolution of modern finance. This book also gives an entertaining account of the discovery of the option pricing formula. We note that some of the material on Louis Bachelier is now out of date in the light of recent research on Bachelier's life

For a general non-technical introduction to the subject of derivatives, it is hard to beat *Essays in Derivatives*, by Don Chance (1998). This book is a compilation of the weekly columns that he posted to an Internet site in 1995 and 1996. He does an excellent job of explaining the basic concepts and the essays are clearly written in plain English.

John Hull's, *Introduction to Futures and Options Markets* (1997), provides a solid introduction to the subject that is a little more technical but still goes gently with the mathematics. Hull has written two books on derivatives and this, the simpler one is often called baby Hull. His more advanced book (Hull (2000)) requires more mathematical background but has won widespread acceptance on Wall Street and in academia.

For readers with some mathematical background, Sheldon Ross's compact introduction should be attractive. The book is only 184 pages long and yet manages to cover a lot of material.

There are many books on derivatives disasters. Michael Lewis (1990) provides an amusing and suitably cynical perspective on Wall Street in the 1980s. Phillipe Jorion (1993), a professor of finance who happens to live in Orange County, lucidly explains the reasons for the Orange County disaster. Nicholas Dunbar and Roger Lowenstein have both produced very readable books on the collapse of Long-Term Capital Management.

Lowenstein provides a more in-depth analysis of the factors that led to the collapse of Long-Term Capital Management.

Finally, Robert McLoughlin (1998) discusses the legal side of derivatives.

REFERENCES

Bernstein, P., 1992, *Capital Ideas: The Improbable Origins of Wall Street* (New York: The Free Press).

Chance, D. M., 1998, *Essays in Derivatives* (New Hope, PA: Frank Fabozzi Associates).

Dunbar, N., 1999, *Inventing Money: The Story of Long-Term Capital Management and the Legends Behind It* (John Wiley and Sons).

Jorion, P., 1995, *Big Bets Gone Bad: Derivatives and Bankruptcy in Orange County* (Academic Press Inc).

Hull, J. C., 1997, *Introduction to Futures and Options Markets, Third Edition* (Prentice Hall Ltd).

Hull, J. C., 1999, *Options, Futures, and Other Derivatives*, Fourth Edition (Longman).

Lewis, M., 1990, *Liar's Poker: Rising Through the Wreckage of Wall Street* (Penguin).

Lowenstein, R., 2000, *When Genius Failed: The Rise and Fall of Long-Term Capital Management* (New York: Random House).

McLaughlin, R., 1998, *Over the Counter Derivative Products: A Guide to Legal Risk Management and Documentation* (New York: Random House).

Ross, S. M., 1999, *An Introduction to Mathematical Finance, Options and Other Topics* (Cambridge University Press).

Shiller, R. J., 2000, *Irrational Exuberance* (Princeton University Press).

Bibliography

Aboody, D., and R. Kasznick, 2000, "CEO Stock Option Awards and the Timing of Corporate Voluntary Disclosures", *Journal of Accounting And Economics* 29(1), pp. 73–100.

Artzner, P., and F. Delbaen, 1990, "Finem Laudem or the Credit Risk in Swaps", *Insurance Mathematics and Economics* 9, pp. 295–303.

Augar, P., 2000, *The Death of Gentlemanly Capitalism* (London: Penguin).

Bachelier, L., 1900, "Théorie de la Spéculation", *Annales Sciences de L'École Normale Supérieur 1018* (Paris: Gauthiers–Villars).

Bernstein, P., 1992, *Capital Ideas: The Improbable Origins of Wall Street* (New York: The Free Press).

Black, F., 1989, "How we came up with the Option Formula", *Journal of Portfolio Management* 15, pp. 4–8.

Black, F., and M. Scholes, 1973, "The Pricing of Options and Corporate Liabilities", *Journal of Political Economy* 81, May–June, pp. 637–54.

Borch, K., 1976, "The Monster in Loch Ness", *Journal of Risk and Insurance* 43, pp. 521–5.

Boyle, P. P., and A. L. Ananthanarayanan, 1979, "The Impact of Variance Estimation on Option Valuation Models", *Journal of Financial Economics* 6(4), pp. 375–88.

Brennan, M. J., and E. Schwartz, 1977, "Savings Bonds, Retractable Bonds and Callable Bonds", *Journal of Financial Economics* 5, pp. 67–88.

Brennan, M. J., 1999, *Financial Markets and Corporate Finance: Selected Papers of Michael J. Brennan* (Northampton, MA: Edward Elgar Publishing Inc).

Callinicos, B., 1999, "Trimming Risk from Microsoft's Corporate Tree", in G. W. Brown and D. H. Chew (eds), *Corporate Risk: Strategies and Management*, pp. 349–66 (London: Risk Books).

Chancellor, E., 1999, *Devil Take the Hindmost: A History of Financial Speculation* (New York: Farrar Straus & Giroux).

Chew, L., 1996, "Not Just One Man-Barings", Case Study prepared for IFCI, URL: http://newrisk.ifci.ch/137550.htm.

Cootner, P. H., 1964, *The Random Character of Stock Market Prices* (Massachusetts Institute of Technology.) Reprinted in 2000 by Risk Books.

Cox, J. C., and S. A. Ross, 1976, "The Valuation of Options for Alternative Stochastic Processes", *Journal of Financial Economics* 3, pp. 145–66.

Cox, J. C., S. A. Ross and M. Rubinstein, 1979, "Option Pricing: A Simplified Approach", *Journal of Financial Economics* 7(3), pp. 229–63.

Cox, J. C., and M. Rubinstein, 1985, *Options Markets* (Prentice Hall).

Derman, E., 1996, "Reflections on Fischer", *Journal of Portfolio Management*, Special Issue, December, pp. 18–24.

Duffie, D., and M. Huang, 1996, "Swap Rates and Credit Quality", *Journal of Finance* 51(3), pp. 921–49.

Duffie, D., and K. Singleton, 1999, "Modeling Term Structure Models of Defaultable Bonds", *Review of Financial Studies* 12, pp. 687–720.

Duffie, D., M. Schroder and C. Skiadas, 1996, "Recursive Valuation of Defaultable Securities and the Timing of the Resolution of Uncertainty", *Annals of Applied Probability* 6, pp. 1075–90.

Dufresne, P. C., and R. Goldstein, 2000, "Do Credit Spreads Reflect Stationary Leverage Ratios?", paper presented at the American Finance Association Meeting, New Orleans, January 2001.

Dunbar, N., 1999, "Sterling Swaptions under New Scrutiny", *Risk* 12(12), pp. 33–5.

Eichengreen, B., and D. Mathieson, 1999, "Hedge Funds: What do we Really Know?", *Economic Issues* 19, September, International Monetary Fund.

Emanuel, D., 1996, "The Peculiar Persistence of Catastrophic Trading Strategies", Working Paper, Chicago Board of Trade Seminar, February.

Falloon, W., 2000, "When Hedging Hurts", *Risk* 13(4), pp. 20–5.

Feller, W., 1968, *Introduction to Probability*, Third Edition, Volume I (New York: John Wiley & Sons).

Fischer, S., 1998, "The IMF and the Asian Crisis", Speech delivered at Los Angeles, March 20.

Froot, K., D. Scharfstein and J. Stein, 1994, "A Framework for Risk Management", *Harvard Business Review*, November–December; reprinted in G. W. Brown and D. H. Chew (eds), 1999, *Corporate Risk: Strategies and Management*, pp. 53–65 (London: Risk Books).

Géczy, C., B. A. Minton and C. Schrand, 1997, "Why Firms use Currency Derivatives", *Journal of Finance* 52(4), pp. 1323–54.

Geman, H., and M. Yor, 1993, "Bessell Processes, Asian Options and Perpetuities", *Mathematical Finance* 3, pp. 349–75.

Goldman, B., H. Sosin and M. Gatto, "Path Dependent Options: Buy at the Low, Sell at the High", *Journal of Finance* 34, pp. 1110–28.

Graham, B., and D. Dodd, 1934, *Security Analysis*, p.86 (New York: McGraw–Hill).

Hathaway, J., 2000, "The Folly of Hedging", Tocqueville Asset Management LP, URL: http://www. tocqueville.com/brainstorms/brainstorm0067.html.

Holmstrom, B., 1979, "Moral Hazard and Observability", *Bell Journal of Economics* 10, pp. 74–91.

Hsu, H., 1997, "Surprised Parties", *Risk* 10(4), pp. 27–9.

Hull, J., 1999, *Options, Futures, and Other Derivatives*, Fourth Edition (Longman).

Itô, K., 1951, "On Stochastic Differential Options", *Memoirs of the American Mathematical Society* 4.

Jacobs, B. I., 1999, *Capital Ideas and Market Realities: Option Replication, Investor Behavior and Stock Market Crashes* (Blackwell).

Jarrow, R., and S. Turnbull, 1995, "Pricing Financial Securities Subject to Credit Risk", *Journal of Finance* 50, pp. 53–85.

Jarrow, R., D. Lando and S. Turnbull, 1997, "A Markov Model for the Term Structure of Credit Risk Spreads", *Review of Financial Studies* 10(2), pp. 481–523.

Jorion, P., 1995, *Big Bets Gone Bad: Derivatives and Bankruptcy in Orange County* (Academic Press Inc).

Jovanovic, F., 2000, "L'Origine de la Théorie Financière: Une Réévaluation de l'Apport de Louis Bachelier", *Revue d' Économie Politique* 100(3), pp. 395–418.

Kemna, A. G. Z., and A. C. F. Vorst, 1987, "Options' Average Asset Values", Working Paper, Economic Institute at Erasmus University, Rotterdam.

Kemna, A. G. Z., and A. C. F. Vorst, 1990, "A Pricing Method for Options based on Average Asset Value", *Journal of Banking and Finance* 14, pp. 113–29.

Krugman, P., 1998, "What happened to Asia?", Working Paper, Massachusetts Institute of Technology.

Kroszner, R. S., 1999, "Can the Financial Markets Privately Regulate Risk? The Development of Derivatives Clearing Houses and Recent Over-the-Counter Innovations", Graduate School of Business, University of Chicago.

Leeson, N., 1996, *Rogue Trader: How I Brought down Barings Bank and Shook the Financial World* (Little Brown and Company).

Lewis, M., "How the Eggheads Cracked", *The New York Times Magazine*, January 24, 1999.

Longstaff, F., and E. S. Schwartz, 1995, "A Simple Approach to Valuing Risky Fixed and Floating Debt", *Journal of Finance* 50, pp. 789–819.

Loomis, C., 1994, "The Risk that won't go Away", *Fortune* 7, March, pp. 40–53.

Lowenstein, R., 2000, *When Genius Failed: The Rise and Fall of Long-Term Capital Management* (New York: Random House).

MacQueen, R., 1996, *Who Killed Confederation Life? The Inside Story* (Toronto: McClelland and Stewart).

Markowitz, H., 1952, "Portfolio Selection", *Journal of Finance* 7, pp. 77–91.

Merton, R. C., 1973, "Theory of Rational Option Pricing", *Bell Journal of Economics and Management Science* 4, Spring, pp. 141–83.

Merton, R. C., 1974, "On the Pricing of Corporate Debt: The Risk Structure of Interest Rates", *Journal of Finance* 29, May, pp. 449–70.

Merton, R, C., 1990, *Continuous Time Finance*, p. xv (Oxford: Basil Blackwell).

Microsoft, 2000, "Annual Report".

Moody, J., 1933, *Wall Street and the Security Markets: The Long Road Home* (Basingstoke: Macmillan).

Niederhoffer, V., 1998, *The Education of a Speculator* (New York: John Wiley & Sons).

Opler, T., and S. Titman, 1997, "The Debt Equity Choice: An Analysis of Issuing Firms", Working Paper, Ohio State University.

President's Working Group on Financial Markets, 1999, "Hedge Funds, Leverage and the Lessons of Long Term Capital".

Rendleman, R. J., 1992, "How Risks are Shared in Interest Rate Swaps", *Journal of Financial Services Research* 7, pp. 5–34.

Rendleman, R. J., and B. J. Bartter, 1979, "Two-state Option Pricing", *Journal of Finance* 34, pp. 1093–1110.

Rendleman, R. J., and R. W. McEnally, 1987, "Assessing the Cost of Portfolio Insurance", *Financial Analysts Journal*, May–June, pp. 27–37.

Report of the Board of Banking Supervision Inquiry into the Circumstances of the Collapse of Barings, 1995, (London: HMSO).

Report of the Financial Economists Roundtable, 1999, "Statement on Long-Term Capital Management and the Report of the President's Working Group on Financial Markets", *The Financier* 6(2 & 3), pp. 6–9.

Rubinstein, M., 1999, *A Derivatives Powerbook*.

Samuelson, P. A., 1965, "Rational Theory of Warrant Pricing", *Industrial Management Review* 6, Spring, pp. 13–31.

Samuelson, P. A., and R. C. Merton, 1969, "A Complete Model of Warrant Pricing that Maximizes Expected Utility", *Industrial Management Review* 10, Winter, pp. 17–46.

Shiller, R. J., 2000, *Irrational Exuberance* (Princeton University Press).

Singh, S., 1999, *The Code Book: The Evolution of Secrecy from Mary, Queen of Scots to Quantum Cryptography* (Doubleday).

Spiro, L. N., 1994, "Dream Team", *Business Week*, August, pp. 50–60.

Steele, M. J., 2000, *Stochastic Calculus and Financial Applications* (New York: Springer–Verlag).

Steyn, A., 2000, "New Rules Needed for Gold Hedging", *Risk* 13(7), pp. 73–8.

Thomson, R., 1998, *Apocalypse Roulette: The Lethal World of Derivatives* (London: Macmillan).

Thorp, E. O., and S. Kassouf, 1967, *Beat the Market* (New York: Random House).

Thorp, E. O., 1969, "Optimal Gambling Systems for Favorable Games", *Review of the International Statistical Institute* 37(3), pp. 273–93.

Tilley, J. A., 1993, "Valuing American Options in a Path Simulation Model", *Transactions of the Society of Actuaries* 45, pp. 83–104.

Treynor, J. L., 1996, "Remembering Fischer Black", *Journal of Portfolio Management*, Special Issue, December, pp. 92–5.

Wilmott, P., J. Dewynne and S. Howison, 1995, *Option Pricing: Mathematical Models and Computation* (Cambridge Financial Press).

World Gold Council, 1999, "A Glittering Future?".

Yermack, D., 1997, "Good Timing: CEO Stock Option Awards and Company News Announcements", *Journal of Finance* 52(2), pp. 449–76.

Yor, M., 1993, "From Planar Brownian Windings to Asian Options", *Insurance Mathematics and Economics* 13(1), pp. 23–34.

Index